**WEIRD, FASCINATING,
THOUGHT-PROVOKING...
UNEXPLAINED PHENOMENA.**

Some of the phenomena in this remarkable book *have* been explained—yet the explanations do not hold up under scrutiny.

HAS THERE BEEN AN ATTEMPT TO SWEEP THESE FREAKS OF NATURE UNDER A SCIENTIFIC RUG . . . HOPING THEY WILL GO AWAY?

The canals of Mars. Enormous mastodons perfectly preserved by an impossible change in climate. Ancient waterworks in Florida that are marvels of engineering. Human footprints in rocks millions of years older than the first men. An eerie lightwheel seen by countless travelers in the Indian Ocean...

ARE THESE STRANGE PHENOMENA THE TIP OF AN ICEBERG THAT WILL REVOLUTIONIZE SCIENCE? READ THIS BOOK AND DECIDE FOR YOURSELF—BUT PREPARE TO BE CHALLENGED IN SOME OF YOUR MOST DEEPLY HELD BELIEFS . . .

The Unexplained:

A SOURCEBOOK OF STRANGE PHENOMEMA

William R. Corliss

BANTAM BOOKS · LONDON · TORONTO · NEW YORK

RLI: VLM 9 (VLR 8–11)
IL 9+

THE UNEXPLAINED:
A SOURCEBOOK OF STRANGE PHENOMENA
A Bantam Book / August 1976

ISBN 0–553–02812–X

Published simultaneously in the United States and Canada

Bantam Books are published by Bantam Books, Inc. Its trade-
mark, consisting of the words "Bantam Books" and the por-
trayal of a bantam, is registered in the United States Patent
Office and in other countries. Marca Registrada. Bantam
Books, Inc., 666 Fifth Avenue, New York, New York 10019.

Contents

IV. GEOLOGY

INDEXES

Preface

I have always been intrigued with the tailings from the mine of science. I mean those facts that do not fit the mold, those anomalies that should not exist, those wild points that lie far off the curve. One of my hobbies is collecting and organizing these homeless facts. These waifs are curious and most intriguing. Either they are all false, or science still has much fundamental work to do. But I leave such probems to the reader; I advance no pet theories. All I have done is collect, categorize, and reproduce this anomalous information. Perhaps you, the reader, can make something out of it. At the very least, I hope you will be excited about the vast unknown territory that still lies ahead.

The vehicle I have selected for presenting these curious tidbits is the "Sourcebook," in which original reports and articles from a wide spectrum of sources are reprinted. I have taken a conservative and "responsible" approach by choosing the majority of the reports directly from the scientific literature. By design I have concentrated on reported facts and avoided articles that advocate sensational hypotheses, such as ancient astronauts and colliding planets. The reader will find, however, that the data I have admitted are very strange indeed and may well support even stranger theories. The cosmos seems a most complex and subtle organism.

To carry on the work of collecting anomalous scientific data from over 200 years of literature, I have formed the Sourcebook Project. The object is to prepare a separate series of sourcebooks in each major field of science. These collections of unexplained and difficult-to-explain data can then be analyzed and cross-correlated to try and make sense out of the disparate data. To my knowledge, this is the first modern, science-wide attempt to collect and organize data that "don't fit." Work is progressing well, and Sourcebooks have already been published in the fields of astronomy, biology, geology, geophysics, and archeology. The present Bantam paperback is a selection of reports from Sourcebooks already published directly by the Sourcebook Project. Further information about the Sourcebook Project and its publications may be obtained by writing the Sourcebook Project, Glen Arm, MD 21057.

William R. Corliss

I

ARCHAEOLOGY

1

Fossil Human Footprints

Geologists have no problem visualizing dinosaurs treading ponderously over a sandbar, leaving in their wakes footprints that are ultimately silted in, petrified, and preserved for men-yet-to-evolve to wonder at. But human footprints in rocks many millions of years old? Impossible!

The word "impossible" is apt because if human footprints in ancient rocks are genuine, either men existed long before evolution stipulates they should or our geological dating schemes are seriously in error. When ostensibly human footprints are discovered in very old sedimentary rocks there are two ways out: (1) declare the footprints to be the distorted tracks of animals; or (2) claim that the tracks were engraved by Indians of yore. The Indian theory has a good deal going for it because ancient man did engrave handprints in abundance plus some fingerprints and footprints on rock walls. The Indian theory collapses, of course, when the prints are found only after the removal of overlying rock strata.

In the accounts that follow, both of the above theories have been introduced in way of explanation. One case, that of the Nicaragua footprints, may be legitimate because man probably did occupy the land in question during the period of recent lava flows. Most of the footprints described here are in much older rock. Furthermore, they represent only a small fraction of the data available. The evidence is so prolific that we may have to face up to some serious inconsistencies in the now-standardized histories of the earth and man.

The prevailing theories of earth and man are based upon seemingly overwhelming, interlocking evidence. But so were Ptolemy's theory of planetary motion and the dogma of fixed continents and ocean basins. Fossil human footprints, the butt of ridicule of geologists and archeologists, may represent but a hairline crack in our Temple of Science. All who appreciate anomalies must therefore welcome fossil human footprints to the arsenal—the more trivial the evidence seems, the bigger the crash when a false edifice topples.

REMARKS ON THE PRINTS OF HUMAN FEET, OBSERVED IN THE SECONDARY LIMESTONE OF THE MISSISSIPPI VALLEY

Schoolcraft, Henry R.; *American Journal of Science*, 1:5:223–230, 1822

I now send you a drawing of two curious prints of the human foot in limestone rock, observed by me last summer, in a detached slab of secondary formation, at Harmony, on the Wabash; together with a letter of Col. Thos. H. Genton, a senator in Congress from Missouri, on the same subject. The slab of stone containing these impressions, was originally quarried on the west bank of the Mississippi river, at St. Louis, and belongs to the elder floetz range of limestone, which pervades that country to a very great extent.

These prints appear to have been noticed by the French soon after they penetrated into that country from the Canadas, and during the progress of settlement at St. Louis, were frequently resorted to as a phenomenon in the works of nature. But no person appears to have entertained the idea of raising them from the quarry with a view to preservation, until Mr. Rappe visited that place five or six years ago. He immediately determined to remove the stone containing them to his village of Harmony, then recently transferred from Butler county in Pennsylvania, to the banks of the Wabash; but this determination was no sooner known than popular sentiment began to arraign his motives, and people were ready to attribute to religious fanaticism or arch deception, what was, more probably, a mere act of momentary caprice, or settled taste. His followers, it was said, were to regard these prints as the sacred *impress* of the feet of our Saviour. Few persons thought of interposing a charitable remark in favour of religious tenets, of which we can judge only by the peaceful, industrious, and devotional lives; the neat and cleanly appearance; and the inoffensive manners of those who profess them. Still less could be conceded in favour of a personal taste for objects of natural history or curiosity, of which this act is, at least, a proof. Be this as it may, Mr. Rappe contracted with a stone mason to cut out the block with the impressions, paying him at the same time a liberal price for his labour, and ordered it to be transported by water to his residence in Posy county, Indiana. Visiting this place during the last summer, in the suite of Governor Cass, Mr. Rappe conducted us to see this curiosity, which has been placed upon mason work in a paved area between his dwelling house and garden. The slab of stone thus preserved, forms a parallelogram of eight feet in length, by three and a half in breadth, and has a thickness of eight inches, which appears to be the natural thickness of the stratum of limestone rock, of which it is a part. This limestone possesses a firm and compact structure, of the peculiar greyish blue tint common to the calcareous rocks of the Mississippi valley, and contains fossil encrinites, and some analogous remains, very plentifully imbedded. It is quarried at St. Louis, both for the purposes of building stone, and for quicklime. It becomes beautifully white on parting with its carbonic acid and water, and those who have used it, observe, that it makes a good cement, with the usual proportion of sand.

The prints are those of a man standing erect, with his heels drawn in, and his toes turned outward, which is the most natural position. The distance between the heels, by accurate measurement, is 6¼ inches, and between the toes, 13½ inches; but it will be perceived, that these are not the impressions of feet accustomed to a close shoe, the toes being very much spread, and the foot flattened in a manner that happens to those who have been habituated to go a great length of time without shoes. Notwithstanding this circumstance, the prints are strikingly natural, exhibiting every muscular impression, and swell of the heel

Impressions of human feet in limestone rock.

and toes, with a precision and faithfulness to nature, which I have not been able to copy, with perfect exactness, in the present drawing. The length of each foot, as indicated by the prints, is 10½ inches, and the width across the spread of the toes, 4 inches, which diminishes to 2½ inches, at the swell of the heels, indicating, as it is thought, a stature of the common size.

This rock presents a plain and smooth surface, having acquired a polish from the sand and water, to which its original position periodically subjected it. Upon this smooth surface, commencing in front of the tracks, there is a kind of scroll, which is two feet and a half in length. The shape of this is very irregular, and not equally plain and perfect in all parts, and would convey to the observer the idea of man idly marking with his fingers, or with a smooth stick, fanciful figures upon a soft surface. Some pretend to observe in this scroll, the figure of an Indian bow, but this inference did not appear, to any of our party, to be justified.

Every appearance will warrant the conclusion that these impressions were made at a time when the rock was soft enough to receive them by pressure, and that the marks of feet are natural and genuine. Such was the opinion of Gov. Cass and myself, formed upon the spot, and there is nothing that I have subsequently seen to alter this view; on the contrary, there are some corroborating facts calculated to strengthen and confirm it.* But it will be observed by a letter which is transmitted with these remarks, that Col. Benton entertains a different opinion, and supposes them to be the result of human labour, at the same period of time when those enigmatical mounds upon the American Bottom, and above the town of St. Louis, were constructed. The reasons which have induced him to reject the opinion of their being organic impressions are these:

"1. The hardness of the rock.

"2. The want of tracks leading to and from them.

"3. The difficulty of supposing a change so instantaneous and apropos, as must have taken place in the formation of the rock, if impressed when soft enough to receive such deep and distinct tracks."

To those who are familiar with the facts of the existence

---

*The following are the facts referred to. At the town of Herculaneum in Jefferson county, Missouri, two supposed tracks of the human foot were observed by the workmen engaged in quarrying stone in the year 1817. These impressions, at the time, attracted the general notice of the inhabitants, and were considered so curious and interesting that the workmen who were employed in building a stone chimney for John W. Honey, Esq. of that place, were directed to place the two blocks of stone containing these marks, in the outward wall, so as to be capable of being examined at all times. It is well known to those who have visited that section of country, that the custom of building the back walls and the pipe of the chimney, in such a manner as to project beyond the body of the house, is prevalent among the French and other inhabitants; and consequently, the above arrangement, while it completely preserves, at the same time exposes the prints to observation, in the most satisfactory manner. I examined them in that position on my first visit to Missouri, in 1818, and afterwards in 1821, when I took drawings of both the prints. They are however the impressions of feet covered with the Indian shoe, and are not so perfect and exquisitely natural as those at Harmony. They were situated in the same range of secondary limestone, and distant from St. Louis 30 miles.

of sea and fresh water shells, ferns, madrepores, and other fossil organic remains, in the hardest sandstones and lime-stones of our continent, the *hardness* of the rock, and the supposed rapidity of its consolidation, will not present objections of that force, which the writer supposes. But the want of tracks leading to and from them, presents a difficulty, which cannot, perhaps be so readily obviated. We should certainly suppose such tracks to exist, unless it could be ascertained that the toes of the prints, when in situ, pointed inland, in which case we should be at liberty to conjecture, that the person making them, had landed from the Mississippi, and proceeded no further into the interior. But no enquiry has enabled me to ascertain this fact, the circumstance not being recollected by Col. Benton; and others, who have often visited this curiosity while it remained in its natural position at St. Louis.

The following considerations, it will be seen, are stated by Col. Benton, as capable of being urged in opposition to his theory of their being of factitious origin.

"1. The exquisiteness of the workmanship.

"2. The difficulty of working such hard material without steel or iron."

The strikingly natural appearance of these prints, has always appeared to me, to be one of the best evidences of their being genuine; for I cannot suppose that there is any artist *now* in America possessed of the skill necessary to produce such perfect and masterly pieces of sculpture: yet, what are we to say of the skill of that people, who are supposed to have been capable of producing such finished pieces of art, without the aid of iron tools? For, let it constantly be borne in mind, that the antiquity of these prints can be traced back to the earliest discovery of the country, and consequently to the introduction of iron tools and weapons among the aborigines. There are none of our Indian tribes who have made any proficiency in sculpture, even since the iron hatchet and knive, have been exchanged for those of flint, and of obsidian. All their attempts in this way are grotesque, and exhibit a lamentable want of proportions, the same which was seen in the paintings, and in the figured vases and pottery of the Asteecks of Mexico, when their towns and temples were first visited by the Spanish conqueror.

HUMAN FOOTPRINTS IN NICARAGUA
Flint, Earl; *American Antiquarian*, 6:112–113, 1884

In a recent trip to Managua for the Peabody Museum, to examine the human footprints found there in one of the quarries, now being worked for building purposes, I uncovered six rows of impressions, breaking through a layer of rock seven inches thick, over a space of six yards by two. Under this was a layer of black sand with an average thickness of one inch, resting on a layer of friable rock from one and one-half to two inches thick, covering the surface of the lowest layer of rock found in the quarry. Below this thin layer was a thin deposit of volcanic sand and gravel, filling up the inequalities caused by the impressions, with an average of one inch in thickness, as seen in the side cuttings.

The rock seems to owe its formation to a volcanic detritus, and ash brought down after the first volcanic eruption. I cannot account in any other way, for its original plasticity, as but little clay could reach the surface, if the eruption covered the neighborhood with rock and ash —evidenced in many places of a large district where this kind of rock occurs. Impressions of leaves and stems occur on the under surface, denoting an absence of forest at the point worked. The upper surface is nearly level, with a barely perceptible dip toward the lake shore—distant some 300 yards, and whose waters must have formerly occupied—or overflowed at times of high water, as some of the aquatic plants, common in the marshy districts, are among the impressions preserved.

The footprints are from one-half to three inches in depth, consequently not made, as some had judged, by a people, fleeing from an inundation. In those exposed there is no length of stride to indicate it, and in the many removed by the owner of the quarry, none exceeded eighteen inches. Some of the impressions are nearly closed, the soft surface falling back into the impression, and a crevice about two inches in width is all one sees, and my first glance at some parallel to one less deep, gave me an idea that the owner of the latter was using a stave to assist him in walking. In some of the substance flowed outward, leaving a ridge around it—seen in one secured for the museum;

the stride is variable, owing to size of person, and the changing nature of surface passed over. The longest one uncovered was seventeen inches, length of foot ten inches, and width four inches, feet arched, steps in a right line, measured from center of heel to center of great toe over three steps. The people making them were going both ways in a direction consonant to that of the present lake shore E. and W. more or less. The nearly level surface extending around the neighborhood of the quarry prevented me from judging as to the nature of or mode of arrival other than that mentioned. As far as worked out, the thickness varied but little from twenty-eight to thirty inches. Following the inequalities of the primitive soil, the perpendicular cuttings on the southern and eastern faces of the quarry above the layers mentioned, show in only one place a barely perceptible dip to the east. The layer removed was covered by one of hard clay, with streaks of white pumice stone beneath and mingled with its lower surface—thickness seen in the cutting twelve inches; above this was a layer of ash, slate colored, very hard, seen in the cuttings along the Masaya road, and also between Granada and Jinotepe—west of latter place, 15 feet in thickness, under 15 feet of loam. In the location worked was only 14 inches, mixed with stems of plants and leaves on and near its under surface. Above this ashy formation are four successive layers of rock, similar to the lower one and are being used for building. The lowest averages 28 inches; the others from 17 to 20 inches. The detritus separating the layers is insignificant. Saw many blocks, and found cavities formerly occupied by stems of plants, but none have leaves like the lowest layer. I think these layers were the results of different eruptions. The clay deposit one of repose.

The depth from the surface of the impressions was 14 feet 10 inches—not counting the surface soil, the strides from 11 to 17 inches. I would mention that later, the purchaser of those remaining uncovered, intends removing them to Europe and will be able to give a correct estimate of each. He kindly gave me permission to remove two. Had he not purchased the site, only the story of their occurrence could be relied on to prove man's antiquity here.

It is useless to speculate on the lapse of time that has passed since their occurrence. Experts in geology may give approximate dates.

Before examining them I was inclined to believe they were coeval with those at San Rafael, but am now convinced that they are in an entirely different formation. The former occurs on sedimentary rock of that locality. One human footprint associated with those of a tiger on hard volcanic rock, on the banks of Grand river, at Pinon, west of Jinotepe is now easily explained. I went in May to cut it out and found the place covered by water, but intend visiting San Rafael to procure specimens from them. Unlike those at Nevada the people of this region needed no covering to protect their feet from a rigorous climate. The discovery is unique and worth recording.

THE PRE-ADAMITE TRACK

McA., A.; *American Antiquarian,* 7:364–367, 1885

In the last issue of your always deeply interesting and instructive journal, I read an article from the pen of Mr. Flint, which aroused some thoughts to which I now take the liberty of giving free expression.

It appears that Mr. Flint, among some really valuable discoveries, came across what he believed to be two impressions of the human foot on a rock in Nicaragua. Finding that the rock contained fossils of a remote era, he has assigned the origin of the "imprints" to a "date" ranging anywhere from 50,000 to 200,000 years ago.

Now, what I desire to say is, that it appears to me to be an error to assume that "footprints" found on the surface of rocks are as old as the fossils beneath. Some of the so-called pre-Adamite tracks are manifestly the work of sculptors, and utterly useless as data by which to calculate the antiquity of our race on this planet.

That sculptors passed through Nicaragua during some period in the remote past is perfectly evident from the images which have been found by travelers. Squier in his admirable book of travels through this region presents us with pictures of chiseled forms in stone that could only have been wrought by masters of the art. Some of the figures represent human bodies with heads of beasts. They are executed with marvelous skill, and nothing is clearer than that those sculptors could, if they pleased, have caused the representation of a footprint on rock.

If the tracks in Nicaragua were made when the rock on

which they appear was in as soft condition as that sea beach on which the startled Crusoe beheld the footprint, then it would be correct to attribute those "footprints in the sand of time" to some pre-Adamite wanderer. But, on the other hand, if the tracks are the work of sculptors, they were, of course, carved after the matter in which they appear had become hard stone; and it would, be absurd and misleading to say that the artist was the contemporary of the fossils found in the sculptured rock. Suppose we find a statue or shell clearly referable to the Tertiary period, would it be wise to conclude that the workman belonged to the same remote era?

I notice that your learned and ingenious correspondent speaks about writings which he has observed on the roofs of caves in the same section of country as that to which the "footprints" belong. It is highly probable that those who carved the tracks also cut the inscriptions. Bradford says: "The most singular of these sculptors [he is telling about the imprints of feet observed in Asia and America] has been discovered on the banks of the Mississippi, near St. Louis. This is a tabular mass of lime stone bearing the impression of two human feet. The rock is compact limestone of grayish-blue color, containing the encrinite, echinite, and other fossils. The feet are quite flattened, but the muscular marks are delineated with great precision. Immediately before the feet lies a *scroll* sculptured in similar style. The opinion sometimes entertained, that these are actual impressions of the human feet, made upon a soft substance subsequently indurated, is incorrect; on the contrary, they are undoubtedly the result of art."—*Am. Antiquities, p. 25.*

On the other hand Priest in his work on "American Antiquities" takes substantially the same ground as Mr. Flint. He says, [speaking of the impressions at St. Louis], "Directly before the prints of these feet, within a few inches, is a well impressed and deep mark, having some resemblance to a scroll, or roll of parchment, two feet long, by a foot in width. To account for these appearances, two theories are advanced; one is, that they were sculptured there by the ancient nations; the other that they were impressed there at a time when the rock was in a plastic state; both theories have their difficulties, but we incline to the latter, because the impressions are strikingly natural, and Mr. Schoolcraft, exhibiting even the muscular marks of the foot, with great precision and faithfulness to nature, and, on this account, weakens, in his opinion, the doctrine of their being sculptured by the ancient nations. But why there are no others going to and from these, is unaccountable, unless we may suppose the rest of this rock, at that time, was buried by earth, brush, grass, or some kind of covering. If they were sculptured, why not other specimens appear; this one isolated effort of the kind, would seem unnatural."

Why doesn't Mr. Priest give us a dozen pictures of the rock at St. Louis? His answer is, because *one* drawing suffices; and in like manner, a single pair of sculptured "imprints" of feet—indicating that certain people had passed that way—served even better than a great number. A multitude of tracks might possibly be mistaken for genuine impressions of the feet of wayfarers belonging to a remote epoch; but a single isolated pair with no trail leading to or from them could not but arrest attention. The perfection of the workmanship merely demonstrates the skill of the artist. And what about the carved scroll? Is it too a fossil? If so it may be a leaf out of the pre-Adamite library.

On page 151 of his profound work, Mr. Priest says: "A few miles south of Braystown, which is at the head waters of the Tennessee river, are found impressed on the surface of the solid rock, a great number of tracks, as turkeys, bears, horses, and human beings, as perfect as they could be made on snow or sand. The human tracks are remarkable for having uniformly six toes each, like the Anakims of Scripture; one only excepted, which appears to be the print of a negro's foot. One, among those tracks, is distinguished from the rest, by its monstrousness, being of no less dimensions than sixteen inches in length, across the toes thirteen inches, behind the toes, where the foot narrows toward the instep, seven inches, and the heel ball five inches."

We can produce no such feet now-a-days. What becomes of the doctrine of evolution in the light of this revelation? Think of feet sixteen inches in length, and bodies and brains in proportion! But I take refuge in the belief that the "imprints" are all carved. True, in Tennessee as in Nicaragua, the tracks of animals are represented. But we know for a fact that the tracks of turkeys, for instance, have been found upon the precipitous rocks, and on the sides of caves. Are we to suppose that the gobblers actually walked up the cliffs at a time when the substance of which the rocks are composed was in a plastic state? And if certain people went to the trouble of representing turkey tracks and letters on vertical rocks, may they not have carved similar impressions and a scroll upon level stones?

Mr. Priest informs us that in addition to the feet of turkeys are those of "bears, horses and human beings." Was it a circus?

"That these are the real tracks of the animals they represent, appears from the circumstance of this horse's foot having slipped several inches, and recovered again; the figures have all the same direction, like the trail of a company on a journey." It must have astonished the natives.

It is interesting to be assured that there were horses in America away back in ancient times. This supports the Danish legend about Bjorn Asbjornson having been seen on horseback by Snorre Sturluson. Moreover, the exiled chief was in command of a troop of horse. And in support of this view we have Priest's testimony: "One also among the tracks of the animals, is distinguished for its great size; it is the track of a horse, measuring eight by ten inches; perhaps the horse which the great warrior led when passing this mountain with his army."

You will note that this hero, whose foot was sixteen inches long, *led* his horse while crossing the mountain. Had he mounted the animal it would probably have gone right through the crust of the earth. Fortunately the immensity of the hoofs of this horse which so admirably matched its master, sustained it above ground while traveling with the show.

The horse was a genuine curiosity. Hoofs ten inches long! It was the only horse in the company, but in quality it atoned for quantity. Mr. Priest even endeavors to belittle it, so anxious is he not to offend our prejudices on the subject of natural history. But let the full truth be told. The track left by the horse is several inches over the ten just mentioned! We are informed that the foot "slipped several inches and recovered again." How does any one know that it slipped? Isn't the track of the monster at least thirteen inches long? What kind of a horse have we here?

Mr. Priest next tells us about the mountains of South America, on whose smooth and perpendicular sides "are engraven [mark the word], at a surprising distance from the base, the figures of animals; also the sun, moon and stars, with other hieroglyphic signs." The thoughtful author concludes that "the stones were once so soft and plastic, that men could easily trace marks on them with their fingers, or with sticks!"

Isn't it much more likely that the sun, moon and stars passed that way, during the procession of the equinox, and left those impressions of their visit on the towering cliffs? To concede that they are mere sculptures opens the door to a world of possibilities which we will not contemplate.

Cannot the slab of Nicaragua be removed north? It is really an interesting object whether viewed as the work of man's hands or feet. Connected with it there is an amazing story.

ON THE SUPPOSED HUMAN FOOT-PRINTS RECENTLY FOUND IN NEVADA
Marsh, O. C.; *American Journal of Science*, 3:26:139–140, 1883

During the past summer, various accounts have been published of the discovery of human foot-prints in sandstone near Carson, Nevada. The locality is in the yard of the State prison, and the tracks were uncovered in quarrying stone for building purposes. Many different kinds of tracks were found, some of which were made by an animal allied to the elephant; some resembled those of the horse and the deer; others were apparently made by a wolf. There were also tracks made by large birds.

The foot-prints occur in series, and are all nearly in the same horizon. Some of the smaller tracks are sharp and distinct, but most of the impressions are indefinite in outline, owing apparently to the fact that the exact surface on which they were made is not usually exposed.

The supposed human foot-prints are in six series, each with alternate right and left tracks. The stride is from two and one-half to over three feet in extent. The individual foot prints are from eighteen to twenty inches in length, and about eight inches wide. The distance between the line of right hand and left hand tracks, or the straddle, is eighteen to nineteen inches.

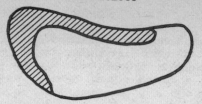

*The Nevada "human" footprints—typical sample from
the several series.*

The form and general appearance of the supposed human tracks is shown in the figure, which is a reduced copy
of one of the impressions represented by Dr. W. H. Hark-
ness, in his paper before the California Academy of Sciences, August 7th, 1882. The shaded portion was restored
by him from other foot-prints of the series. A copy of this
impression was given, also, by Professor Joseph LeConte,
in his paper before the same society, August 27th, 1882.

The size of these foot-prints, and especially the width between the right and left series are strong evidence that they
were not made by men, as has been so generally supposed.

A more probable explanation is that the impressions are
the tracks of a large Sloth, either *Mylodon* or *Morotherium*, remains of which have been found in essentially the
same horizon. In support of this view it may be said that
the foot-prints are almost exactly what these animals would
make, if the hind feet covered the impressions of those in
front. In size, in stride, and in width between the right and
left series of impressions, the foot-prints agree closely with
what we should expect *Mylodon* or *Morotherium* to make.

The geological horizon of these interesting foot-prints is
near the junction of the Pliocene and Quaternary. The evidence, at present, appears to point to the Equus beds of
the upper Pliocene as the nearest equivalent.

Since the above communication was read, the writer
has had an opportunity of examining photographs and
casts of the Carson foot-prints, and is confirmed in his
opinion that the supposed human tracks were made by
large Edentates. The important fact has recently been determined that some of these tracks show impressions of
the fore feet. The latter are somewhat outside of the
large foot-prints, as would naturally be the case, if the
animal changed its course.

2

The Mexican Messiah

This is one of the two one-article chapters of the book. This is not because there is not abundant material available but rather because Daly's contribution is so fascinating that it cannot be cut to less than chapter size. It is a superb summary of legends and history regarding Quetzalcoatl and pre-Columbian American messiahs.

The mystery of these irrepressible tales of the white messiahs of pre-Columbian days can be solved in several ways: (1) by attributing the legends to an actual pre-Columbian contact from Europe, such as St. Brendan (Daly's theory); (2) by denying that the Quezalcoatl stories are anything more than the babbling of primitive peoples; (3) by asserting that Quetzalcoatl was merely a particularly wise native American and that his achievements have been embellished by fictitious near-miraculous happenings; and (4) by going to the extraterrestrial extreme and proclaiming that Quetzalcoatl was the equivalent of a modern, UFO-riding "space brother" who dispersed the same platitudes that messiahs have for many centuries all over the world. Take your choice or construct your own explanation.

THE MEXICAN MESSIAH
Daly, Dominick; *American Antiquarian*, 11:14–30, 1889

There are few more puzzling characters to be found in the pages of history than Quetzatcoatl, the wandering stranger whom the early Mexicans adopted as the Air-God of their mythology. That he was a real personage; that he was a white man from this side of the Atlantic, who lived and taught in Mexico centuries before Columbus; that what he taught was Christianity and Christian manners and morals—all these are plausible inferences from facts and circumstances so peculiar as to render other conclusion well-nigh impossible.

When, in 1519, Cortez and his 600 companions landed in Mexico they were astonished at their coming being hailed as the realization of an ancient native tradition, which ran in this wise: Many centuries previously a white man had come to Mexico from across the sea (the Atlantic) in a boat with wings (sails) like those of the Spanish vessels. He stayed many years in the country and taught the people a system of religion, instructed them in principles of government, and imparted to them a knowledge of many industrial arts. He won their esteem and veneration by his piety, his many virtues, his great wisdom and his knowledge of divine things. His stay was a kind of golden age for Mexico. The seasons were uniformly favorable and the earth gave forth its produce almost spontaneously and in miraculous abundance and variety. In those days a single head of maize was a load for a man, the cotton trees produced quantities of cotton already tinted in many brilliant hues; flowers filled the air with delicious perfumes; birds of magnificent plumage incessantly poured forth the most exquisite melody. Under the auspices of this good white man, or god, peace, plenty and happiness prevailed throughout the land. The Mexicans knew him as Quetzatcoatl, or the green serpent, the word green in this language being a term for a rare and precious thing. Through some malign influence—brought about by the enmity of a rival deity—Quetzatcoatl was induced or obliged to quit the country. On his way to the coast he stayed for a time at the city of Cholula, where subsequently a great pyramidal mound surmounted by a temple was erected in his honor. On the shores of the gulf of Mexico he took leave of his followers, soothing their sorrow at his departure with the assurance that he would not forget them, and that he himself or some one sent by him would return at some future time to visit them. He had made for himself a vessel of serpents' skins, and in this strange contrivance he sailed away in a northeasterly direction for his own country, the holy island of Hapallan, lying beyond the great ocean.

Such in outline was the strange tradition which Cortez found prevalent in Mexico on his arrival there, and powerfully influencing every inhabitant of the country from the great Montezuma, who ruled as king paramount in the city of Mexico, to the humblest serf who tilled the fields of his lord. Equally to their surprise and advantage the Spaniards found that their advent was hailed as the fulfilment of the promise of Quetzatcoatl to return. The natives saw that they were white men and bearded like him, they had come in sailing vessels such as the one he had used across the sea; they had clearly come from the mysterious Hapallan; they were undoubtedly Quetzatcoatl and his brethren come, in fulfilment of ancient prophecy, to restore and permanently re-establish in Mexico the reign of peace and happiness of which the country had had a brief experience many centuries before.

The Spaniards made no scruple of encouraging and confirming a belief so highly favorable to their designs and it is conceded by their writers that this belief to a large extent accounts for the comparative ease and marvelous rapidity with which a mere handful of men made themselves masters of a great and civilized empire and subjugated a warlike population of millions. To the last the unfortunate emperor Montezuma, in spite of much evidence of the ungodlike character of the Spaniards held to the belief that the king of Spain was Quetzatcoatl and Cortez his lieutenant and emissary under a sort of divine commission.

The Mexicans had preserved a minute and apparently an accurate description of the personal appearance and habits of Quetzatcoatl. He was a white man, advanced in years and tall in stature. His forehead was broad; he had a large beard and black hair. He is described as dressing in a long garment, over which there was a mantle marked with crosses. He was chaste and austere, temperate and abstemious, fasting frequently and sometimes inflicting severe penances on himself, even to the drawing of blood. This is a description which was preserved for centuries in the traditions of a people who had no intercourse with or knowledge of Europe, who had never seen a white man, and who were themselves dark skinned with but few scanty hairs on the skin to represent a beard.

It is therefore difficult to suppose that this curiously ac-curate portraiture of Quetzatcoatl as an early European ecclesiastic was a mere invention in all its parts—a mere fable which happened to hit on every particular and characteristic of such an individual. Nor is it easier to understand why the early Mexicans should have been at pains to invent a messiah so different from themselves, and with such peculiar attributes. Yet in spite of destruc-tive wars, revolutions and invasions—in spite of the break-ing up and dispersal of tribes and nations once settled in the vast region now passing under the name of Mexico—the tradition of Quetzatcoatl and the account of his per-sonal peculiarities survived among the people to the days of the Spanish invasion. Everything therefore tends to show that Quetzatcoatl was an European who by some strange adventure was thrown amongst the Mexican peo-ple and left with them recollections of his beneficent in-fluence which time and change did not obliterate. But time and change must have done much in the course of cen-turies to confuse the teachings of Quetzatcoatl. These would naturally be more susceptible of mutation than the few striking items of his personal appearance which (if only on account of their singularity) must have deeply impressed the Mexicans, generation after generation. Not-withstanding such mutation enough remained of the teach-ings of Quetzatcoatl to impress the Spaniards of the six-teenth century with the belief that he must have been an early Christian missionary as well as a native of Europe. They found that many of the religious beliefs of the Mexi-cans bore an unaccountable resemblance to those of Christians. The Spanish ecclesiastics, in particular, were astounded at what they saw and knew not what to make of it. Some of them supposed that St. Thomas, "the apostle of India," had been in the country and imparted a knowl-edge of Christianity to the people; others with pious hor-ror and in mental bewilderment declared that the Evil One himself had set up a travesty of the religion of Christ for the more effectual damning of the souls of the pagan Mexi-cans.

The religion of the Mexicans as the Spaniards found it was in truth an amazing and most unnatural combination of what appeared to be Christian beliefs and Christian vir-tues and morality with the bloody rites and idolatrous prac-

tices of pagan barbarians. The mystery was soon explained
to the Spaniards by the Mexicans themselves. The milder
part of the Mexican religion was that which Quetzatcoatl
had taught them. He had taught it to the Toltecs, a people
who had ruled in Mexico some centuries before the arrival
of the Spaniards. The Aztecs were in possession of power
when the Spaniards came and it was they who had introduced that part of the Mexican religion which was in such
strong contrast to the religion established by Quetzatcoatl. It appeared further that the Toltec rule in the land
had ceased about the middle of the eleventh century. They
were a people remarkably advanced in civilization and
mental and moral development. Somewhere between the
latter part of the fourth century and the middle of the
seventh century they were supposed to have come into
Mexico from the Northeast—possibly from the Ohio valley, where vast remains of a strange character have been
found. They were versed in the arts and sciences, and their
astronomical knowledge was in many respects in advance
of that of Europe. They established laws and regular government in Mexico during their stay in the country, but
about the year 1050 A. D. they disappeared south by a
voluntary migration, the cause of which remains a mystery. They are supposed to have been, subsequently, the
builders of the great cities the marvelous remains of which
are found in the wilds of Central America. In the migration of the Toltecs some remained behind from choice or
necessity, but no attempt appears to have been made at
reestablishing a Toltec empire and government in Mexico.

After the lapse of a century or more from the era of
the great Toltec migration the first bands of Aztecs began
to appear. They were wanderers from the Northwest, the
Pacific slopes of North America, and were a fierce and
warlike people, possessing little capacity for the mental and
moral refinement and high civilization of their Toltec predecessors. It was not until the middle of the fourteenth
century that the Aztecs acquired sufficient settled habits to
enable them to found states and cities, and by that time they
seem to have adopted so much of what had been left of
Toltec civilization and Toltec religion as they were capable
of absorbing, without, however, abandoning their own
ruder ideas and propensities. Hence the incongruous mixture of civilization and barbarism, mildness and ferocity,

gentleness and cruelty, refinement and brutality, presented by Mexican civilization and religion to the astonished contemplation of the Spaniards when they entered the city two centuries later. "Aztec civilization was made up" (as Prescott, the author of the History of Mexico, says), "of incongruities apparently irreconcilable. It blended into one the marked peculiarities of different nations, not only of the same phase of civilization, but as far removed from each other as the extremes of barbarism and refinement."

* * * * * * * * * * * * * * *

All that was savage and barbarous in the religious rites of the Mexicans was attributed by the Mexicans themselves to the Aztecs; all that was gentle and humanizing to the Toltecs, and probably with substantial justice in each instance. To a Toltec origin was assigned those doctrines and practices which struck the Spaniards as remnants of an

Aerial view of a cross in Pickaway County, Ohio, probably built by the pre-Columbian moundbuilder Indians. Did very early trans-Atlantic crossings introduce Christian symbols before 1492?

early knowledge of Christianity. The Aztecs only came into the inheritance of those doctrines and practices at second hand—that is from the remnants of the Toltec people. The new-comers were probably little disposed to submit wholly to the influence of alien religious ideas essentially different from their own gloom and sanguinary notions of divine things. Some they adopted, while still retaining their own national observances, and hence the extraordinary mixture of brutality and gentleness presented to the wondering contemplation of the Spaniards by the Mexican cult as they found it in the early part of the sixteenth century. The better, that is the Toltec side of this mixed belief included amongst its chief features a recognition of a supreme God, vested with all the attributes of the Jehovah of the Jews. He was the creator and the ruler of the universe, and the fountain of all good. Subordinate to him were a number of minor deities, and opposed to him a father of all evil. There was a paradise for the abode of the just after death, and a place of darkness and torment for the wicked. There was an intermediate place which was not perhaps so much a purgatory as a second-class heaven. There had been a common mother of all men, always pictorially represented as in company with a serpent. Her name was Cicacoatl, or "the serpent woman," and it was held that "by her sin came into the world." She had twin children, and in an Aztec picture preserved in the Vatican at Rome those children are represented as quarreling. The Mexicans believed in a universal deluge, from which only one family (that of Coxcox) escaped. Nevertheless, and inconsistently enough with this, they spoke of a race of wicked giants, who had survived the flood and built a pyramid in order to reach the clouds; but the gods frustrated their design by raining fire upon it. Tradition associated the great pyramid at Cholula with this event. This was the pyramid which had been erected to Quetzatcoatl, and which had a temple on the summit dedicated to the worship of him as the god of air. The Mexicans regarded Cholula as the one holy city—the Jerusalem or Mecca of their country—from having been the place of abode of Quetzatcoatl. The pyramid in a dilapidated condition still remains, and is surmounted by a chapel for Christian worship. It is scarcely necessary to suggest that the traditions of Cicacoatl, Coxcox, the giants and the pyramid at Cholula, are extremely like a confused acquaintance with biblical narratives.

The foregoing are merely specimens of the more remarkable features of Mexican belief, and they are so special and peculiar in character as to leave no reasonable alternative to the supposition that the Mexicans must have had imparted to them at one time a knowledge of the bible. This has induced in some quarters the opinions that the Mexicans are descendants of the lost tribes of Israel; but whatever may be the arguments for or against this theory, the still more abundant knowledge of a Christian-like character

possessed by the ancient Mexicans is strongly suggestive of
Christian teaching, which would sufficiently account for
familiarity with narratives contained in the Old Testament.

Whether due to such teaching or to accidental coincidence, it is certain that the Mexicans held many points of
belief in common with Christians. They believed in the
Trinity, the Incarnation, and apparently the Redemption.
One of the first things which struck the Spaniards on their
arrival in Mexico was the spectacle of large stone crosses
on the coast and in the interior of the country. These were
objects of veneration and worship. One cross or marble
near one of the places the Spaniards named Vera Cruz was
surmounted by a golden crown, and in answer to the curious inquiries of the Spanish ecclesiastics the natives said
that "one more glorious than the sun had died upon a
cross." In other places the Spaniards were informed that
the cross was a symbol of the god of rain. At any rate it
was an object of divine association and consequent adoration. In the magnificent pictoral reproduction of Mexican
antiquities published by Lord Kingsborough there is a remarkable sketch of a monument representing a group of
ancient Mexicans in attitudes of adoration around a cross
of the Latin form. The leading figure is that of a king or
priest holding in his outstretched hands a young infant,
which he appears to be presenting to the cross.

Further acquaintance with the people and their religious
ideas disclosed to the Spaniards additional evidence of
Christian-like beliefs. They believed in original sin and
practiced infant baptism. At the naming of the infant the
lips and bosom of the child were sprinkled with water and
the Lord was implored to "permit the holy drops to wash
away the sin that was given to it before the foundation of
the world, so that the child might be born anew."

Confession to the priests, absolution and penance, were
also features of the Mexican religion. The secrets of the
confessional were esteemed inviolable. Absolution not only
effaced moral guilt but was held to free the penitent from
responsibility for breaches of the secular law. Long after
the Spaniards had established their rule in the country it
was a common thing for native culprits, especially in the
remoter districts, to demand acquittal on the plea that they
had confessed their crimes to the priest.

The Mexican prayers and invocations were strongly

Christian in character. The priestly exhortation, after confession, was—"Feed the hungry and clothe the naked according to your circumstances, for all men are of one flesh." Another form of exhortation was—"Live in peace with all men; bear injuries with humility; leave vengeance to God, who sees everything." Among the invocations to the deity was the following—"Wilt thou blot us out, O Lord, forever? Is this punishment intended not for our reformation but for our destruction?" Again, "Impart to us, out of Thy great mercy, Thy gifts, which we are not worthy to receive through our own merits." A still more striking similarity to scriptural morality and expression is contained in the admonition—"He who looks too curiously on a woman commits adultery with his eyes."

The Mexicans believed in the doctrine of transubstantiation in its strictest form, and even in its Roman Catholic peculiarity of communion under one kind. Communion and administration of the eucharist took place at stated intervals. The priest broke off morsels from a sanctified cake of maize and administered it to the communicant as he lay prostrate on the ground. Both priest and communicant regarded the material as the very body of God himself. The religious consumption of a horrible mixture of maize and human blood, and sometimes flesh, has already been alluded to as associated with the worship of the Aztec war god, Huitzilopochtli, and is suggestive of an Aztec perversion of the Christian, and apparently Toltec, idea of transubstantiation. On some occasions a model of the god was formed out of a paste of maize flour tempered by the blood of young children sacrificed for the purpose, the figure being subsequently consumed by the worshipers.

The Mexicans priesthood had much in common, and little in conflict, with the priesthood of the papacy. Celibacy was esteemed a merit and was observed by certain orders, though not by all; but all were governed by rules of a monastic character, very similar and quite as severe as those in force in the earlier ages of the Christian church. Thrice during the day and once at night the priests lodging in the great temples were called to prayer. They also mortified the flesh by fasting and abstinence, by severe penances, flagellations, and piercing the flesh with sharp thorns. They undertook the entire education of the young and devoted themselves to works of charity. The great cities and rural districts were divided into parishes, each presided over by a priest. These priests were of a different order and had different functions from the priests who lived and served in the temples, and seem to have been in all important respects similar to the regular parochical clergy of Christian countries. The inference to be drawn by students of early Mexican history from these apparent remnants of Christian teaching is very much a matter of personal capacity and individual idiosyncrasy. Probably the majority will conclude that the Mexicans must have had Christian enlightenment from some source at a time long antecedent to the Spanish invasion. That such enlightenment should have become obscure and confused in the lapse of centuries, through the operation of revolutions, and by contact with Aztec idolatry, would not be surprising; the only wonder would be that so much that was still Christian-like should remain at the beginning of the 16th century. Was it then remains of Christianity which the Spaniards found? There is no reason to doubt the concurrent testimony of their writers and historians, lay and clerical, as to what they *did* find. There could be no adequate motive for a general conspiracy amongst them to manufacture evidence and invent fables for the purpose of making it appear that the people whom they were about to plunder, enslave and slaughter were a sort of Christian. On the contrary, their expressions of surprise and horror at finding Christian doctrines and Christian practices, intermingled with the grossest idolatry and most barbarous and bloody rites, are too natural and genuine to be mistaken. They—the direct observers and with the best opportunities for judging—had no doubt that what they saw was a debased form of Christianity. The points of resemblance with real Christianity were too numerous and too peculiar to permit the supposition that the similarity was accidental and unreal. With them the only difficulty was to account for the possession of Christian knowledge by a people so remote and outlandish—or rather to trace the identity of Quetzatcoatl, the undoubted teacher of the Mexicans. Their choice lay between the devil and St. Thomas. However respectable the claims of the former, it is clear enough that the St. Thomas was not Quetzatcoatl and had never been in Mexico. He was dragged in at all because the Spaniards long clung to the idea that America was a part of India, and St. Thomas was styled "the Apostle of India," on the authority of an ancient and pious but very doubtful tradition. The weakness of the case for St. Thomas secured a preference for the claims of the devil, and the consensus of Spanish opinion favored the idea that Quetzacock [sic] was indeed the devil himself, who, aroused by the losses which Christ had inflicted upon him in the old world, had sought compensation in the new, and had beguiled the Mexicans into the acceptance of a blasphemous mockery of the religion of Christ infinitely more wicked and damnatory than the worst form of paganism.

Another theory as to the identity of Quetzatcoatl may here be noticed. Lord Kingsborough makes the startling suggestion that Quetzatcoatl was no other than Christ himself, and in support of this maintains that the phonetic rendering, in the Mexican language, of the two words "Jesus Christ" would be as nearly as possible "Quetzat Coatl." He does not mean to say that Christ was ever in Mexico, but his suggestion is that the Mexicans, having obtained an early knowledge of Christianity, and become acquainted with the name and character of its Divine Founder, imagined in subsequent ages that Christ had actually been in Mexico, and so built up the tradition of Quetzatcoatl. But this theory does not get rid—on the contrary makes essential—the presence of a missionary in Mexico through whom the people were instructed in the truths of Christianity, and from whom they obtained a knowledge of Christ. It is of course possible that in the lapse of ages the Mexicans might have transferred to this missionary the name of the great founder of his religion, but that there was no confusion of personalities is obvious, for in age and in many personal peculiarities Quetzatcoatl is represented as very different from the earthly figure of Christ. It may further be noted that the term "Quetzatcoatl" has a clear and appropriate significance ("Green Serpent") in the Mexican language, and this is somewhat inconsistent with the supposition that it is a close phonetic rendering of the words "Jesus Christ." In fact Lord Kingsborough's ingenious and not wholly improbable theory in no degree helps to the identity of the early Christian missionary called Quetzatcoatl.

But whoever Quetzatcoatl may have been, and whatever might be the right designation of the religion which he taught, it is clear beyond question that he was the medium through which the Mexicans obtained their curious Christianlike knowledge. To him there is no rival. The Aztecs claimed the honor of being the importers of the terrible Huitzilopochtli and all the unholy rites connected with his worship. They, and all other Mexicans, agreed in assigning the milder features of Mexican worship to the teachings of Quetzatcoatl. To him also they attributed the foundation of the monastic institutions and clerical systems, and the introduction of baptism, confession, communion, and all the beliefs, ceremonies, and practices, having a greater or less resemblance to those of the Christian religion.

It is, therefore, hard to understand what it was that Quetzatcoatl taught if it was not Christianity, and equally hard to conceive what he could have been if he were not a Christian missionary. His personality and attributes are altogether, and without a single exception or the slightest qualification, those of an early Christian missionary. A white man, with all the peculiarities of an European, teaches to a remote and isolated pagan people *something,* the remnants of which in after centuries bears an extraordinary resemblance to Christianity. Could that "something," coming from such a source, be other than Christianity? The teacher himself is depicted as a perfect and exalted type of a Christian missionary, though the Mexicans could have had no model to guide them in their delineation of such a character. The "Lives of the Saints," the "Annals of the Faith," any records of the lives and labors of pious and devoted Christian missionaries, supply no more perfect nor more Christian-like character than that of Quetzatcoatl. Long, earnestly and successfully he preached the worship of the great unseen but all present God, and taught the Mexicans to trust in an omnipotent and benevolent Father in heaven. He preached peace and good will amongst men, and he "stopped his ears when war was spoken of." He encouraged and taught the cultivation of the earth, and the arts and sciences of peace and civilization. He conferred upon the Mexicans, through the great influence he seems to have obtained over them, so many material benefits that in after ages they exaggerated the period of his rule into a veritable golden age, and impiously exalted himself into a deity of the most benevolent attributes. The impression he made was indeed so profound that the memory of his virtues and good works survived and were exaggerated through centuries of change and trouble, and made him acceptable as a god even to the rude intruding barbarians, who only learnt of him remotely and at second hand, ages after the completion of his mission. Chaste, frugal, earnest, self denying, laborious, he stands depicted in Mexican tradition as the highest specimen of an apostolic saint or early Christian missionary. Can he then be an imaginary person? Could the early Mexican pagans have evolved such a character from their own fancy, or created it out of pagan materials? The thing seems incredible. It would indeed be a curious thing if the Mexicans—never having seen a white man, and wholly ignorant of European ideas and beliefs—had invented a fable of a white man sojourning amongst them; it would be still more curious if, in addition to this, they had invented another fable of that white man instructing them in European religion and morals. The white man without the teaching might be a possible but still a doubtful story; the teaching without the white man would be difficult to believe; but the white man and the teaching together make up a complete and consistent whole almost precluding the possibility of invention.

Three points in relation to Quetzatcoatl seem well established: (1) He was a white man from across the Atlantic; (2) he taught religion to the Mexicans; (3) the religion he taught retained to after ages many strong and striking resemblances to Christianity. The conclusion seems unavoidable—that Quetzatcoatl was a Christian missionary from Europe who taught Christianity to the Mexicans or Toltecs.

Accepting this as established, the possibility of fixing the European identity of Quetzatcoatl presents itself as a curious but obviously difficult question. To begin with, the era of Quetzatcoatl is not known with any precision. It has a possible range of some six and a half centuries—from before the beginning of the fourth century to the middle of the tenth century—that is from about A. D. 400 to A. D. 1050, which is the longest time assigned to Toltec domination in Mexico. The era of Quetzatcoatl may, however, be safely confined to narrower limits. The Toltecs must have been well established in the country before Quetzatcoatl appeared amongst them, and he must have left some considerable time before their migration from Mexico. The references to Quetzatcoatl's visits to the Toltec cities prove the former, and the time which would have been required to arrange for and complete the great pyramid built at Cholula in his honor, and after his departure, proves the latter. From a century to two centuries may be allowed at each end of the period between A. D. 400 and A. D. 1050, and it may be assumed with some degree of probability that Quetzatcoatl's visit to Mexico took place some time between (say) A. D. 500 and A. D. 900.

If attention is directed to the condition of Europe during that time it will be found that the period from about A. D. 500 to A. D. 800 was one of great missionary activity. Before the former date the church was doing little more than feeling its way and asserting itself against the pagan supremacy in the basin of the Mediterranean and elsewhere. After the latter date the incursions and devastations of the northern barbarians paralyzed European missionary efforts. But from the beginning of the fifth century to the beginning of the eighth there was no limit to missionary enterprise, and if even a Christian missionary had appeared in Mexico all probability favors the theory that he must have gone there during those centuries. The era of Quetzatcoatl may therefore be narrowed to those three hundred years, and the task of tracing his identity thus simplified to some slight extent.

It may now be asked: Is it reasonable to expect that there are, or ever were, any European records of the period from A. D. 500 to A. D. 800 referring to any missionary who might have been Quetzatcoatl? It is a long time since Quetzatcoatl, whoever he was, sailed from the shores of Europe to carry the truths of Christianity into the unknown regions beyond the Atlantic, but the literary records of his assumed period are numerous and minute and might possibly have embraced some notice of his undertaking. It seems unlikely that his enterprise would have escaped attention altogether, especially from the ecclesiastical chroniclers, who were not given to ignoring the good works of their fellow religionists. Moreover, the mission of Quetzatcoatl was not one which could have been launched quietly or obscurely, nor was there any reason why it should be. The contemplated voyage must have been a matter of public knowledge and comment in some locality; it could not have been attempted without preparations on some scale of magnitude; and such preparations for such a purpose must have attracted at least local attention and excited local interest. It is thus reasonable to suppose that the importance and singularity of a project to cross the Atlantic for missionary purposes would have insured some record being made of the enterprise. *A fortiori* if the venturesome missionary ever succeeded in returning—if he ever came back to tell of his wonderful adventures—the fact would have been chronicled by his religions confreres and made the most of, then and for the benefit of future ages. It comes therefore to this—accepting Quetzatcoatl as a Christian missionary from Europe we have right and reason to expect that his singular and pious expedition would have been put upon record somewhere.

The next step in the inquiry is to search for the most likely part of Europe to have been the scene of the going forth and possible return of this missionary. The island of Hapallan, says the Mexican tradition, was the home from whence he came and whither he sought to return. The name of the country afforded us assistance, and it might not be safe to attach importance to its insular designation. But in looking for a country in Western Europe— possibly an island—which, from A. D. 500 to A. D. 800, *might* have sent out a missionary on a wild trans-Atlantic expedition, one is soon struck with the possibility of Ireland being such a country. To the question, "Could Ireland have been the Hapallan, or Holy Island, of the Mexican tradition?" an affirmative answer may readily be given, especially by any one who knows even a little of the ecclesiastical history of the country from A. D. 500 to A. D. 800. In that period no country was more forward in missionary enterprise. The Irish ecclesiastics shrunk from no adventures of land or sea, however desperate and dangerous, when the eternal salvation of heathen peoples was in question. On land they penetrated to all parts of the continent, preaching the gospel of Christ and founding churches and religious establishments. On sea they made voyages for like purposes to the remotest known lands of the northern and western seas. They went as missionaries to all parts of the coast of Northern Britain, and visited the Hebrides, the Orkneys, and the Shetland and Faro Islands. Even remote Iceland received their pious attention, and Christianity was established by them in that island long before it was taken possession of by the Norwegians in the eighth century.

Prima facie, then, Ireland has not only a good claim, but really the best claim to be the Hapallan of the Mexicans. It is the most western part of Europe; it is insular, and in the earlier centuries of the Christian era was known as the "Holy Island"; between A. D. 500 and 800 it was the most active centre of missionary enterprise in Europe, and its missionaries were conspicuous above all others for their daring maritime adventures. It is natural therefore to suspect that Ireland may have been the home of Quetzatcoàtl, and, if that were so, to expect that early Irish records would certainly contain some references to him and his extraordinary voyage. Upon this the inquiry suggests itself: Do the early Irish chronicles, which are voluminous and minute, contain anything relating to a missionary voyage across the Atlantic at all corresponding to that which Quetzatcoatl must have taken from some part of Western Europe?

To one who, step by step, had arrived at this stage of the present inquiry, it was not a little startling to come across an obscure and almost forgotten record which is, in all its main features, in most striking conformity with the Mexican legend of Quetzatcoatl. This is the curious account of the trans-Atlantic voyage of a certain Irish ecclesiastic named St. Brendan in the middle of the sixth century—about A. D. 550. The narrative appears to have attracted little or no attention in modern times, but it was widely diffused during the Middle Ages. In the Bibliotheque at Paris there are said to be no less than eleven MSS. of the original Latin narrative, the dates of which range from the eleventh to the fourteenth centuries. It is also stated that versions of it, in old French and Romance, exist in most of the public libraries of France; and in many other parts of Europe there are copies of it in Irish, Dutch, German, Italian, Spanish and Portuguese. It is reproduced in Irsher's "Antiquities," and is to be found in the Cottonian collection of MSS.

This curious account of St. Brendan's voyage may be altogether a romance, as it has long been held to be, but the remarkable thing about it is the singularity of its general concurrence with the Mexican tradition of Quetzat-coatl.

St. Brendan—called "The Navigator," from his many voyages was an Irish bishop who in his time founded a great monastery at Cloufert, on the shores of Kerry, and was the head of a confraternity or order of 3,000 monks. The story of his trans-Atlantic voyage is as follows: From the eminence now called after him, Brendan Mountain, the saint had long gazed upon the Atlantic at his feet and speculated on the perilous condition of the souls of the unconverted peoples who possibly inhabited unknown countries on the other side. At length, in the cause of Christianity and for the glory of God, he resolved upon a missionary expedition across the ocean, although he was then well advanced in years. With this purpose he caused a stout bark to be constructed and provisioned for a long voyage, a portion of his supplies consisting of five swine. Taking with him some trusty companions he sailed from Tralee Bay, at the foot of Brendan Mountain, in a southwesterly direction. The voyage lasted many weeks, during several of which the vessel was carried along by a strong current without need of help from oars or sail. In the land which he ultimately reached the saint spent seven years in instructing the people in the truths of Christianity. He then left them, promising to return at some future time. He arrived safely in Ireland, and, in after years (mindful of the promise he had made to his trans-Atlantic converts) he embarked on a second voyage. This, however, was frustrated by contrary winds and currents, and he returned to Ireland, where he died in 575 at the ripe age of 94 and "in the adorn of sanctity."

It would be idle to expect a plain matter of fact account of St. Brendan's voyage from the chroniclers of the sixth century. The narrative is, in fact, interwoven with several supernatural occurrences. But eliminating these there remains enough of apparently real incident worthy of serious attention. The whole story, as already suggested, may be a mere pious fable promulgated and accepted in a noncritical and ignorant and credulous age. If substantially true the fact could not be verified in such an age; if a pure invention its falsity can not now be demonstrated. All that can be said about it is that it is in wonderful agreement with what is known or may be inferred from the Mexican legend. The story of St. Brendan's voyage was written long before Mexico was heard of, and if forged it could not have been with a view to offering a plausible explanation of a singular Mexican tradition. And yet the explanation which it offers of that tradition is so complete and apropos on all material points as almost to preclude the idea of accidental coincidence. In respect to epoch, personal characteristics, race, religion, direction of coming and going—the Mexican Quetzatcoatl might well have been the Irish saint. Both were white men, both were advanced in years, both crossed the Atlantic from the direction of Europe, both preached Christianity and Christian practices, both returned across the Atlantic to an insular home or Holy Island, both promised to come back and failed in doing so. These are at least remarkable coincidences, if accidental.

The date of St. Brendan's voyage—the middle of the sixth century—is conveniently within the limits which probability would assign to the period of Quetzatcoatl's sojourn in Mexico, namely from about the fifth to the eighth centuries. The possibility of making a voyage in such an age from the Western shores of Europe to Mexico is proved by the fact that the voyage was made by others at about the same time. The probability of St. Brendan designing such a voyage is supported alike by the renown of the saint as a "navigator," and by the known maritime enterprises and enthusiastic missionary spirit of the Irish of his time; the supposition that he succeeded in his design is countenanced by the ample preparations he is said to have made for the voyage.

There is a disagreement between the Mexican tradition and the Irish narrative in respect to the stay of the white man in Mexico. Quetzatcoatl is said to have remained twenty years in the country, but only seven years—seven Easters—are assigned to the absence of St. Brendan from his monastery. Either period would probably suffice for laying the foundations of the Christianity the remnants of which the Spaniards found in the beginning of the sixteenth century. On this point the Irish record is more likely to be correct. The Mexican tradition was already very ancient when the Spaniards became acquainted with it—as ancient as the sway of the vanished Toltecs. For centuries it had been handed down from generation to generation, and not always through generations of the same people. It is therefore conceivable that it may have undergone variations in some minor particulars, and that a stay of seven years became exaggerated into one of twenty years. The discrepancy is not a serious one, and is in no sense a touchstone of the soundness of the theory that Quetzatcoatl and St. Brendan may have been one and the same person.

A curious feature in the Mexican tradition is its apparently needless insistency upon the point that Quetzatcoatl sailed away from Mexico in a vessel made of a serpents' skins. There seems no special reason for attributing this extraordinary mode of navigation to him. If the design were to enhance his supernatural attributes some more strikingly miraculous mode of exit could easily have been invented. The first impulse accordingly is to reject this part of the tradition as hopelessly inexplicable—as possibly allegorical in some obscure way, or as originating in a misnomer, or in the mis-translation of an ancient term. But further consideration suggests the possibility of their being more truth in the "serpents' skins" than appears at first sight. In the absence of large quadrupeds in their country the ancient Mexicans made use of serpents' skins as a substitute for hides. The great drums on the top of their temple-crowned pyramids were, Cortez states, made of the skins of a large species of serpent, and when beaten for alarum could be heard for miles around. It may therefore be that Quetzatcoatl in preparing for his return voyage across the Atlantic made use of the skins of serpents or crocodiles to cover the hull of his vessel and render it water-tight. The Mexicans were not boat-builders and were unacquainted with the use of tar or pitch, employing only canoes dug out of the solid timber. When Cortez was building the brigandines with which he attacked the City of Mexico from the lake, he had to manufacture the tar he required from such available trees as he could find. Quetzatcoatl may have used serpents' skins for a similar purpose, and such use would imply that the vessel in which he sailed away was not a mere canoe, but a built-up boat. If he was really St. Brendan nothing is more likely than that he would seek for a substitute for tar or pitch in skins of some sort. Coming from the west coast of Ireland, he would be familiar with the native currahs, couracles, or hide-covered boats then in common use (and not yet wholly discarded) for coasting purposes, and sometimes for voyages to the coasts of Britain and continent of Europe. Some of these were of large size and capable of carrying a small mast, the body being a stout frame work of ash ribs covered with hides of oxen, sometimes of threefold thickness. It may have been a vessel of this kind which Quetzatcoatl constructed for his return voyage, or it may be that he employed the serpents' skins for protecting the seams of his built-up boat in lieu of tar or pitch. In any case the tradition makes him out a navigator and boat-builder of some experience, and if he were really St. Brendan he would have had a knowledge of the Irish mode of constructing and navigating sea-going crafts and would probably have employed serpents' skins, the best Mexican substitute for ox-hides, at either of the ways suggested.

It would be presumptuous to claim that the identity of Quetzatcoatl and St. Brendan has been completely established in this essay, but it may reasonably be submitted that there is no violent inconsistency involved in the theory herein advanced, and an examination of the evidence upon which it is based discloses many remarkable coincidences in favor of the opinion that the Mexican Messiah *may* have been the Irish saint. Beyond that it would not be safe to go, and it is not probable that future discoveries will enable the identity of Quetzatcoatl to be more clearly traced. It is a part of the Mexican tradition that Quetzatcoatl, before leaving Mexico, concealed a collection of silver and shell objects, and other precious things, by burial. The discovery of such a treasure would no doubt show that he was a Christian missionary, and would probably settle the question of his nationality and identity. But the deposit may have been discovered and destroyed or dispersed long ago, and if not there is little probability now that it will ever see the light of day. It would be equally hopeless to expect that Mexican records may yet be discovered containing references to Quetzatcoatl. A thousand years may have elapsed from the time of that personage to the days of Cortez, and since then nearly another four hundred years have contributed to the further destruction of Mexican monuments and records. In the earlier days of the Spanish Conquest, all the memorials of the subjugated races were ruthlessly and systematically destroyed, and so effectually that but comparatively few scraps and fragments remain of native historical materials which formerly existed in great abundance. Even these remnants are for the most part useless, for in a single generation or two of Spanish fanaticism and Spanish egotism destroyed all use and knowledge of the native Mexican languages and literature. It may, therefore, be concluded that we know all we are ever likely to know of the history and personality of the Mexican Messiah, and what we do know is this—that he was a Christian missionary from Europe, and is more likely to have been St. Brendan than any other European of whom we have knowledge.

3

Ancient Canals and Waterworks

Sensational Archaeology dwells upon the Pyramids, Stonehenge, Easter Island, and the other stone architecture of the ancient world. How were these great stones cut and moved? What marvelous feats of engineering! The same awe and wonder could well be applied to the more prosaic water-handling structures built by these supposedly unsophisticated peoples. The quantities of earth moved in these enterprises were stupendous even in these days of mountain-chomping diesel-powered machines. In addition, the engineering know-how displayed in the design of Britain's dew ponds and Arizona's canal system deserves our admiration. Equally impressive waterworks can be found all over the world: North Africa's irrigation network, South America's ridged fields, Ohio's artificial terraces, and so on. Here, space allows us to serve only a few hors d'oeuvres.

Why did ancient man undertake such massive tasks? Mostly to grow more food. Banish the thought that primitive populations were always sparse. The adobe buildings constructed by the Arizona canal builders reached five and more stories and contained hundreds of rooms. To feed such dense populations, agriculture had to be intensive. Some canals, such as those in Florida, may have been simply waterways. We cannot be certain, but why else would anyone dig huge trenches miles long connecting two bodies of water? Perhaps the big mystery is the nature of the commerce that required such canals.

THE HOHOKAM CANALS AT PUEBLO GRANDE, ARIZONA

Woodbury, Richard B.; *American Antiquity,* 26:267–270, 1961

Interest in the surviving, visible remains of ancient irrigation canals in southern Arizona and northern Sonora has been long and intense, going back at least to Manje's careful notes on the canal at Casa Grande ruin in 1697 (Karns 1954), and including such observant travelers as Rusling (1877) and the records of several local residents, particularly Patrick (1903) and Turney (1929). Nevertheless, the body of information available has consisted largely of unsystematic comments on the surface appearance of these canal remnants, and the investigation of Hohokam irrigation by archaeological techniques has proceeded very slowly. The work that Cushing directed at Los Muertos was reported by Hodge (1893) and supplemented by Haury's monograph (1945) which also summarized the available information on the subject. The only thorough excavation of a Hohokam canal that has been reported is the cross sectioning at Snaketown in 1935 which provided clear association between the stages of construction and use of the canal and the ceramic sequence being worked out at the site. On this basis it was possible to assign the beginning of the Snaketown canal to about A.D. 800 and suggest that it was in use for about 500 years. Careful mapping of the entire surviving Hohokam canal system, making use of aerial photographs, was begun by the Smithsonian Institution in 1930 but never completed due to the pressure of other activities and the lack of funds.

The interdisciplinary program in the utilization of arid lands which is being carried on at the University of Arizona with financial support from the Rockefeller Foundation of New York has made it possible to examine several surviving Hohokam canals, including (during October and November, 1959) the well-known pair of canals in the Park of Four Waters, Phoenix. This city park, of about 10 acres extent, is located just across the modern Grand Canal and the Southern Pacific tracks from the Pueblo Grande Museum, in the stockyards area of eastern Phoenix. Although the location is far from scenic, surrounded as it is with industrial activities, it has been protected from the encroachments that have destroyed all trace of most prehistoric canals in the Salt River Valley.

Prior to this recent excavation, which is reported in preliminary form here, the canals at Pueblo Grande were marked by two pairs of conspicuous parallel ridges, the remains of the banks which several centuries of erosion had not yet leveled. The actual channels were filled to about the level of the surrounding land, although the height of the banks gave the illusion of two deep channels. Both canals trend to the west and northwest, gradually swinging away from the Salt River which lies nearby on the south. At their eastern ends they are so close together that their adjacent banks merged into a single bank. This has been thought in the past to indicate that either (a) they forked just to the east from a common parent canal, now entirely destroyed by recent floods of the Salt, or (b) they both headed here, at a time when the Salt flowed closer to the spot than it does now. As will be shown, both of these beliefs are almost certainly wrong. The canals, at the point investigated, run along a low terrace of the river, only a couple of meters above the present channel, which is here nearly a half mile wide but flowing only in rare floods.

Excavation of a cross section of these canals was greatly aided by the generous loan of a Gradall, with its two operators, by the Salt River Valley Water Users Association. The 60-m. trench with sloping sides which the Gradall dug to a depth of two to three meters was further deepened by hand where it crossed the filled channels of the two canals, and one wall was cleaned to permit observation of the stratigraphy.

One of the most impressive revelations of this trench was the size of the original canals, about 10 and 6 m. wide at the former ground level, and about 26 and 18 m. wide from crest to crest of the banks. Also, the fact that subsequent filling of the channels had raised the level between the banks to slightly higher than the original ground level is of interest, since it vitiates inferences that have been made in the past concerning the relationship of river channel elevation and canal elevation. Such inferences have been based only on observations of present surface indication, which this cross section shows to be inadequate for estimating original depth (or profile).

The North and South canals proved to be quite different in profile, the North Canal being flat-bottomed with the sides sloping at about 35°, the South Canal V-shaped in profile with the lower part of the sides sloping at 50° to 60°. Nevertheless, they contained rather similar fills, ranging from coarse sand through fine sand to silt, much of it laminated and indicating successive phases of deposition, with either periodic intentional cleaning or natural removal of the deposits. Both canals were dug through an otherwise undisturbed layer of fine-grained, river-laid sand ranging in thickness from 1.5 to 2.0 m., and both were dug into underlying coarse gravel, a most unpromising material for holding the water that the canals were constructed to carry. There is, of course, a possibility that the water table was high enough in ancient times for the canal bottom to have penetrated it, and thus considerably reduced the loss of water in transit. However, in the North Canal, the remains of a substantial clay lining were found resting on the lowest of the sandy fills in the channel. The lining consists of a compact, homogeneous layer of chocolate brown clay, from 5 to 9 cm. thick, with a cracked and uneven upper surface as though exposed to the sun. Careful examination revealed no lamination or horizontal structure within the clay, such as would indicate that it was naturally deposited in standing water. Furthermore, although the layer of clay was not traceable across the bottom of the canal, where it had probably eroded away, it was well preserved for a considerable distance up the sides; if this were the remnant of a water-laid layer it would have originally been over a meter thick, a wholly unreasonable deposit in such circumstances. Instead, the evidence points clearly to its having been laid by hand, with clay brought from a source not yet identified but possibly within a few miles. The total extent of this clay layer can only be guessed, but its presence was verified in test pits 40 and 145 m. to the west. With an observable width of at least 8 m., and assuming a minimum thickness of 5 cm., such a lining would have needed at least four-tenths of a cubic meter of clay for every linear meter of canal. Only a very critical need could have justified bringing in such a quantity of material. The need was undoubtedly for a canal bottom that would lose less of its water in transit, as the channel is here dug into coarse material into which water would percolate easily. Many modern irrigation canals are, of course, lined with concrete for the same purpose, the cost being more than offset by the saving in water. No other Hohokam canal has been found with an identifiable lining, although some early and unsubstantiated reports mention the use of adobe or clay for this purpose. It is doubtful if this was ever a common practice but in this instance there seems little doubt that at least part of a large canal was carefully lined to render it practically watertight, even though the cost in labor must have been enormous. It should be noted that the canal saw use for at least a short time prior to the addition of the lining, as shown by the deposit underlying it.

The canal banks are made up, as would be expected, initially of the material excavated from the channels during construction. All three banks contain at the base, unstratified sandy material identical with the undisturbed material below it except for the latter's laminated condition. The presence of a few sherds at the contact between the stratified and the homogeneous material helped in determining the position of the original ground level. As the construction of the canals progressed and the diggers encountered coarse gravel, this was piled on the banks above the finer, sandy level. This gravel, being the last material dug out of the channels, should have formed the tops of the banks, and probably did at first. But the banks were further augmented by fine material, silt and sand, cleared from the channels, so that today the banks still stand 2.0 to 3.0 m. high even after enough material has been washed down from them to completely refill the canals. This should, then, be a rough indication of the quantity of sand and silt dredged from the channels during the years that they were kept in use.

It was hoped that clear evidence would be found in the central bank, shared by both canals, for the priority of one canal or the other. This proved difficult to determine, as no clear line could be found separating the material piled onto the bank from the North and South canals. Nevertheless, the position of the gravelly zones in this central bank suggests that the larger zone, extending from 44 to 48 m. in the profile, comes from the South Canal, and is overlain by finer material at its north end as a result of the subsequent excavation of the North Canal. The position of two smaller gravelly zones high in the north side of the central bank also suggests that the North Canal was dug after the South Canal had been in use long enough to require considerable clearing. Therefore, it is probable but not certain that the South Canal is the older.

The difference in elevation between the bottoms of the canals is of considerable interest. If the two canals were branches of a parent canal (now destroyed by the river), they would have to be approximately the same elevation. Therefore, this widely-held belief must be discarded. The bottom of the South Canal is about 1.5 m. below the bottom of the North Canal, and is about the same elevation as the dry bed of the Salt immediately to the south. It is possible, therefore, that the South Canal headed only a short distance to the east; the North Canal would have had to head some little distance further upstream to gain its higher elevation. It is much less probable that both canals headed nearly to the east, and that lowering of the river channel by erosion resulted in abandonment of the higher, northern channel and digging of the new channel to a greater depth. Much less labor would have been required for the deepening of the already existing channel.

The successive fills of the two canals could not be correlated with each other, and there is no way to determine at what point in the history of the South Canal the North Canal came into use—if, as we suspect, they were used in this sequence, their spans of use may, of course, not have overlapped at all. The fills, as observed in cross section, are separated by fairly clearly defined discontinuities. However, the material of one fill is very similar to another, the variation being in fineness of particles and in changes in the thickness and dip of the bedding planes that record each layer's manner of deposition. A detail of excavation technique is of interest in connection with these fills; observation of details was made easier by the passage of a few days because the loss of color difference due to drying was less important than the clear and delicate etching that was produced by the strong winds that blew nearly every day. The relief that was developed between the more compact and less compact laminae could be only partly achieved by gentle jabbing with a fine-bristled paint brush, but this substitute for a few days' wind action was helpful in making possible immediate interpretation of exposed portions of the profile.

The fill of both channels shows one characteristic shared with modern irrigation channels and permanent streams. When the rate of flow is increased by an increase in the volume of water, previously deposited materials are removed, but mainly from the bottom of the channel and to a lesser extent from the sides. This can be easily observed in the cross section of the North Canal; the deposits labeled 1, 3, and 4 are entirely absent at the center of the canal but remain at one or both sides. In the South Canal, the oldest fill, No. 1, appears to have been two or three times as thick as the remaining portion at the center of channel, with all but a small portion against the south side cut away prior to deposition of fill 2.

Dating the construction and use of the canals has proved difficult. Their proximity to Pueblo Grande would suggest use during its occupation, which probably extended from the 12th century to the end of the 14th, with a large part of its construction during the Soho phase, approximately 1150 or 1200 to 1300. However, examination of the few sherds found in and under the canal banks and in the canal fills shows no evidence of construction before the Soho phase or of use after it. The small number of sherds makes such a conclusion somewhat less than final, and the possibility cannot be eliminated of a much earlier canal having been completely cleaned out or totally re-excavated and enlarged, thus removing evidence of its original date.

The total extent of these canals was recorded by both Patrick (1903) and Turney (1929), Turney probably depending heavily on Patrick's much earlier first-hand observations. The North Canal is shown as extending for about 9 miles, the South Canal about seven. Both are shown heading about a half mile east of the Park of Four Waters. There is an apparently reliable local recollection, however, that before the end of the last century one of these canals could be traced another two miles eastward, to a point opposite Tempe Butte (O. S. Halseth, personal communication). It may never be possible to establish the original length of these canals precisely, but the general order of magnitude suggested here is undoubtedly correct. Both canals are comparable in length to some of the modern canals in use today. It might be expected that canals of such size, involving substantial and probably protracted labor in their construction, would have been used for more than the century or so suggested by the ceramic evidence. On the other hand, many causes may have been responsible for their abandonment after a relatively brief span of service—excessive silting, water-logging of the fields they served, or changes in the river.

It is too early in the current study of prehistoric land- and water-use in the Southwest to attempt answers to the many questions posed by Hohokam irrigation. Its origins, its extent, and the reasons for its decline need much further study, and the social and economic implications of this extensive system of large canals are not yet understood. As this study progresses it is hoped that all of these aspects of Hohokam irrigation will become better known. A more detailed report on the canals at the Park of Four Waters, and reports on the other investigations now in progress will be presented in the future.

ANCIENT CANALS ON THE SOUTH-WEST COAST OF FLORIDA
Douglass, Andrew E.; *American Antiquarian*, 7:277–285, 1885

While exploring the South-west coast of Florida, I was much interested in two ancient canals which I examined, and whose object seemed quite inexplicable. The first occurs about three miles north of Gordon's Pass, an inlet thirty-three miles south of Punta Rasa, and twenty miles north of Cape Roman.

. . . .

I entered Gordon's Pass, and for some days was occupied in examining the evidences of Indian occupation in the shell and earth mounds to be found there, and while awaiting a fair wind for Punta Rasa, devoted a day to the examination of the Canal. With two of my men I walked northward along the beach, which was a perfectly straight line to the next Pass. For the first half mile this beach was skirted by a beautiful grove of cabbage palmetto, under whose shade was the ranch of Mr. Madison Weeks, an intelligent settler, who was cultivating the surface of an extensive shell mound, just north of the Inlet, and who courteously gave me much information about the country. The Palm Grove was on a plateau about eight feet above the sea level, but beyond the grove the land sank into a low marsh not more than half that elevation. The storms of many years had created a levee of sand, which defended this morass from the sea, and was at least one hundred feet in breadth. It was apparent, however, that erosion of the coast had here occurred to a great extent, for stumps of dead palms could be seen a hundred yards or so to sea, and suggested the probability of great change in the contour of the land during not remote years. One of our party followed the line of embankment or sand-dune while the other two kept along the beach. At a distance of three and a-half miles from the Inlet the former announced the Canal, and we soon joined him and saw the object of our search before us. Where we stood it was buried in the sand embankment, but from that it was plainly visible straight as an arrow, crossing the low intervening morass and penetrating the sandy pine ridge, half a mile, or nearly so, away. The bottom was moist and full of tall grass; the sides and summit of the embankment covered with a dense chapparal of oak scrub and scrub palmetto. Its direction from our stand-point was about one point South of East. We could see in the distance, pines growing upon the inner and outer sides of its banks. With infinite labor we worked our way through the dense scrub for a hundred yards or so, and took our measurements. The width from the summit ridge upon each bank was 55 feet, and the depth from that summit level to centre of the excavation 12 feet. At the bottom the width was 12 feet, the banks being almost perpendicular for some 5 feet, and then receding on an easier angle at the summit. This summit was about eight feet above the level of the meadow, through which for nearly half a mile it was excavated, till it reached the higher level of the sandy pine land beyond. Owing to considerable indisposition on my part, this was the end of our exploration for that day, but on the day following we rowed up the Interior Lagoon with a view of examining its eastern terminus. Mr. Weeks, the resident settler, kindly accompanied us and gave us all the information he possessed as to its structure and peculiarities. He had often hunted through the pines, and had crossed it at various points not at present accessible to us. A long pull of about four miles from the Inlet along the Lagoon brought us to a little bay on the west shore where we landed, and penetrating the thickets reached a swamp of saw grass and water, where we found the Eastern terminus of the canal, though much reduced in dimensions, as probably it was here more exposed to the wash of the Lagoon in the rainy season. The banks were covered with a growth of cabbage palms, and as it progressed toward the pine barren, it increased in size and height. We found that at this end the trench curved to the South as it approached the Lagoon, and about two hundred yards from the shore it was intersected by a cross ditch or trench, as if to allow it to receive the waters from the level on either side. If this cross opening has not been a modern adjunct, designed to allow the swamps to discharge into the Lagoon, as we found was now the case, it would seem to indicate that the whole of these interior waters were expected to find an outlet to the sea by means of this very considerable drain or canal. Mr. Weeks gave us the following information about the canal in its passage through the pine land. The whole canal is about one mile and a half in length, reaching from the Lagoon to the Sea. With the exception of the curve at the Eastern terminus it is perfectly straight. In passing through the pine woods it intersects sand ridges, in which it is excavated to a depth of forty feet. The bottom is everywhere of the same width I have described, but at points where he has crossed it in hunting, he finds a trench about four feet in breadth, and at present, two feet deep running along the center, leaving a breadth of about four feet on each side. Mr. Weeks was of the impression that this supplementary trench was designed to accommodate the keel of a boat as it ran along the conduit. Leaving the Canal, we crossed the Lagoon and found and ascended a creek with rocky banks and bottom for some two miles, into the pine woods of the mainland. Mr. Weeks was of the opinion that it formerly connected with the Canal, and the latter was constructed to carry it to the sea, but I see no indication of that being even remotely possible, though it is as good a guess as any other that can be made in the apparent absence of any more plausible theory. The trench in the middle of the main canal appears to me to indicate that the canal has been made by civilized men, and within a comparatively recent period. It is a work of enormous labor indeed, but in trenching through the sands of these regions, it is quite usual to make an interior ditch, that the tables left on each side may intercept the drifting sands brought down the sides by heavy weather, rains or wind. But the question is, what was the purpose of such an expense of labor, and who in this sparsely settled country could have undertaken it. As regards drainage, the Lagoon already empties into the Inlet, and through that into the sea. If for the admittance of vessels, the Inlet of Gordon's Pass gives far greater accommodation. And who would not be aware that an opening of the kind at right angles to the shore, without some very massive artificial breakwater and continually dredged channels, would be choked up by the sand on the first storm, and show the same obstruction at its mouth as we have just seen. My own idea is that by whomsoever constructed, it was designed to relieve the lowlands to the eastward of great accumulations of fresh water in the rainy season, at some remote period when there was no Gordon's Pass, and when the exterior conformation of the coast was far different from what it is at present. Inlets in the Florida coast, particularly on the Atlantic side, open and close unexpectedly. In St. Johns County a couple of miles south of Mantanzas Inlet, an inlet, known as Hughes', closed up in heavy gales a hundred years since, and that region was rendered very unhealthy by the stagnant fresh water. A few Spanish soldiers with shovels, opened a channel through the marsh back of the Sand Dunes, and in a short time the waters had worn a course into the Matanzas river, which has so remained ever since. Heavy storms on the Gulf Coast may have choked up several Inlets on the west coast, and filled up channels among the Mangrove Islands, or on the other hand, the mainland which now confronts Gordon's Pass only a mile or so to the eastward, may have reached the sea in bygone ages, and enclosed a fresh water lake where is now the Northern Lagoon. Who were the constructors, is a question, even more difficult to settle. There is no record of such a work in any local tradition, or in any history that we now possess. Indeed, there is nothing more obscure than the history whether ancient or modern, of the South-west Coast of Florida.

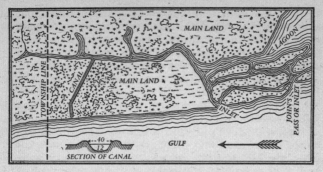

*Map of one of the ancient canals on the
West Coast of Florida.*

• • • • • • • • • • • • • •

The other canal I visited, is quite as inexplicable, and
even more surprising for its extent and dimensions than
this. It has been occasionally noticed in accounts of hunt-
ers and sportsmen, who have not infrequently encountered
it in a more accessible and better known region. The sheet
of water on the coast north of Caloosahatchee river known
as Charlotte Harbor, Charlotte Sound and Carlos Bay,
has on its eastern border a long island known as Pine
Island. It is about 18 miles long, and from three to five
miles broad, extending in a direction nearly north and
south. On its east side it is separated from the mainland
by a shoal channel, obstructed by oyster and sand bars,
from half a mile to a mile in width. On the west, Charlotte
Sound intervenes between it and the outside or coast-line
of keys, with a width of from three to five miles. Just on
the verge of Pine Island, a maze of mangrove keys or
islets stretch along the entire distance, and some of these
have been occupied by the Muspa Indians as late as fifty
years since. Pine Island itself is clothed in pines, and is a
sandy level fringed along the water by mangrove thickets.
Some of the adjacent islets are occupied here and there,
by a solitary settler, who finds cultivatable ground on the
shell mounds left by the Indian inhabitants of prehistoric
or more recent days. One of the largest of these shell
mounds which I have ever seen, is found on the west

coast of Pine Island, some four miles from its northern end. The heaps cover a space of several acres, and rise in steep ridges to the height of, in some instances, twenty-five feet. Their flanks run off frequently on very slight inclinations, and have been dwelt on by Indian residents long subsequent to the era of original construction, until the debris accumulated over the shells has resolved itself into a very fertile mould, tempting to the settler of the present day. This shell heap had been so utilized, that around the steep ridges, rows of lime and lemon trees, with pomegranates and fig trees, spread out on the long levels. But all was now deserted and on landing I found it a maze of wild luxuriance; briars and the American Aloe, and cacti innumerable, filled up every vacant space, and these with the "Spanish bayonet," render it a danger as well as labor to explore.

I had but little time to spare, owing to the delays forced upon us by a long period of unusually inclement weather, and could only make a hasty inspection. We had expected to find two settlers at the ranch, but it was vacant, and our work had to be done without the aid of a guide. We made for the mangrove swamps to the south, and the tide fortunately being out, we worked through the damp thickets till we emerged into the tangle of scrub palmetto which covered the surface of the sandy upland of the Island. Catching a glimpse of a sand mound glistening with whitened crest, among the pines a quarter of a mile away to the eastward, we plunged in through the chapparal and made for that object. On our way we rose upon a slight ridge and then descending into a hollow level for some thirty feet, again surmounted a ridge and then realized that this was the Canal. It was thus we found it, much to our surprise. A thin growth of tall pines covered it and the surrounding sand level, an occasional palmetto rose here and there along the bottom, all else was a thicket of scrub palmetto. The position of this end of the canal was of some interest, as enabling us to estimate how far it was coeval with the sand or shell mounds at its western terminus. So far as it can be described without the aid of a diagram, the arrangement of these objects was as follows: On the western verge of the Island in a mangrove swamp, rose the various masses of shells constituting the Shell mound spreading over an area of eight or ten acres; due east of these ridges at a distance of some 300 feet, but upon the sand level of the Island, rose a sand mound 35 feet in height and 200 feet in base diameter, (one of the largest of these constructions which had come under my observation anywhere in Florida.) Looking eastward from its summit, we could discern about 460 yards distant, the sand mound we had first descried. It was a twin or double-headed mound, as I afterward ascertained, 20 feet in perpendicular height, with a depression of 8 feet between the two summits, and the longest diameter of its base 300 feet. While these two mounds lay on a line due east and west, the canal passed between them angularly, coming from the south-east. The dimensions of the latter were at this point 30 feet in width from the bottom of the opposite banks, and seven to eight feet in height to the summit of the banks, which was also at an elevation of some three or four feet above the level of the adjacent sand of the Island surface.

Far as the eye could reach, we could trace this canal in a direct line through the sparse pine woods; its course being especially marked by the tall fronds of the cabbage palms, which the moisture of the depression tempted to grow within the banks, and were confined to that level. After passing between the two sand mounds in an angular direction, the western terminus of this interesting construction, faded away in the general level of the surface to the north of the larger mound, and this level, within a few rods, sank into a creek which continued straight through the mangroves into Charlotte Sound, emptying two hundred yards north of the ranch where I had landed. These were all the local characteristics of this Canal that I was able personally to inspect. I was assured by an old settler that it crosses the entire Island in a direct line on the course which I observed. At this point, the direct width of Pine Island is three and a half miles. The Canal however, crossing at the angle indicated, must exceed five miles in length. It was a source of great regret that indisposition on one hand and delays incident to an unusually rough and inclement winter on the other hand should have prevented my making a more thorough survey of this interesting and inexplicable work.

PRIMITIVE WATER-SUPPLY
Hubbard, A. J., and Hubbard, G.; *Nature,* 71:611–612, April 27, 1905

[A book review]

The mighty earthworks that still crown so many of our hills fill the archaeologist alike with wonder and despair—wonder that prehistoric man, with the most primitive tools, was equal to the task of raising them, and despair that so little can ever be known about them, despite the most laborious and costly excavation. Plenty of books, however, of the kind now under notice would do much to solve the mystery and increase our admiration for Neolithic man, for it is to the period before bronze was known in Britain that the authors assign the stupendous works of Cissbury and Chanctonbury on the South Downs.

This is an open-air book that gives life to the dry bones of archaeology, and reads like the record of a well-spent holiday. A keen eye for country is one of the qualifications possessed by one or both the authors, and evidence of ramparts long since levelled is wrung from the very daisies as they grow. The construction of dew-ponds by the early inhabitants of Britain has often been glibly asserted, but few, if any, have furnished such clear and circumstantial evidence as the authors of this short treatise. The water-supply for the occupants of our huge prehistoric "camps" has always been somewhat of a mystery, and it has been suggested that they were only temporary refuges, when the country was "up," so that a permanent supply was not regarded as a necessity. But the watering of men and animals on the scale indicated by the areas enclosed would be a formidable task even for a day, and another explanation must be sought. The late General Pitt-Rivers, for example, held that the water-level of the combes was higher then than now, and streams would have been plentiful on the slopes; but, feeling the inadequacy of this view, he also had recourse to the dew-pond theory. To those familiar with the process, this might seem an obvious expedient, but the interesting account given of the formation of such reservoirs might make us chary of crediting prehistoric man with such scientific methods.

An exposed position innocent of springs was selected,

and straw or some other non-conductor of heat spread over the hollowed surface. This was next covered with a thick layer of well puddled clay, which was closely strewn with stones. The pond would gradually fill, and provide a constant supply of pure water, due to condensation during the night of the warm, moist air from the ground on the surface of the cold clay. Evaporation during the day is less rapid than this condensation, and the only danger is that the straw should be sodden by leakage. It is for this reason that springs or drainage from higher ground are avoided, as running water would cut into the clay crust.

Some ponds of this kind, no doubt of very early, and perhaps of Neolithic date, may still be seen in working order: others are of modern construction; but to and from the ancient dew-ponds (or their sites) can sometimes be traced the hillside tracks along which the herds were driven, one leading from the camp, or cattle-enclosure hard by, to the watering-place, another leading back, to avoid confusion on the road. These and other details as to guard-houses and posts of observation are brought to our notice in the description of selected strongholds in Sussex and Dorset; and verification, if, indeed, such is demanded, must be sought on the spot by any who have doubts or rival theories.

The banks, that enclosed pasture-areas sometimes of vast extent, were no doubt stockaded against man and beast, and may be compared with the base-court defences of the Norman burh; but the excavator of Wansdyke had an alternative theory that such banks were sometimes erected for driving game. Incidentally, the authors discountenance the view that the "camps," not to mention the outworks, were ever efficiently manned. Their extent would necessitate for this duty a vast number of fighting men within call.

Possibly, in a few instances, the ridges on the hill-slopes may be due to outcropping strata, and others might suggest terrace-cultivation; but there seems ample evidence for the view taken that Neolithic cattle-tracks have survived to this day around certain of our most imposing "camps."

4

Scotland's Vitrified Forts

Vitrifaction is the process of fusing stone or glass. It requires a high temperature (about 2800°F), the precise value being dependent upon the material involved. Glassmaking was evidently mastered by the Egyptians and has a long, not-very-mysterious history. Given wood fuel and a good hearth, glassmaking is not too difficult. The question is not whether the ancients could make glass but whether they could vitrify large stone walls to a depth of several feet.

The Scottish vitrified forts are described below in quaint detail in a 200-year-old article by Anderson. This is followed by a more modern report that makes the vitrified forts seem less anomalous, as if anyone could melt a pile of rocks together.

Those who have been at a hot campfire know that the intense heat blackens stones but does not fuse them. However, intense house fires will occasionally melt foundation stones. Thus it is not beyond comprehension that ancient men could pile seasoned timber against a pile of rocks, fire it in a good wind, and fuse some of the rocks together. A more significant question is "Why bother?" An enemy can storm a vitrified fort just as easily as an unvitrified one.

Vitrified forts are important in Sensational Archaeology because they were obviously created when the ancients turned their laser weapons upon Scotland. (Of course, the great rock-cutting feats of yore were also consumated with lasers.) A connection also exists with the vitrified areas found in such places

as the Libyan Desert. These are supposed to be the
sites of pre-Alamagordo nuclear explosions.

Less sensationally, Scottish vitrified forts could well
have an origin and purpose more mysterious than
precocious laser guns. The point here is that lasers
are not absolutely necessary to explain fused stone
walls. The real mysteries of ancient man may be
much more subtle.

ANCIENT FORTIFICATIONS OF SCOTLAND
Anderson, James; *Archaeologia*, 5:241–266, 1777

Nothing seems to be so well calculated for throwing
light on the origin of nations, as an attention to the radical
construction of the language of the people, and to the nature of those monuments of remote antiquity that have
escaped the ravages of time.

Much has been written about the origin of the Scottish
nation. And although some attention has been paid to the
nature of the language of the natives, the antiquities of the
country have been in a great measure disregarded; though
it should seem that the last would be of greater utility in
this discussion than the first of these particulars. For, a
language may have been spread through so many nations
at a very remote period, and is subject to such perpetual
variations, and it is so difficult to trace these variations before the discovery of letters, that there is no possibility of
pointing out by any unequivocal peculiarities of language,
the particular nation from which any particular tribe may
have descended. But the mechanic arts discovered by any
particular nation, especially before commerce was generally practised, were in a great measure confined to the
original discoverers themselves, or their immediate de-
scendents; and therefore they serve more effectually to
distinguish the countries that were occupied by particular
tribes of people. It is with this view that I suggest the following remarks on some of the remains of antiquity that
are still discoverable in Scotland.

All the antiquities that I have yet heard of in this
country may be referred to one or other of the following
general classes, (not to mention Roman camps, or other

works of later date) of each of which I shall speak a little, according to the order in which they occur.

I. Mounds of earth thrown up into a fort of hemispherical form, usually distinguished by the name of *mote* or *moat*.

II. Large heaps of stones piled upon one another, called *cairns*.

III. Large detached stones fixed in the earth in an erect position.

IV. Large stones fixed likewise in an erect position in a circular form.

V. Circular buildings erected of stone without any cementing matter, usually distinguished by the adjunct epithet *dun;* and

VI. Walls cemented by a vitrified matter, usually found on the top of high mountains.

[The first two categories are of little interest and are omitted here.]

III. The long stones set on end in the earth are, with still greater certainty, known to be monuments erected to perpetuate the memory of some signal event in war. These are probably of later date than the cairns; for there is hardly one of them whose traditional history is not preserved by the country people in the neighbourhood: nor is it difficult on many occasions to reconcile these traditional narratives with the records of history. On some of these stones is found a rude kind of sculpture; as on the long stone near Forress in the shire of Murray, and on that at Aberlemno in the shire of Angus; but in general the stones are entirely rude and unfashioned, just as they have been found in the earth.

It is probable that this kind of monument has been first introduced into Britain by the Danes; as almost all the traditional stories relate to some transaction with the Danes, or other memorable event since the period when that Northern people infested this country; and I have never heard of any of them in the internal parts of the Highlands, though they are numerous along the coasts every where. It is certain, however, that the Britons adopted this method of perpetuating the memory of remarkable events, as appears by Piercy's cross in Northumberland, which is a modern monument belonging to this class.

IV. The stones placed in a circular form, as being less known than the former, and confined to a narrower district, deserve to be more particularly described.

These, from their situation and form, have been evidently places destined for some particular kind of religious worship. They are for the most part placed upon an eminence, usually on that side of it which declines towards the South, and seem to have been all formed after one plan with little variation. I have examined, perhaps, some hundreds of them in different places, and find, that by restoring the parts that have been demolished they would all coincide very exactly with the plan annexed to this, which was drawn from one that is still very entire in this neighbourhood, at a place called *Hill of Fiddess*, which I believe you once saw.

This particular temple, 46 feet in diameter, consists of nine long stones, placed on end in a circular form, at distances nearly equal, though not exactly so. The area within this circle is smooth, and somewhat lower than the ground around it. By this means, and by a small bank carried quite round between the stones, which is still a little higher than the ground about it, the circular area has been very distinctly defined. Between two stones that are nearest the meridian line, on the South side of the area, is laid on its side, a long stone, at each end of which are placed two other stones smaller than any of those that form the outer circle. These are a little within the circle, and at a somewhat greater distance from one another; and still farther, within the circular line, are placed two other stones. Behind the large stone the earth is raised something more than a foot higher than the rest of the circular area. It is probable that on this stage the priest officiated at the religious ceremonies, the large stone supplying the place of an altar.

There is not the smallest mark of a tool on any of these stones; but they are sometimes found of surprisingly large dimensions, the horizontal one on the South side especially, which seems to have been always chosen of the largest size that could be found. They are seldom less than six or eight feet in length, usually between ten and twelve; and I met with one that was near sixteen feet in length, and not less than eight feet in diameter in any of its dimensions. It appears to us amazing how in these rude times stones of such a size could have been moved at all; and yet they are so regularly placed in the proper part of the circle, and so much detached from other stones, as leaves not a possibility of doubting that they have been placed there by design.

It does not seem, however, that they have been confined to any particular size or shape of any of the stones in these structures, for they are quite irregular in these respects; only they seem always to have preferred the largest stones they could find to such as were smaller. Neither does there seem to have been any particular number of stones preferred to any other; it seems to have been enough that the circle should be distinctly marked out. In the shire of Nairn, where flat thin stones much abound, I saw some structures of this kind where the stones almoust touched one another all round. It appears also by the plan annexed, that exact regularity in the distance between the different stones were not much regarded.

I have never seen or heard of any temples of this kind in Scotland to the South of the Grampian mountains, nor to the North of Inverness. They abound in Aberdeenshire, and along the Grampian mountains themselves.

Stonehenge in Wiltshire, is without doubt a monument referable to this general class, although differing from the above in many particulars.

There are some vestiges of these four kinds of antiquities in South Britain; but it is doubtful if there are any of a similar nature with those of the other two classes that remain to be taken notice of. I shall, therefore, be a little more particular with regard to them.

V. The first of these in order are the circular buildings, consisting of walls composed of stones firmly bedded upon one another without any cement; some of which have been so firmly built as to be able to withstand the ravages of time for many centuries.

I have seen many of these more or less entire, and have heard of others that are still more perfect than any of those that I have seen. By the description I have got of these, the structure, when entire, seems very much to have resembled one of our modern glass-houses; the walls having been gradually contracted to a narrow compass at top, which was left open.

This account of the upper part of these buildings I give merely from hear-say, as the walls of the most entire one that I have seen did not, as I imagine, exceed twenty feet in height, and was at top very little narrower than at the base. This was at a place called *Dun Agglesag* in Rossshire, about ten miles West from Tain, on the South bank of the firth of Dornoch, which was, in summer 1775, in the following condition.

The walls appeared to be perfectly circular. The internal diameter, (as nearly as I can recollect, having lost my notes of this tour) was about fifty feet. The walls were about twelve feet in thickness, and the entry into it was at one place by a door about four feet wide: the height I could not exactly measure, as the passage as well as the inside of the building was choaked up in some measure with rubbish, so that we could not see the floor. The coins of the door consisted of large stones carefully chosen, so as exactly to fit the place where they were to be put; but neither here, nor in any other part of the building, could I discover the smallest mark of a hammer or any other tool. The aperture for the door was covered at top with a very large stone in the form of an equilateral triangle, each side being about six feet in length, which was exactly placed over the middle of the opening. This stone was about four feet in thickness. We must here be again surprized to think in what manner a stone of these dimensions could be raised to such a height by a rude people, seemingly ignorant of the powers of mechanism, and carefully placed above loose stones, so as to bind and connect them firmly together, instead of bringing down the wall, as would have inevitably happened without much care and skill in the workmen. Nor could I help admiring the judgement displayed in making choice of a stone of this form for the purpose here intended; as this is perhaps at the same time more beautiful to look on, and possesses more strength for the same bulk and weight than any other form that could have been made choice of.

The outside of the wall was quite smooth and compact, without any appearance of windows or other apertures of any kind. The inside too was pretty uniform, only here and there we could perceive square holes in the wall, of no great depth, somewhat like pigeon-holes, at irregular heights.

I have been informed that there is in many of these buildings a circular passage about four feet wide, formed in the centre of the wall that goes quite round the whole, on a level with the floor. I looked for it, but found no such thing in this place. At one place, however, we discovered a door entering from within, and leading to a kind of stair-case that was carried up in the centre of the wall, and formed a communication between the top and bottom of the building, ascending upwards round it in a spiral form. The steps of this stair, like all the other stones here employed, discovered no marks of a tool, but seemed to have been chosen with great care of a proper form for this purpose. At a convenient height over head, the stair-case was roofed with long flat stones going quite across the opening, and this roof was carried up in a direction parallel with the stair itself, so as to be in all places of an equal height. It was likewise observable, that the stair was formed into flights of steps; at the top of each of which there was a landing-place, with an horizontal floor about six feet in length; at the end of which another flight of steps began. One of these flights of steps was quite compleat, with a landing-place at each end of it, and two others were found in an imperfect state; the lowermost being in part filled up with rubbish, and the highest reached the top of the wall that is now remaining before it ended. Whether these flights were regularly continued to the top, and whether they contained an equal number of steps or not, it was impossible for me to discover; but these remains show that the structure has been erected by a people not altogether uncivilized.

About twenty years ago, a gentleman in that neighbourhood, who is laird of the spot of ground on which this beautiful remnant of ancient grandeur is placed, pulled down eight or ten feet from the top of these walls, for the sake of the stones, to build a habitation for its incurious owner. It may perhaps be a doubt with some whether the builders or the demolishers of these walls most justly deserve the name of a savage and uncivilized people?

By whatever people this has been erected, it must have been a work of great labour, as the collecting the materials alone, where no carriages could pass, must have been extremely difficult to accomplish. It must, therefore, have been in all probability a public national work, allotted for some very important purpose. But what use these buildings were appropriated to it is difficult now to say with certainty.

Most persons whom I have conversed with on this subject seem to think, that they have been intended as places of defence; which conjecture seems to gain some probability from the name; as it is said, by those who understand the *Erse* language, that *dun* signifies a place of strength, or a rock. But there are many reasons that satisfy me that this could not have been their original use. For, not to mention any other reason, these buildings are, all of them that I have seen, save that at Dun-robin alone, placed in a valley; and many of them are commanded by adjoining heights, from whence stones might have been thrown through the aperture at top with ease. Neither is there in any of them that I have seen, the least appearance of a well within the walls; from which circumstances alone we may be satisfied that they must have been appropriated to some other use than that of defence.

It appears to me, that they have been places of religious worship, which is also confirmed by the name these places still bear among the vulgar. For although every place where one of these is found has the syllable *dun* added to the original name of the place; as Dun-robin, Dunbeath, &c. yet the particular building itself is always called the *Druids house*, as the Druids house of Dunbeath, &c.

Ossian mentions the horrid circle of Brumo as a place of worship among the ancient Scandinavians, unknown in his own country in those times. Possibly he may here allude to structures of this fort, which may have been introduced into this country along with the religious worship peculiar to the Scandinavians, during the period that the Western isles and Northern provinces of Scotland were under the dominion of Norway. This conjecture gains an additional degree of probability when we observe, that although thousands of ruins of this species of buildings are found in the shire of Caithness, and in the Western and Northern islands, yet not one of them has hitherto been heard of in Scotland to the Southerward of Inverness. That at Dun-agglesag is the Southermost of the East coast, and another at Glenelg, opposite to the Isle of Sky, the Southermost that has hitherto been observed on the

West coast. But it is well known that the county of Caithness was so long under the dominion of Norway, that the inhabitants of that country still use a language, the greatest part of whose words are immediately derived from Norwegian roots, and many of the customs of Norway still prevail there as well as in the Northern isles, which were annexed to the crown of Scotland not many centuries ago.

If this conjecture is well founded, similar buildings to these will certainly still be discoverable in Norway or Denmark, and this is no improper subject of enquiry.

You will probably recollect the building called Arthur's Oven, which stood upon the banks of the Carron near Stirling, and was demolished not long ago. A drawing of it is preserved in Sibbald's "Scotia illustrata"; from which it appears that in its general form, and several other particulars, it much resembled the buildings of this class; and if it should be admitted as one of them, it would be an exception to the foregoing rule, and tend to invalidate the reasoning I have employed. But although in some particulars it did resemble these buildings, in other respects it was extremely different. Its size is the first observable particular in which it differed from them, as there is hardly one of them which has not been many times larger than it was. These buildings are always composed of rough stones, without any mark of a tool. It consisted entirely of hewn stones squared and shaped by tools, so as exactly to fit the place where they were to be inserted. The walls of Arthur's Oven were thin without any appearance of a stair within them. In short, it bore evident marks of Roman art and Roman architecture, and resembled Virgil's tomb near Naples more than it did the structures we now treat of; on which accounts it has always been, with seeming justice, supposed a small temple, erected by the Romans when they occupied that station, and very different from the ruder but more magnificent temples of these Northern nations.

The temple (for so I will venture to call it) at *Dunagglesag* has no additional buildings of any kind adjoining to it, although I had occasion to observe, from many others, that it has been no uncommon thing to have several low buildings of the same kind, joining to the base of the larger one, and communicating with it from within, like cells. The most entire of this kind that I have seen is at Dun-robin, the seat of the Earl of Sutherland. The late Earl was at great pains to clear away the rubbish from this building, and secure it as much as possible from being farther demolished. Unfortunately it is composed of much worse materials than that I have described.

The only particular relating to the situation of this kind of building that occurred to me as observable, was, that they were all situated very near where water could be obtained in abundance. The side of a lake or river is therefore a common position; and where another situation is chosen, it is always observable, that water in considerable quantities from a rivulet, or otherwise, can be obtained near. It seems, however, to have been a matter of indifference, whether that water was salt or fresh, stagnant or running; from whence it would seem probable, that water, in considerable quantities, must have been necessary for performing some of the rites celebrated there.

In Caithness, as I have already hinted, the ruins of this kind of buildings are exceedingly numerous; but many of them are now such a perfect heap of rubbish, that they have much the same appearance with the *cairns* already mentioned, and might readily be confounded with them by a superficial observer. The names in this case will be of some use to prevent mistakes, as every building of this kind seems to have been distinguished by the syllable *dun* prefixed to the word; so that whenever this is found to be the case, there is reason to suspect at least that it is not a cairn.

Dr. Johnson, in his late tour to the Hebrides, was carried to see one of these buildings in the Isle of Sky, which he seems to have surveyed rather in a hasty manner. He conjectures, that these structures have been erected by the inhabitants as places of security for their cattle, in case of a sudden inroad from their neighbours. A thousand circumstances, had he bestowed much attention upon the subject, might have pointed out to him the improbability of this conjecture. We shall soon see that the inhabitants knew much better in what manner to secure themselves or cattle from danger than they would have been here.

VI. The most remarkable of all the Scottish antiquities are the vitrified walls, which I come now to mention.

It is not yet three years since I got the first hint of this species of building, from a gentleman who had examined them with attention; and who was, I believe, the first person who took notice of them in Scotland. This was Mr. John Williams, who was for several years employed by the honourable board of trustees for managing the forfeited estates in Scotland, as a mineral surveyor on these estates. Since that time I have seen and examined them myself, and have made the following observations upon them.

These walls consist of stones piled rudely upon one another, and firmly cemented together by a matter that has been vitrified by means of fire, which forms a kind of artificial rock, (if you will admit this phrase,) that resists the vicissitudes of the weather perhaps better than any other artificial cement that has ever yet been discovered.

All the walls of this kind that I have yet seen or heard of, have been evidently erected as places of defence. They, for the most part, surround a small area on the top of some steep conical hill of very difficult access. It often happens that there is easier access to the top of one of these hills at one place than at any other; and there they have always had the entry into the fort, which has always been defended by outworks more or less strong according to the degree of declivity at that place. If the form of the hill admitted of access only at one place, there are outworks only at one place; but if there are more places of easy access, the outworks are opposed to each of them, and they are proportioned in extent to the nature of the ground.

The first fortification of this kind that I saw was upon the top of a steep hill called *Knock-serrel*, two miles west from Dingwal in Rossshire. And as an idea of all the others, may be formed from this one, I shall here subjoin a particular description of it.

The hill is of a longish form, rising into a ridge at top, long in proportion to its breadth. It is of great height and extremely steep on both sides; so that when it is viewed at a distance from either end, it appears of a conical shape, very perfect and beautiful to look at; but, when viewed from one side, one of the ends is seen to be much steeper than the other.

The narrow declivity of the hill is of easy access, and forms a natural road by which you may ascend to the top on horseback; and at this end has been the entry into the fort. This fort consists, as I guessed by my eye, of a long elliptical area of near an acre, which is entirely level, excepting towards each end, where it falls a little lower than in the middle. The fortification of vitrified wall, is continued quite round this area; being adapted to the form of the hill, so as to stand on the brink of a precipice all round, unless it be at the place where you enter, and at the opposite end; both which places have been defended by outworks. Those at the entry had extended, as I guessed, about a hundred yards, and seem to have consisted of cross walls one behind another, eight or ten in number; the ruins of which are still plainly perceptible. Through each of these walls there must have been a gate, so that the besiegers would be under the necessity of forcing each of these gates successively before they could carry the fort; on the opposite end of the hill, as the ground is considerably steeper, the outworks seem not to have extended above twenty yards, and consist only of two or three cross walls. Not far from the further end was a well, now filled up, but still discoverable.

To assist you in forming an idea of this structure, I subjoin a plan of the hill with its fortification, as if it were compleat. This is drawn entirely from memory, and is not

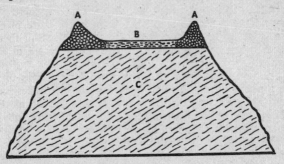

A Scottish "vitrified" fort. In this cross section, the outer layer of stones in the ring (A) are fused together as if by heat.

pretended to be exact in proportions; but it has the general form, and is sufficiently exact for our purpose here.

The wall all round from the inside, appears to be only a

mound of rubbish, consisting of loose stones now buried among some earth, and grass that has been gradually accumulated by the dunging of sheep, which resort to it as a place of shelter. The vitrified wall is only to be seen on the outside.

Nor are these walls readily distinguishable at a distance, because they are not raised in a perpendicular direction, but have been carried sloping inwards at top, nearly with the same degree in inclination as the sides of the hill; so that they seem, when viewed at a small distance, to be only a part of the hill itself.

It appears at first sight surprizing that a rude people should have been capable of discovering a cement of such a singular kind as this is. It is less surprizing that the knowledge of it should not have been carried into other countries, as distant nations in those periods had but little friendly intercourse with one another. But it is no difficult matter for one who is acquainted with the nature of the country where these structures abound to give a very probable account of the manner in which this art has been originally discovered, and of the causes that have occasioned the knowledge of it to be lost, even in the countries where it was once universally practised.

Through all the Northern parts of Scotland, a particular kind of earthy iron ore of a very vitrescible nature much abounds. This ore might have been accidentally mixed with some stones at a place where a great fire was kindled; and being fused by the heat would cement the stones into one solid mass, and give the first hint of the uses to which it might be applied. A few experiments would satisfy them of the possibility of executing at large what had been accidentally discovered in miniature.

This knowledge being thus attained, nothing seems to be more simple and natural than its application to the formation of the walls of their fortified places.

Having made choice of a proper place for their fort, they would rear a wall all round the area, building the outside of it as firm as they could of dry stones piled one above another, the interstices between them being filled full of this vitrescible iron ore; and the whole supported by a backing of loose stones piled carelessly behind it.

When the wall was thus far compleated, with its facing all round reared to the height they wished for, nothing more was necessary to give it the entire finishing but to kindle a fire all round it sufficiently intense to melt the vitrescible ore, and thus to cement the whole into one coherent mass, as far as the influence of that heat extended. As the country then abounded with wood, this purpose would be readily effected by building a stack of wood round the whole outside of the wall, and then setting it on fire. It was probably with a view to enable them to build this stack of wood with the greater ease, and to suffer the fire to act more forcibly and equally upon the different parts of the wall as it gradually consumed, that they were induced to incline the walls so far from a perpendicular position. In an after period, when the woods had gradually been destroyed, and before it was well known how to manufacture peat for fuel, it would be such a difficult matter to procure fuel in abundance, that buildings of this kind would come to be disused, and the art in a short period, among a people ignorant of letters, be entirely forgotten.

You will perhaps imagine that the above account of the manner in which these walls have been formed, is only an ingenious conjecture, entirely destitute of proof. But that they have indeed been formed in this manner, can, I think, be demonstrated in as clear a manner as the nature of the subject will admit.

The ingenious Mr. Williams, already mentioned, by the permission of the board of trustees, caused a section to be made across the top of the Hill of Knockferrel, which was carried quite through the walls on each side, so that any person has now an opportunity of observing the nature of these walls, and may judge of the manner in which they have been constructed.

It appears by this section that the wall all round is covered on the outside with a crust of about two feet in thickness, consisting of stones immersed among vitrified matter; some of the stones being half fused themselves where the heat has been greatest, and all of them having evidently suffered a considerable heat. This crust is of an equal thickness of about two feet from top to bottom, so as to lie back upon and be supported by the loose stones behind it.

Within that crust of vitrified matter is another stratum of some thickness running from top to bottom, exactly parallel to the former, which consists of loose stones that have been scorched by the fire, but discover no marks of fusion. The stones that are nearest the vitrified part of the wall being most scorched, and those behind becoming gradually less and less so, till at length they seem not to have been affected by the heat in the smallest degree.

It deserves to be remarked, that these different crusts or strata, as I have named them, for want of a more appropriated term, do not consist of separate walls disjoined from one another, but are parts of one aggregate mass; as it frequently happens that one stone has one end of it immersed among the vitrified matter in the wall, and the other end of it only scorched by heat; and in the same manner it often happens, that one end of a stone is scorched by heat while the other end appears never to have suffered in the smallest degree from the action of the fire. This affords the clearest proof that the heat has been applied to them after they have been placed in the wall.

In carrying the section across the level area in the middle of the fortification, there was found a stratum of black vegetable mold, lying above the solid rock. This mold has probably been formed in the course of ages by the dunging of sheep which resort often to this place for shelter.

Nothing seems to be more judicious or simple than this mode of fortification adopted by our forefathers. The stones for forming the walls were probably dug from the top of the rock that formed the ridge of the hill, and therefore served at once to level the area of the fort, and to erect the massy walls without any expence of carriage. The walls too, although rude in form, and inelegant in appearance, were extremely well adapted for the only mode of defence that their situation rendered necessary. For as they were always placed upon the brink of a precipice, no weapon could have been so destructive to an assailant as a stone rolled down the hill: but as the inside of the wall consisted in every part of it of an immense heap of loose stones, the defendants could never be at a loss for weapons wherever the attack was made.

I have been told, that on some of the hills which have been fortified in this manner, there is another circumvallation drawn round the hill nearer the base, which has been defended by a wall of dry stones only. But as I never saw any of these myself I cannot describe them particularly. It is probable these were intended as places of security for cattle, in case of any sudden inroad from an enemy of no great force. If so they will naturally be placed on the extremity of some swelling part of the hill so as to include an area of as little declivity as possible immediately behind them.

Many hills are fortified in this manner through all the northern parts of Scotland. I have heard of none of this kind that have as yet been discovered farther South than the shire of Angus; but it is possible that others of the same kind may be yet discovered that have not hitherto been taken notice of. I think Governor Pownal mentions some in memoir lately given in by him to the Antiquary Society. I have not the memoir here and therefore cannot consult it; but a little attention will soon discover if it is of the same kind with that which is here described.

I am much disposed to believe that this has been entirely a British invention, and think it probable that the art was never carried out of this country. That it was not known by the Danes at least seems extremely probable, from a curious fact that I shall now take notice of; and if it was not known by the Danes, it seems probable, that it would not be known by the other Northern nations on the continent. The fact I allude to is as follows:

It is well known that the Danes made frequent inroads into Scotland, for several centuries, with various degrees of success. During that period they seized upon a peninsulated rock in the Murray Firth, about four miles from Elgin, which is now called *Brough head*. As this was a place naturally strong, and formed besides a kind a harbour, by means of which supplies could be brought to it by sea, they thought it a very convenient station to be occupied as a place of arms, and accordingly fortified it for that purpose. Three large and deep parallel ditches were drawn across the neck of the Isthmus that joined it to the land; and within the innermost of these a large wall has been erected, which has been continued quite round the peninsula, as the ruins of it at this day clearly show.

The circumstance that made me here take notice of this Danish fortification is, that all the stones on the outside of the wall appear to have been scorched in the fire, insomuch that they appear almost as red as bricks on that side, although the stone is naturally of a very white kind, and some of them are almost burnt to a powder. Between these stones, on digging among the ruins of the wall is found a good deal of reddish dust, exactly resembling dry clay that has been burnt to ashes. But in no part of this fortification is there the smallest appearance of vitrified matter, and the stones in the inside are every where of their natural colour.

From these circumstances it appears to me extremely probable, that the Danes, from having seen in their incursions some of the vitrified fortifications, have admired the invention and wished to imitate them. We may suppose they might have been able to learn in general that they consisted of walls of stone intermixed with dry clay in powder, which was afterwards converted into a vitrified mass by surrounding the whole with a stack of wood or other combustibles, and then setting it on fire. But having been ignorant of the necessity of employing only that particular substance already described, which, from its general appearance, might be on some occasions mistaken for a kind of clay, they have probably taken some ordinary clay and employed that in its stead. But as ordinary clay is hardly at all vitrescible, they have not been able to succeed in their attempt, but instead of that, the stones, by the great heat applied to them, have been scorched in the manner they now appear, and the clay between them has been burnt to ashes. This so perfectly accounts for the peculiarity observable in the ruined walls of this fortification, and it is so difficult to assign any other reason for the singular appearance of them, that I could not avoid throwing out this probable conjecture to direct towards other researches.

Although it is only of late that the real nature of these vitrified walls has been known, it is long since the vitrified matter has been observed; but it was always supposed that these were the natural production of volcanos; from whence it was inferred that volcanos had been very common in Scotland at some very distant period. But if no better proof can be adduced in support of this last hypothesis it will hardly be admitted.

From the foregoing account it appears, that these works

are purely artificial. At the same time it must be owned, that the natural appearance of the places where these vitrified masses are usually found, is well calculated to favour the opinion that they have been produced by volcanos.

The vitrified matter is usually first discovered by travellers around the bottom, and on the sides of steep hills, frequently of a conical shape, terminating in a narrow *apex,* exactly resembling the hills that have been formed by the eruptions of a volcano. It is therefore very natural to think that these may have been produced in the same way.

Let us suppose that a traveller, strongly impressed with this idea, should resolve to examine the top of the mountain more nearly, and for this purpose ascends to the summit; would not his former conjecture be much confirmed when at the top he should find himself in a circular hollow, surrounded on all sides by matter rising gradually higher to the very edge of the precipice, which is there entirely environed with vitrified matter of the same kind with that he had found at the bottom? Could such a man be called unreasonably credulous if he should be induced by so many concuring circumstances to believe that this had been a real volcano? But would he not be reckoned sceptical in extreme if he should entertain the smallest doubt of the truth of this opinion if he should likewise see the very opening itself in the centre of the hollow, through which the boiling *lava* had been sprewed out? Yet strong as all these appearances are, we know that they may, and actually do all concur on many occasions to favour the deceit. The formation of the hollow basin has been already explained; and the well, with which every one of these forts has been provided, and which is still discoverable in all of them, though for the most part now filled up with stones to prevent accident, might very readily be mistaken for the mouth of the volcano.

In these circumstances a casual visitor might be excused if he should believe in such strong appearances without enquiring minutely into the matter. But a philosophical enquirer who resolved cooly to investigate the matter, would soon find reason to doubt that he might be mistaken. The vitrified masses themselves are of a nature extremely different from real *lava;* so different indeed, that nothing but the difficulty of accounting for the way in which they could be otherwise produced would ever have occasioned them to be confounded with one another. In real *lava,* the heat has been so intense as to fuse almost all matters, and reduce them into one heterogeneous mass; but in the matter, of which we now treat, the heat has been so slight as to vitrify scarce any of the stones, but barely to fuse the vitrescible matter that was interposed between them; which alone points out a very essential difference between the nature of the two. But if he should proceed farther in this investigation, he would also discover, on digging into the hill in any part, that no *lava,* or any other matters that show marks of having been in the fire, are to be found; but that they consist of rock or other strata of mineral matter similar to what is found in other parts of the country. Neither has there ever been found in Scotland any appearance of pumice stones, nor large beds of ashes like those which are always found in the neighbourhood of volcanos. There is not (for the most part) even any appearance of *basaltes* in the neighbourhood of these fortified hills; a substance which is now thought to be invariably generated by volcanos alone, although it does not seem that the proofs upon which this opinion is founded are so conclusive as to leave no room to doubt of the fact. Unfortunately too for Scotland, the parallel fails in another respect; for, instead of the extraordinary fertility of soil that for the most part is found near volcanos, we here find that sterility which is invariably produced by the vitrescible iron ore above alluded to wherever it abounds.

If this account of the *artificial* curiosities, found in the Highlands of Scotland, should afford you any entertainment, I may, perhaps, on some future occasion, make a few observations on the natural curiosities of these unknown regions, which are more numerous and more generally interesting to philosophic enquirers than the former. I know no way in which a philosopher, who wants to view nature undisguised, and to trace her gradual progress for successive ages, could do it with half so much satisfaction as in the Highlands of Scotland. Half a day's ride there would do more to give such an enquirer a proper idea of the changes produced on this globe, and the means by which they are effected than twenty years study in the closet could produce; as any one who shall attentively view these, after reading the writings of Buffon, will readily allow.

A VITRIFIED FORT AT DUNAGOIL, BUTESHIRE
Anonymous; *Nature,* 119:213, February 5, 1927

Excavations carried out at a fort at Dunagoil, Buteshire, from 1913 until 1915 and again in 1919, have yet to be described in detail; but a summary of the results has been published by Mr. L. M'Lellan Mann, in the *Transactions of the Buteshire Natural History Society* for 1925. The exploration of the fort is not quite complete. Vitrified forts are so called from the fact that the rubble core of the walling has been intentionally burned to form a hard vitrified mass to which the stones of the external walls adhere, thus giving great strength and power of resistance. Such structures are almost entirely lacking in fortified sites outside Scotland, where they occur chiefly near the seashore, ranging from the Solway up to the central west Highlands and thence in a belt across country to Invernessshire as well as on a portion of the north-east coast. Dunagoil fort is entirely pre-Roman and was occupied from about 200 B.C. until A.D. 100. It is situated on a knife-edge ridge at the south end of the island of Bute. The construction of a crescentic wall on the less precipitous side in order to give a fairly secure platform for the habitations of the occupiers, caused an accumulation of refuse which afforded a rich harvest for the excavators. The walls of the building were some twelve feet thick. They were built in stages of two or three feet, the rubble being burned at each stage until a height of fifteen feet had been reached. The rampart probably had two parapets and the fort two entrances, protected apparently by massive timber doors held by wooden bars which, when not in use, lay in horizontal holes in the interior of the walling. The objects found, which are very fully illustrated, included stone axes, hammers, knives, anvils, and other tools of stone, saddle querns imperfectly converted into rotary querns, utensils and personal ornaments of imported soapstone and lignite, an inferior hand-made pottery, many objects of bone and antler including a peculiar pin or bodkin, square in section with ornamented sides; bracelets of jet, lignite, and glass, the last-named multi-coloured, and a large variety of iron objects.

5

Echoes of Stonehenge

It is common knowledge that Europe is liberally dotted with stone circles, dolmens, menhirs, and other megalithic structures. Actually, these fascinating constructions have worldwide distribution; they are found almost everywhere, even the remotest Pacific islands. Stonehenge, Long Meg, the great alignments in Brittany; these structures get all the attention. What is not generally recognized is that North America has its own megalithic monuments, although they are much scarcer than and not as sophisticated as those in Europe.

The first colonists of North America found a heavily wooded land peopled by Indians who were scarcely the Stonehenge type. Yet bit by bit the colonists discovered stone circles, rocking stones, and the like. Many labeled these finds freaks of nature, but others declared they were proof that the megalith builders had come this way too. Finch's charming summary article reproduced below is of 1824 vintage. In it he ascribes the North American megaliths to the Druids, as was then the custom in ascribing European stone monuments. Finch's survey covers just the tiny corner of our continent known in 1824. The Mystery Hill site of New Hampshire is not mentioned, nor is the great pyramidal Cahokia mound, the Povery Point works, and the Big Horn Medicine Wheel. Still, Finch describes a primeval countryside we do not know, for in our day most traces of ancient man have long been obliterated by plow and bulldozer.

What people or peoples traveled the whole globe

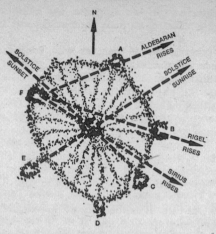

Big Horn Medicine Wheel, showing some of the pre-sumed astronomical alignments. The rim, spokes, and cairns are constructed of piled rocks.

dragging huge stones hither and yon, erecting strange structures from them? The worldwide megaliths may be the surviving traces of some great prehistoric re-ligious movement or perhaps a global empire of some sort. All we know is that these people came and went, that they had some unique conception of the universe, and that they constructed the monuments required by their system. When archaeologists 10,000 years hence carefully excavate our Interstate Highway Sys-tem, they will doubtless write learned dissertations about the religious import of concrete trackways which will be just as close to the truth as our discus-sions of megalithic sites.

ON THE CELTIC ANTIQUITIES OF AMERICA
Finch, John; *American Journal of Science,* 7:149–161, 1824

From our earliest infancy we are accustomed to ad-mire every thing connected with ancient times. The senti-ment seems implanted in our nature, and if the monu-ments we see, or those we read of, belong to our native country, or even to one which we have made our home, the interest becomes more intense, and every faculty of the mind is exerted, to trace their origin and investigate their use.

With communities of men, as with individuals, great importance is attached to a long line of glorious ancestry, and the first desire of all civilized nations has been, to investigate the history of the tribes who first visited the countries they inhabit, and it is an honorable feeling which prompts men to ascertain the history and migrations of the ancient inhabitants of the earth.

While the people of Europe boast their descent from the Goths, the Celts, and a hundred other barbarous tribes which the page of history has immortalized; the natives of America are considered as *"novi homines,"* because their existence can be traced only during two or three centuries of years. It is the duty of Americans to refute this groundless accusation, and at the same time fill up a chasm in the early history of their country; this may be effected by calling their attention to the rude stone monuments with which their country abounds, although they have hitherto escaped their notice, or been passed over as unworthy of regard.

Who is there within the limits of the wide world, that has not heard of the name and fame of the Druids, of their religious sacrifices, and of their instruments of gold, with which they severed the sacred mistletoe from the venerable father of the forest, the wide-spreading oak. The object of the present essay is to extend their empire a little farther than has hitherto been imagined, and to suggest that the Aborigines of America were of Celtic origin, that their monuments still exist in the land, and are the most ancient national memorials which America can show, and that if antiquity is to be a boast, this continent can produce monuments nearly as old as any in Europe, and derived from the same common ancestry.

Man lives a few years; but he erects monuments, and thus survives in the recollection of posterity, and the various tribes who have successively inhabited the world may be traced by the peculiar features of their architecture. That of barbarous nations was distinguished by its simplicity, and large massy stones were the first objects of attention and respect. The primitive families of the earth were destitute of tools with which to shape and polish masses of rocks; and the first national monuments we read of in sacred writ, were rude stones, either placed alone, formed into a circle, or piled into a heap.

These shapeless stones are proofs of the highest antiquity in any nation where they are found, and were erected by men of whom tradition has scarcely preserved even the name; they remind us of times to which our calculations and our history do not reach.

The Celts or Scythians, who gradually migrated from the borders of Assyria and Palestine, have left remains of their language and religion, in the central and northern regions of Asia, in England, France, Germany, Russia, and Scandinavia. Let us ascertain if no memorials of their residence can be traced in this country.

The monuments which they erected, while in distinct hordes they successively traversed the various quarters of the world, may be divided into five species. 1st. Cromlechs. 2d. Stones of memorial or sacrifice. 3d. Circles of memorial. 4th. Rocking Stones. 5th. Tumuli or Barrows.

1. We begin with the ancient and venerable cromlechs, by which, as an unerring guide, the tribes of men who erected them may be identified; they are of a peculiar structure, one huge stone, elevated two feet or more above the ground, higher at one end, and supported by several stones placed underneath. In England, some of the top stones, or rather rocks, are of an enormous size, and similar structures are found in various parts of Europe and Asia. These majestic and durable stone monuments appear built to defy the knowledge and foil the curiosity of the present race of men; the purpose for which they were erected is unknown, and various have been the opinions upon this subject.

They have successively been called tombs, small temples for the residence of country divinities, and altars contaminated with the dreadful sacrifice of human victims.

"The barbarous priests some dreadful God adore,
    And sprinkle every stone with human gore."

The voice of history, with perhaps too just a decision, affixes the perpetration of this enormity upon all the tribes who departed from the land of Scythia; but whether these were the altars consecrated for such purposes, is one of those secrets which perhaps even time can never solve.

On my arrival in this country, I thought I had left the land of Celts and Druids far behind me, and great was my astonishment, on a perusal of Silliman's Philosophical Journal, when I read in the second volume, page 200, to which the reader is requested to refer, the description of a most noble cromlech, although the writer, the Rev. Elias Cornelius, is evidently not aware of the valuable relic of antiquity which he has described. It is mentioned by that gentleman on account of a geological fact supposed to be connected with it; the highest stone is of granite, and the pillars which support it are of primitive limestone, which is therefore supposed to be of equal age with the granite above; but in fact, it is a magnificent cromlech, and the most ancient and venerable monument which America possesses, and establishes a common origin between the Aborigines who erected this monument, and the nations who erected similar cromlechs in other parts of the world.

It is thus described:—"In the town of North-Salem, and State of New-York, is a rock which, from the singularity of its position, has long attracted the notice of those who live in its vicinity; and being near the public road, seldom escapes the notice of the passing traveller. Although weighing many tons, its breadth being ten feet, and greatest circumference forty feet, it stands elevated in different parts, from two to five feet above the earth, resting its whole weight upon the apices of seven small conical pillars. Six of these, with their bases either united or contiguous, spring up like an irregular group of teeth, and constitute the support of one end of the rock. The remaining pillar supports the other end, and stands at the lowest part of the surface over which the rock is elevated.

"Notwithstanding the form of the rock is very irregular, and its surface uneven, its whole weight is so nicely adjusted upon these seven small points, that no external force yet applied, has been sufficient to give it even a tremulous motion. There is no mountain or other elevation near it, from which the rock could have been thrown."

The Geologists in Europe have made an attack upon some of these ancient monuments, and assert that they were produced by the decomposition of rocks of granite; but in this instance, the pillars underneath being of limestone, and the large stone on the top of granite, we cannot consider it as the production of nature, because those rocks seldom or never occur in that relative situation. It may also be supposed that it is a bowlder of granite, deposited by diluvian torrents in its present situation; but against this opinion, it may be asserted with some confidence, that primitive limestone never appears above the surface of ground in the shape of small conical pillars, but in large massy blocks, which may be readily seen at some distance. Others may suppose that some ardent admirer of Celtic antiquities erected this monument for his own amusement, but the immense weight of the upper stone renders this improbable.

2. *Stones of Memorial or Sacrifice.*—Mr. Kendall, who travelled in the northern parts of the United States, seems to have had a very correct idea of the value of these monuments in an historical point of view; and mentions some of those which occur in Massachusetts. He says: "In different parts of the woods are six or seven masses of stone, on which the few Indians who still hover around their ancient possessions, make offerings; and on this account the name is given to them of Sacrifice Rocks. Two of these are on the side of the road leading from Plymouth to Sandwich; one of them is six feet high, the other four, and they are ten or twelve feet in length. They differ in nothing as to their figure from the masses of granite and other rocks, which are scattered over the surface of the surrounding country. All that distinguishes them are the crowns of oak and pine branches which they bear, of which some are fresh, others are fading, and the rest decayed."

Captain Smith, in his description of Virginia, relates that the Indians had certain altar stones, which they call Pawcorances; these stand apart from their temples, some by their houses, others in their woods and wildernesses, where they met with any extraordinary accident or encounter. As you travel by them, they will tell you the cause of their erection, wherein they instruct their children as their best records of antiquity, and sacrifices are offered upon these stones when they return from the wars, from hunting, and upon many other occasions.

Charlevoix mentions the worship of rocks as one of the superstitions of the Northern Indians.

In Messrs. Lewis & Clark's Travels there are noticed several of these rocks.

Stone Idol Creek, on the Missouri, derives its name from three rude stones which the Ricaras, a tribe of Indians, worship. Whenever they pass by, they stop to make some offering of dress, in order to propitiate these sacred deities.

On the bank of the Chissetaw Creek is a rock which is held in great veneration by the neighbouring savages, and is visited by parties who go to consult it as to their own and nation's destinies.

The fate of the Mandan tribes depends upon the oracular responses of another sacred rock, whose commands are believed and obeyed with the most implicit confidence. Every spring, and on some occasions during the summer, a deputation from the savages visits the sacred spot where there is a large porous stone, twenty feet in circumference.

In Major Long's Tour to the Rocky Mountains, it is stated, that the Minnitaree Indians worship the Me-mo-ho-pa, a large, naked, and insulated rock in the midst of a small prairie, about two days' journey from the village of that nation. In shape in resembles the steep roof of a house; and the Minnitarees resort to it for the purpose of propitiating their Great Spirit by presents, fasting and lamentation, which they continue for a space of three or five days.

Under this class of Indian monuments may be a arranged the figured rock at Dighton, in the State of Massachusetts, which has been described in various publications; also the sculptured rocks that occur in many parts of the American continent, at Tiverton, Rutland, Newport, Scaticook, Brattleborough, Ohio, &c. &c.

It is to be regretted that a manuscript of the late Dr. Stiles, which is in the possession of the American Academy of Arts and Sciences, and contains an account of many of these remains, has not yet been published.

Perhaps the intricate question of American ancestry might be solved by the annals of Mexico, or the histories of Peru, and a deep research into the books of those countries, would no doubt amply repay the toil.

Acosta relates that, amongst the ancient Mexicans, worship was paid to rocks or large stones, and that in the highways they found great heaps of them, which had been offered to the gods; but he adds, that in his time this superstition of worshipping great stones had altogether ceased.

Gomara, in his account of Peru, mentions the same practice as still continued amongst the old inhabitants in that country.

Thus in the various regions of America, the natives had carefully preserved the stones of memorial and sacrifice, in the use of which they had been instructed by their Celtic ancestors, and which in some instances may have been the individual monuments erected by that people.

If accurately examined, there can be little doubt that America contains an abundance of these rude stones, which were erected by the ancient inhabitants as memorials of their history and exploits in war, or as altars on which to sacrifice to the Deity. The books of the first historians of America, contain many accounts of the homage which was paid by the natives to shapeless rocks, and the sacrifices offered upon them; but in the lapse of time, the Indians being nearly destroyed by diseases or by war, and these stones offering no particular feature to the common observer, scarcely a trace of their present position can be distinctly marked; but to the historian these rude stones are objects of the highest interest, and every exertion should be made to identify the situations where they occur.

3. *Circles of Memorial* were the next monuments erected by the ancient Celtae; they consist of nine, twelve, or more rude stones, placed so as to form a circle, and were generally placed upon an eminence.

They answered several purposes; they were dedicated to religious services, and sacrifices were made either within the sacred circle, or in its vicinity; at the election of chiefs and leaders, the nations assembled here, and public business was supposed to be sanctioned by the gods, if transacted within the boundary of their temples. They were also used by the priests for astronomical purposes.

There appear to be at least three of these sacred circles in America. I have been informed of one by Dr. E. James, the scientific tourist to the Rocky Mountains. It is situated upon a high hill, one mile from the town of Hudson, in the State of New-York, and attracted his notice many years ago, on account of the remarkable size of the stones, and their position.

In Mackenzie's tour from Quebec to the Pacific ocean, there is noticed a circle of stones, artificially laid on a high rock, upon the banks of the river Winnipigon, which discharges itself into a lake of the same name. The Indians are accustomed to crown this circle of stones with wreaths of herbage, and with branches; for this reason, the carrying place which passes it has received the appellation of Le Portage de Bonnet.

In Purchas' Collection of Voyages, vol. 3, page 1052, one of the historians of Peru, in describing the manners and customs of the children of the sun, says: "To make the computation of their year sure and certain, they did use this industry; upon the mountains which are about the city of Cuzco, where the kings held their court, there were twelve pillars set in order, and at such distance the one from the other, as that every month one of these pillars did note the rising and setting of the sun. They were called Succanga, and by means of these stones, they taught the seasons fit to sow and reap, and other things; they did certain sacrifices to these pillars of the sun."

These are no doubt connected in their history with the other Celtic remains, and resemble those druidical circles, which are so common in Europe and Asia, and which from their immense size and the majesty of their appearance, received from Tacitus the expression "rudes et informes saxorum compages," and from Cicero the appellation "mirificae moles." But the scientific assistance of individuals who reside near these monuments is requested, that an accurate account of them may be published, and thus a small ray of light be thrown over the history of the Aborigines of America.

Tradition sometimes conveys along the stream of time a name attached to these stone monuments, which informs us of their use. In Erin's bright green isle, which was a favorite resort of the Druids, these stone circles, placed upon an eminence, are called in the Irish language

Carrich Brauda; and in Wales, similar structures have retained the name Cerrig Brudyn, to the present time; the appellation is the same in both countries, and means Astronomer's circles. And thus in ages long since past, perhaps at the same instant of time, though under different skies, the Druids of England, and the priests of Cuzco, the astronomers of Ireland, Hudson, and Winnipigon, seated upon the lofty hills, and surrounded by their sacred circles of stone, were calculating the progress of the seasons, the revolutions of the planets, and the eclipses of the sun, by the same formulae which their ancestors had first practised in the central plains of Asia.

4. *Rocking Stones*, are memorials raised by the same people, and the same race of men, who elevated the cromlechs; they consist of an enormous stone so equally poised upon its base, that a very small force is sufficient to move it; sometimes even the touch of a finger will cause it to vibrate.

Granite rocking stone north of Peekskill, New York. The stone can be moved easily by hand and is 31 feet in circumference (American Journal of Science, 1:5: 253, 1822).

There are several of these memorials of a former race, in the United States of America, but of the origin of the whole of them we cannot be certain, until an accurate account is published of their size, appearance, and situation, and it would be desirable if they were illustrated by correct drawings. In the State of New-York there are probably three or more. Professor Green has described one, in the American Journal of Science, vol. 5 page 252. It is situated near the top of a high hill, near the village of Peekskill, in Putnam county; the moveable stone is thirty-one feet in circumference; the rock is of granite, but the mica contained in it being schistose, gives it some resemblance to gneiss, and it is supported by a base of the same material. This rocking stone can be moved by the hand, although six men with iron bars were unable to throw it off its pedestal. From the drawing which accompanies the description in Silliman's Journal, this rock presents every appearance of an artificial monument, and may perhaps with safety be classed amongst the Celtic antiquities of North-America.—Putnam's rock, which was thrown from its elevation on one of the mountains in the Highlands during the revolutionary war, may have been a rock of this description.

There is also a rocking stone in Orange County, State of New-York, of which no account has yet been published.

In the State of Massachusetts, I have heard of some near Boston, between Lynn and Salem, but do not vouch for the accuracy of the statement, until they undergo a careful examination.

There is one at Roxbury, near Boston, described in the Journal of Science, edited in that city.

A small rocking stone occurs at Ashburnham in the same State.

In New-Hampshire there are two; one at Andover, weighing fifteen or twenty tons, and the other at Durham. This was a short time since a very splendid rocking stone, weighing between fifty and sixty tons, and so exactly poised, that the wind would move it, and its vibrations could be plainly seen at some distance. But, two years ago, a party from Portsmouth visited it, and after several hours of labor succeeded in moving it from its position. A proper feeling on the part of the persons who effected this mischief, would cause them to restore it to its original place. The rock is forty-five feet in circumference and seven in thickness.

5. *Tumuli* or *Barrows*, are found in every part of the immense expanse of American territory, from the Lakes of Canada to the Mexican sea, from the shores of the Atlantic, to the borders of the Pacific ocean, and they may be considered merely a continuation of the same monuments which extend from the icy promontories of Kamschatcka, through the barren steppes of Tartary, the level plains of Russia, and all the northern regions of Europe.

These tumuli were the simple repositories of the Celtic dead, the tombs of their warriors, the last resting place of those who were wise in council and valiant in war, and an enlightened people should respect the remains of the former chieftains of North America.

It is a spot upon the escutcheon of Virginia that a tumulus which had belonged to an ancient Indian nation, and been described by the pen of the philosophic Jefferson, should now be nearly destroyed by the encroaching spirit of agriculture, and the bones of Celtic warriors allowed to blanch under a meridian sun, but in the western states this may be said to occur every day, and thus the vestiges of former times are effaced by the advance of the plough, and even Antiquarians have assisted to open and rifle these sanctuaries of the dead. Surely the land has been acquired cheap enough from its aboriginal possessors, and humanity might dictate that their tumuli, their mounds, their camps, their altars, and the bones of their warriors should be allowed to rest in peace.

It seems probable that if these untutored nations wished, in a more particular manner, to perpetuate the memory of some one, who was near and dear to them, who had given his nation important councils in peace, or raised the fame of his country in war, then they thought the mound of earth too humble a covering for his remains, and raised high a pile of stones, to mark to future times, the tomb of their favorite chief. In the Celtic language, these were called Cairns.

J. C. Atwater mentions them as occurring near Newark, and in the counties of Perry, Pickaway and Ross.

In Dr. Dwight's travels in Connecticut, there are noticed two of these stone tumuli, which appear to have been erected over offenders against the law.

Adair, in his History of the North American Indians, says, "in the woods we often see innumerable heaps of small stones in those places, where according to tradition, some of their distinguished people were either killed or buried. There they add stone to stone, still encreasing every heap, as a lasting monument and honor to the dead and an incentive to great actions in the survivors."

In the same volume it is said, "the Cherokees continue to raise and multiply heaps of stones, as monuments for their deceased warriors."

Mr. Jefferson says they occur in Virginia;—they are also mentioned by other historians, and tradition relates that the Indians in passing these tumuli still add a stone to the heap to shew their respect to the memory of the heroes of other times, the ancient Celtic chiefs.

These monuments of the aborigines, carry with them undoubted evidence of their Celtic origin, and although few are at present described, yet when the country is fully explored, many other remains of the same character may be observed. Moderns build their temples in crowded cities, and the talent of eminent architects is put in requisition, to erect the most splendid edifices that skill and taste can produce, but the wild and untutored Goth, Celt, Scythian, Indian, and Druid, thought it a disgrace that their Gods, who created the immensity of the heavens should be confined in buildings made by the hands of men. They worshipped them in the solitude and silence of retired groves and woods, and it is there we must look for the remains of their altars and cromlechs, their kistvaen and Tolmin.

It may be asked if these are really druidical remains, where are the Stonehenge, or the Abury, or the Carnac of America, the reply is that the insular situation of Britain, and the mountainous country of Bretagne were favorable to the institutions and genius of the Celts, and it was in those countries alone that the Druids erected those more splendid monuments of their religion, which have attracted the most powerful feelings of admiration and awe from passing ages.

What connexion can there be between the ancient Celts

and Germans, who have been described by the pencil of a Tacitus, and the wandering tribes who now inhabit the interior parts of America?

Beneath the majestic language of the Roman historian, you may discover a picture of uncivilized tribes, varying not much from the North American Indians. But these scorned even the slight trammels, which must be the bond of any civilized society, and wished to be as free as the air they breathed; the love of liberty was to these poor savages a meteor light, which divided them into weak, independent tribes, who were continually at war.

Before I close this essay, may I be allowed to say one word to plead for the preservation of these monuments, which should be to all Americans a subject of the most anxious care.

In other climes, superstition and despotism have contributed to the overthrow of many a noble Celtic monument, but in this land of freedom, it would be well, if legislative power, or better still, if public opinion would throw its shield around these remains, and protect the last monuments of a former race. Americans should consider that one of these cromlechs or Cairns, does more to elucidate the history of their native country, than the learning of Robertson, or the genius of Buffon.

The Celts erected these monuments in order that they might speak to their chilren.

> "Quid nobis dicunt isti lapides?
> Positi sunt in monumentum."

They prove that a nation of Celtic origin once inhabited this continent.

II

ASTRONOMY

6

Enigmatic Objects

Astronomers usually have little difficulty in classifying objects seen in the heavens as stars, planets, comets, or meteors. The speeds with which these objects move across the sky and the paths they take are generally diagnostic. However, every once in a while some object passes into the telescope's field of view that does not meet the criteria for any of these "acceptable" denizens of the solar system—in short, it is an "enigmatic object."

Enigmatic objects may be bright or dark; if the latter, they are seen passing in front of the sun or moon. Their proper motions are often large; that is, they move quickly across the field of fixed stars. Likewise, their trajectories may be unusual. They are here one day and almost invariably gone a day or two later.

The last two centuries have seen many enigmatic objects. Most are named after their discoverers: Huth's star, Wilk's object, and so on. It is also characteristic of enigmatic objects that only one or two observers see them before they disappear forever. The reputations of these observers must be unquestionable or the observation will be discarded. Heaven knows how many observations of enigmatic objects have never seen print because their observers were not judged completely trustworthy with the telescope.

What then are the enigmatic objects; those interlopers cruising strange solar system paths? Some observations are undoubtedly erroneous and others can probably be written off as "abnormal" comets, meteors, and the like. In other words, the criteria for identification can be stretched enough to accommodate them. The remainder, though, a substantial number, must be objects, natural or artificial, that are just "passing through." The import of enigmatic objects is that they comprise a population of unknown astronomical entities that come from somewhere unknown and move out of our ken before they can be legitimatized.

HUTH'S "MOVING STAR" OF 1801–2
Anonymous; *Nature*, 14:291–292, August 3, 1876

At the beginning of the present century, when, although Bode and some few others had been looking forward to such a discovery, astronomers generally were startled by Piazzi's accidental detection of the small planet Ceres, we read of observations of more than one so-called "moving star," which, after progressing slowly for a short interval, finally disappeared. The most singular narrative refers to an object said to have been remarked by Hofrath Huth, at Frankfort-on-the-Oder, on the night from December 2 to 3, 1801, particulars of which were communicated to Bode in several letters during the ensuing five weeks. If the observations are *bona fide,* there is yet a mystery attaching to the object to which they relate. Huth was one of the three independent discoverers of the periodical comet now known as Encke's, on October 20, 1805, Pons and Bouvard sharing with him an almost simultaneous discovery, and he did other astronomical work. Writing to Bode on December 5, he says: "In the night from the 2nd to the 3rd of this month, I saw with my 2½ feet Dollond, in a triangle with θ and δ Leonis to the south-west, a star with faint reddish light, round, and admitting of being magnified. I could not discern any trace of it with the naked eye; it had three small stars in its neighbourhood." He writes again on the 15th, that unfavourable weather had allowed of his observing the object only on three occasions, which appear to be on the early mornings of the 3rd, 13th and 14th, and he concludes from his observations that it had a slow retrograde motion to the south-west. From the 13th to the 14th, by eye-estimate, it had retrograded 4' of arc, and from the 3rd to the 13th at most 30'. He forwarded to Bode at this time a diagram of the neighbouring telescopic stars. On December 21 he writes again that he had only succeeded in observing his moving star on one additional night, that of December 19–20, when he found it "near four stars apparently situate to the westward, about half a diameter of the full moon below a smaller one." Its path appeared directed towards *i* Leonis and towards the ecliptic. He adds: "Of the motion of this planet-like star I can now no longer doubt, since I have observed a difference of ⅚° nearly, between its positions on the 3rd and 20th." In a fourth letter, dated 1802, January 12, he informs Bode that he had seen the star on two later nights, those of the 1st and 2nd of the same month from 11h. to 14h., with many telescopic stars in its vicinity, of which he enclosed a diagram, by eye-estimate only, with the path of the object.

He mentions that on January 1 the star was even smaller than one of the satellites of Jupiter, and on the following night he had difficulty in perceiving it in close proximity to a star towards which it was moving. On the 5th he could discern only now and then, to the right of the star, on the left of which it was situated on the 1st and 2nd of January, and at a very small distance from it, a glimmer, but the star's former place on the left was vacant. He concludes that the object must have been receding from the earth, and might perhaps have been more distinct and larger before December 3. On the night of January 6 there was no trace of it. He closes this final letter by saying that he would have gladly learned that some other astronomer had observed this star and confirmed its motion, and expressing his regret that Bode had not succeeded in finding it.

CACCIATORE'S SUPPOSED PLANET OF 1835
Anonymous; *Nature*, 18:261, July 4, 1878

It might have been expected that long ere this, if the object twice observed at Palermo in May, 1835, were really a planet, it would have been recovered by one or other of the astronomers who have occupied themselves with the examination of the ecliptical region of the sky.

The particulars of the Palermo observations were communicated by Cacciatore to Valz in a letter dated September 19, 1836, and at an earlier period to the late Admiral Smyth, as will be known to readers of the "Cycle of Celestial Objects." Valz sent a copy of Cacciatore's letter to Schumacher, who published it in No. 600 of the *Astronomische Nachrichten*. When observing the star 503 of Mayer's catalogue with the Ramsden circle, on May 11, 1835, it was noted down that a smaller star of the eighth magnitude followed Mayer's star two seconds of time, and was about 2½′ to the south. Such entries were frequently made by Piazzi, when observing with the same instrument, as may be seen from his catalogue, but although No. 503 occurs there, no mention is made of a star near it. On the next fine night, May 14, observing Mayer's star again, the assistant, according to custom, read out the note made on May 11: "Seguita da una altra di 8 per 2″ circa di A. R. circa 2½′ al sud." No star was then visible in this position even in a dark field, but one of the eighth magnitude *preceded* Mayer's star nine seconds of time, only 1⅓′ to the south. Cacciatore says he intended to repeat the observation on the following evening, the weather promising to continue fine. Returning to the library he found that no one of the four small planets known at that time was in the observed position, and he appears to have considered the object either a planet beyond Uranus or a comet, remarking: "Onde con impazienza attendeva il dimani." But the night of May 15 proved unfavourable, rain setting in, followed by clouded skies for upwards of a fortnight, and not until June 2 could an observation be attempted, "Ma la stella era involta nel crepusculo, feci varj [sic] tentativi fuori del meridiano, non transcurai ogni mezzo per riconoscere la mia osservazione." Cacciatore says his assistants were unsuccessful on other evenings to the end of June. The search was repeated in the first five months of 1836, but to no purpose.

Valz first showed that a body with the observed positions on May 11 and 14, could not be a distant planet, as Cacciatore had conjectured, but rather a pretty near member of the minor-planet group, which, on the hypothesis of a circular orbit, might have a period of revolution of about three years, with the ascending node of the orbit in longitude 339° 36′ and an inclination of 3° 22′ to the plane of the ecliptic. In 1849 Dr. Luther repeated the calculation with the following results:—Radius or orbit, 2.1055; ascending node, 343° 20′; inclination, 3° 37′; period, 1,116 days; and from these elements Oeltzen computed a *zodiac* for the planet, or a table indicating with right ascension as argument, the northern and southern limits of declination (*Astron. Nach.*, No. 662). It is certain that any determination of the position of the orbit from Cacciatore's data must be open to considerable uncertainty, and hence a search for his supposed planet amongst the one hundred and eighty-eight planets now discovered would not be decisive one way or the other if confined to similarity in the position of the nodes and the inclination; places must be calculated for the epoch of Cacciatore's observation for such planets as could by possibility pass near Mayer's star. An attempt in this direction has failed to identify the object. That a minor planet which so far from opposition attains the brightness of stars of the eighth magnitude can still remain unknown to us is, to say the least, very improbable. Must we leave Cacciatore's star in the same category as those reported to have been observed by Huth in 1801 and Reissig in 1803, to which reference has been made in this column?

WILK'S COMETARY OBJECT
Anonymous. *Popular Astronomy*, 34:538–539, 1926

A cablegram from Professor E. Stromgren announced the discovery by Wilk, at Cracow, of a comet in the following position: September 1. 9069 U.T., R. A. 15h. 53m. 12s., Dec. 3° 55′. Magnitude 6. "Direct motion one degree in four minutes." A radiogram was received at Harvard College Observatory, direct from Cracow, confirming the announcement.

We had no success here in locating this unusual cometary object. The magnitude 6 given by the discoverer placed it at the limit of naked-eye visibility near Serpentis. But the unusual remark "direct hourly motion 15°″" showed at once that this was a very uncommon appearance. In fact on receiving the message in the evening of September 2, I thought there was some erroneous interpretation and that 15° per day instead of per hour was already exceptional enough. Through haze and clouds I therefore exposed a pair of plates centered about 20° east of *e*

Serpentis with a wide-angle Ross lens. Only stars down to 8^M were recorded but no unexpected object was noticed. Cloudy weather interfered with further search the next few days but in the meantime the rapid angular motion was confirmed by a card from the Harvard College Observatory. I do not think there is any record of a celestial object, other than a meteor, showing such a rapid apparent motion across the sky. At that rate it was next to impossible to tell in what direction the object would have to be expected on the following days. If we consider it as a comet passing close to the earth its speed must have been about 42 km/sec. Taking into account the component of the earth's velocity I made a rough estimate showing that the object must have been at a distance from the earth less than twice the distance of the moon! I had supposed the object to move at right angles to the line of sight; otherwise the distance had to be still smaller. Under that assumption it was found that after an interval as short as twenty-four hours the object would have slowed down almost to a standstill somewhere in Aquila, but that at the same time it would have decreased in brightness by at least five magnitudes. On September 7 a plate was exposed for two hours by Messrs. Bobrovnikoff and Morgan on the region thus indicated but nothing suspicious was found.

Possibly more detailed information will enable computers to predict more closely where the object was to be expected; unless this can be done no further search of the plates can be attempted with any chance of success.

The object reminds us of the strange cometary appearance that was noticed May 4, 1916, at Cordoba by Perrine and Miss Glancy (*Pub. A. S. P.*, 28, 176, 1916). Its displacement amounted to 10° per hour. The object might of course have been an unusual form of meteor; some of these have sometimes been followed for several hours. I cannot refrain from thinking also of a terrestrial source as a conceivable explanation. It is curious to note in this connection that from the time given for the observation the altitude of the object is found to have been only 4° above the horizon of Cracow, and that any stationary source of light (pilot light of a captive balloon, automobile headlight on a mountain, mirage of a terrestrial light, or what not) would have shown relatively to the stars an hourly motion of 15° in the direction indicated by the discoverer.

But it may be better not to anticipate anything about Wilk's unusual discovery until further information about the circumstances of the observation are available. Such information is awaited with great interest.

STRANGE OBJECTS TRANSITING THE SUN'S DISC
Anonymous; *Nature*, 94:401–402, December 10, 1914

[The "telescopic meteors" mentioned below form a whole class of curious astronomical observations. Some seem windblown, like seeds, or under their own power, like birds and insects. Many, however, remain enigmatic.]

In scanning the solar surface observers have often remarked that they have seen bright objects passing across the sun's surface, and have concluded that they were meteors in the absence of any other plausible explanation. Attention may be directed to two interesting letters dealing with this subject which are communicated to the *Observatory* for November by Prof. Barnard and Mr. Denning. They put before the reader a large number of instances when such objects were observed, and decide conclusively that these daytime showers are not meteors. Mr. Denning in a series of conclusions, sums up the reasons why the objects seen were nothing like telescopic meteors, and these are as follows:—They require a longer focus than the sun; they did not move in parallel directions; their general direction agreed with the direction of the prevailing wind; they were objects of irregular shape and light filamentous material; their vagaries of motion while in sight were greatly dissimilar to that of true telescopic meteors seen at night; and, finally, on one occasion Mr. Denning followed them on several successive days and a change occurred in the directions. These showers, they state, are purely local terrestrial events. In most cases they are seeds or the down of various plants carried by the wind at high elevations. In some cases snowflakes are the cause of the phenomenon, whilst insect-swarms, gossamer-threads, etc., are sometimes observed. Prof. Barnard states that at certain seasons of the year they can be seen in abundance when the telescope is pointed within a few degrees of the sun, giving the greatest angle of reflection, and if moving slowly appear like minute stars.

THE UNIDENTIFIED BRIGHT OBJECT SEEN NEAR THE SUN

Pearce, J. A.; *Royal Astronomical Society of Canada, Journal,* 15:364–367. 1921

The object seen near the setting sun on the evening of August by observers in both hemispheres has been the subject of much discussion and the following brief account of it may be of interest to the readers of the *Journal.*

On Sunday evening August 7, a party, which included Professor Henry Norris Russell, of Princeton, Major Chambers, Capt. Rickenbacher and Director Campbell, were observing the setting sun from the porch of the latter's residence upon Mt. Hamilton, Cal. Just at sunset (14h. 50m. G.M.T.) Major Chambers said: "What star is that to the left of the sun?" Capt. Rickenbacher said that he had been watching that star for several minutes but had not mentioned it because he supposed it was well known. All agreed that the body was star-like. Its appearance still seemed stellar when a minute later Director Campbell observed it through binoculars, not more than two seconds before it disappeared behind the cloud stratum at the horizon.

Upon consulting the *Nautical Almanac* it was evident that the object seen could not have been the planet Mercury, as was at first supposed. Professor Russell and Director Campbell concluded that it was brighter than Venus would have been under similar circumstances. After a comparison of notes the following telegram was sent to the Harvard College Observatory:—"Star-like object, certainly brighter than Venus, three degrees east, one degree south, of sun seen several minutes before and at sunset by naked eye. Five observers. Set behind low clouds. Unquestionably celestial object. Chances favour nucleus bright comet, less probably nova." This information was distributed by telegraph the following day and is contained in H. C. O. *Bulletin* 757 of August 9.

The object was not seen again, although careful searches

were subsequently made. The position assigned by Campbell was R. A. 9h. 22m., Decl. 15½° N; or in ecliptic coordinates, Long. 139°, Lat 0°. 4N. For his account of the observation see the October number of the *Publications of the Astronomical Society of the Pacific.*

Two observations were made in England on August 7. Lieut. F. C. Nelson Day and others at Ferndown, Dorset, saw the object at sunset (7h. G.M.T.), estimating its position as 4° from the sun and its magnitude as -2. Mr. S. Fellows observed it at Wolverhampton with binoculars shortly after sunset. He noted it as reddish, elongated towards the sun, which was distant 6°.

Astronomische Nachrichten No. 5118, contains an observation on this object made at Plauen, Vogtland, Lat. 50° 30′ N., Long. 12° 7′ E.; by the daughter of Professor E. Kaiser and several others. It appeared like Venus at its greatest brilliancy, low in the evening sky shortly after sunset. The time was 7h. 35m. G.M.T. Its azimuth was determined as 98° 27′.6 from south to west, and its apparent altitude as 2° 35′.9, or 2° 21′.9 when corrected for refraction. Professor Wolf, of Heidelberg, deduces that the R. A. was 11h. 6.7m. and Decl. was 7° 9′ N., or Long. 165°, Lat. 1° 20′ N.

Nature, October 6, gives the following report:—"Dr. W. Bell Dawson of Ottawa, claims he saw a bright object low in the west in unusually clear air just before sunset on September 4, which he assumes to be the same as that observed at Mt. Hamilton, on August 7."

One other observation may be mentioned. Part of H. C. O. *Bulletin* 759 of October 14, is as follows:—"Dr. H. C. Emmert, of 3403 Warren Ave. West, Detroit, Michigan, states that he saw a bright object in the western sky on August 6, at 5h. 50m. E.S.T. Its altitude was 14°.5 to 15° and its azimuth 85°, the sun's altitude was 15°, and azimuth 90°. The object was fully as bright as Venus in twilight at her greatest brilliancy, and the light was perfectly steady." The date of August 6, was later confirmed by Dr. Emmert.

The writer plotted the above observations upon a celestial sphere from which the following deductions were drawn. The positions of the planets on August 6, at 5h. 50m. p.m. E.S.T. were as follows:—Venus (-3.6) had just set; Mercury (-1.0) and Mars (1.7) were too near the sun to be visible; Jupiter (-1.2) and Saturn (1.4) were within 3° of each other in azimuth 55° and altitude 35°, the moon being in conjunction with each on that day. All planets were north of the ecliptic except Venus.

Dr. Emmert's observation was made in broad daylight two hours before sunset. The altitude and azimuth he assigned gives a position of Long. 139° and Lat. 8° S., the object being 11° from the sun. Clearly some discrepancy in his observation exists, for on that day when the sun's altitude was 15°, its azimuth was 99°; and when its azimuth was 90°, its altitude was 25°, and not 15°, as stated by Dr. Emmert. Moreover, there is the difference of one day to be accounted for.

It is very probable that Dr. Bell Dawson saw one of the planets which set soon after the sun on September 4. At sunset Mercury (-0.7) had an azimuth of 89° and an altitude of 4°; while Jupiter (-1.2) had an azimuth of 86° and an altitude of 6°, either of which would agree with his statement.

Miss Kaiser's observation was made one hour after sunset. According to the position given by Professor Wolf, its azimuth and altitude at sunset were 87° and 11°, respectively, which differs considerably from the observation made in England half an hour earlier, the azimuth of the sun when setting being 116°. It would be interesting to know more details concerning Miss Kaiser's observation as the position of the body is so accurately stated. It should be pointed out that Jupiter at the time of the observation had an altitude of 3°, and an azimuth of 93°, which is indeed very near the position assigned by her. It is therefore not unlikely that she observed Jupiter. Otherwise it is difficult to account for the great difference between the position of her object and the position as stated by the English and Californian observers.

To account for the great motion along the ecliptic of 27° in 8 hours, if the Plauen and the Lick objects are to be assumed identical, the distance of the body from the earth on August 7, was, according to Professor Wolf, 0.005 astronomical units, or about twice the moon's distance. It appears unlikely that a comet at this distance would have had such a well-defined stellar appearance.

The English observations agree very closely with Russell's and Campbell's. Although the estimates of distances are probably too rough to be used for a deduction of motion, it would appear that during the interval of 8 hours the body had moved a degree or two closer to the sun.

What was it then, a nova or a comet? Being 40° from the Galactic plane would almost certainly rule out the former. A comet is more feasible. It may be noted that a comet with retrograde motion, near the plane of the ecliptic, and approaching the sun from behind might remain in close proximity to it the whole time it was bright. This was the case with the Tewfik comet of May 17, 1882. Although this hypothesis seems the most likely, the object still remains somewhat of a mystery.

Note:—On August 8, at 12h. G.M.T., luminous bands were seen at Konigstuhl, (Heidelberg) and Sonneberg, and it was subsequently reported that the earth had passed through the tail of a comet on the night of August 7–8. *Astronomische Nachrichten* No. 5116 contains full particulars of the luminous bands seen and which now are believed to have been auroral.

7

Vulcan: The Lost Intramercurial Planet

It is astounding that astronomers attach so much importance to the tiny specks of matter that circle the sun. This preoccupation with the planets must be a heritage from many generations of sky-watching astrologers. Of what terrestrial import is a minuscule bit of matter in orbit between Mercury and the sun? An object smaller and nearer to the sun than Mercury would be almost impossible to see and (supposedly) of no physical consequence to the earth; yet anyone who discovered an intramercurial planet would be famous forever.

A French physician named Lescarbault apparently discovered an intramercurial planet in 1859. Lescarbault's planet filled an astronomical need. It helped explain the advance of Mercury's perihelion and did not throw Bode's law out of joint. Lescarbault's sighting was not unexpected and was even welcome. Many famous astronomers saw it; so many, in fact, that it was given an honored place in the astronomical tables of the day under its new name, Vulcan.

The situation began to unravel late in the last century. Vulcan did not transit the sun when it should. In vain astronomers searched for it. It had vanished. Planets are not supposed to be temporary residents, and the credibility of past observers, famous in their time, was brought into question. The whole Vulcan episode was downgraded and its history rewritten in terms of the fumblings of inexperienced observers.

Einstein's theory of relativity, which also seemed to explain the advance of Mercury's perihelion, was the coup de grace. Anyone who saw an intramercurial planet in this century was looked at askance. Reports naturally dropped to a near-zero level.

Bright objects were still seen near the sun, however, and strange black spots that transited the sun. Even today objects that could well be intramercurial planets are reported. Whatever these objects are, they are here one day and gone the next. They seem to be part of that population of enigmatic objects that pervade the solar system. Without much doubt, considerable debris, including some chunks large enough to be labeled planets, circulates through the solar system. The two moons of Mars, even our own moon, may be captured interlopers. There could be a large reservoir of such objects unseen beyond Pluto's orbit. Whatever their source, whenever they penetrate the inner solar system, some discordant noise is heard with the music of the spheres.

LESCARBAULT'S PLANET (?)
Anonymous; *Astronomical Register,* 2:161, 1864

A correspondent at London, Canada, has forwarded to us a slip from an American paper, containing an account of the observation by a Mr. Samuel Beswick, of New York, of a planet which he saw cross the sun's disc on the 12th of February last, at 20 minutes past 8 in the morning: it was then 10′20″ from the eastern limb and 14′20″ from the southern limb of the sun; its motion was exactly 711″.66 in 100 minutes, and the whole time of transit was 4 hours 33.5 minutes. The size of the object was 8″; and its rate of progress across the disc exceeded that of Venus, and was less than that of Mercury. Mr. Beswick considers that this is a planet moving in an orbit between Mercury and Venus, and that from his computations it agrees with several appearances of small bodies crossing the sun, more particularly with that of Lescarbault, March 26, 1859; that of Schmidt, Oct. 11, 1847; Stark and Steinhubel, Feb. 12, 1820; Stark, Oct. 9, 1819; Fritsch, Oct. 10, 1802; and Schentan and Crefield, June 6, 1824. From these Mr. Beswick calculates the period of the planet at 126 days. He also considers that this planet will account for the supposed satellite of Venus, and that it was seen and taken for such a satellite by Cassini, Aug. 28, 1686; by Short, Oct. 23, 1740; and by Montaigne on four occasions between May 3 and 11, 1761. Mr. Beswick adds that it may be expected to cross the sun's disc on June 18, early in the morning. Our correspondent says, "I shall not attempt to speak of the merits of this paper, trusting to hear of it in the *Register*." We regret that our correspondent's communication reached us too late for our June number.

OBSERVATION OF A SUPPOSED NEW INFERIOR PLANET
Anonymous; *Astronomical Register*, 3:214, 1865

The following letter, dated Constantinople, May 10, 1865, has been addressed to M. Leverrier, by M. Aristide Coumbary:—

"I take advantage of an opportunity of communicating with you which has unexpectedly occurred, to make you acquainted with an observation made by me on May 8.

"It is my custom to direct my telescope from time to time on the sun for the purpose of observing the solar spots; and during the month of May, in particular, my scrutiny is very constant, for, to tell you the truth, the temperature at the period of the year indisposes me to active exertion. On May 8, I was observing the sun according to my custom, and about 9h. 28m. I fancied I saw a little black point detach itself from a certain spot. I did not feel quite confident that that was the case, and thinking my eye might be at fault, I rested awhile; again examining the disc, a further proof awaited me that I had not been deceived, for I found that the black point had departed from the spot to the extent of twice its former distance. This time I discovered that the black point had a circular outline, and moved minute by minute. The power I was using was 140, but I changed this for a higher one, to wit, 280. This enabled me to distinguish very plainly the movement of the black body, but the loss of light rendered the outline less clear. From the time I first saw the object till its final disappearance off the sun's limb, a period of about 48 min. elapsed. Just before the disappearance the outline became oval, and seemed to show a central separation as if there were two bodies in close contiguity, but of this I am not certain, for perhaps my eye, being fatigued, was at fault, or the eyepiece had something to do with it.

"I deem it my duty to lay this observation before you as it may serve as a basis for further observation."

THE PLANET VULCAN
Kirkwood, Daniel; *Popular Science*, 13:732–735, 1878

The discovery of an intra-Mercurial planet during the total eclipse of July 29, 1878, has given new importance to any previous speculations on the question of its existence. A brief historical review of the subject will not be without interest.

In an article by the writer, "On the Probable Existence of Undiscovered Planets," written immediately after the discovery of Neptune, and published in the *Literary Record and Journal of the Linnaean Association of Pennsylvania College*, the question was thus considered:

"The distance from the centre of Jupiter to the nearest satellite is about three times the equatorial diameter of the primary. If, therefore, we suppose the distance of the nearest primary planet to have the same ratio to the diameter of the sun, the orbit of such planet will be somewhat less than 3,000,000 miles from the sun's centre. Consequently, in the interval of 37,000,000 miles there may be four planets, the orbit of the nearest having the dimensions above stated, and their respective distances increasing in the ratio of Mercury's distance to that of Venus. Such bodies, however, in consequence of their nearness to the sun, could hardly be detected except in transiting the solar disk."

It is well known that the disturbing influence of the other planets causes an advance in the position of Mercury's perihelion. In a century this change amounts to 10°43″, which, according to Leverrier, is 38″ more than can be accounted for by the influence of the known planets. This great astronomer inferred, therefore, that a planet, or possibly a zone of extremely small asteroids, must exist within the orbit of Mercury.

The conclusions of Leverrier were communicated to the French Academy in the autumn of 1859. Soon after their publication Dr. Lescarbault, an amateur astronomer as well as a medical practitioner of Orgeres, some forty miles southwest of Paris, announced that, on March 26, 1859, he had observed the passage of a dark circular spot across the sun's disk, which he thought might have been the transit of an intra-Mercurial planet. He stated further that he had delayed the publication of the fact in the hope of obtaining confirmatory observations. On the appearance of this statement Leverrier at once determined to seek an interview with the observer, in order to test the truth of his discovery. With the details of this interview the public is familiar. After a thorough examination of Lescarbault's original memoranda, as well as of his instruments and methods of observation, Leverrier was satisfied that the amateur astronomer of Orgeres had really observed the transit of an intra-Mercurial planet. From the notes furnished by Lescarbault, the director of the Paris Observatory estimated the period of the planet at nineteen days seventeen hours; its mean distance from the sun, 13,000,-000 miles; the inclination of its orbit, 12°10′; and the greatest elongation of the body from the sun, 8°. The apparent magnitude of the solar disk, as seen from Vulcan's estimated distance, is fifty times greater than as seen from the earth.

The sun was again watched during the last days of March in 1860 and 1861, in the hope of reobserving the new member of the system. The search, however, was unsuccessful until March 20, 1862, when Mr. Lummis, of Manchester, England, between eight and nine o'clock a.m., observed a perfectly round spot moving across the sun. Having satisfied himself of the spot's rapid motion, he called a friend, who also noticed its planetary appearance. From these imperfect observations two French astronomers, MM. Valz and Radau, computed elements of the planet: the former assigning it a period of seventeen days thirteen hours; the latter, one of nineteen days twenty-two hours. From 1862 to 1878 the planet was not seen, or at least no observation was well authenticated. The transit of Mercury, however, on May 6, 1878, afforded new evidence of the truth of Leverrier's theory that Mercury's motion is disturbed either by a planet or a zone of planetary matter within his orbit.

We must now refer to a very unpleasant incident in the history of this interesting discovery. This is nothing less than the charge, by an eminent astronomer, that the observations and measurements claimed by Dr. Lescarbault were a pure fabrication. M. Liais, a French astronomer employed at Rio Janeiro by the Brazilian Government, claimed to have been engaged in an examination of the sun's surface with a telescope of twice the power of Dr. Lescarbault's, at the very time of the latter's alleged discovery of the planet. M. Liais says, therefore, that "he is in a condition to deny, in the most positive manner, the passage of a planet over the sun at the time indicated." The weight of this negative testimony has, perhaps, been over-estimated; and Lescarbault, who for eighteen years has quietly submitted to the charge of falsehood and dishonesty, may perhaps yet retort that, if M. Liais was examining the sun at the time referred to his merit as an observer cannot be highly rated.

But the astronomer of Brazil did not stop with denying the truth of Lescarbault's observations. He boldly called in question the conclusion derived by Leverrier himself from a laborious discussion of the observed transits of Mercury. It now appears, however, that in this case also his position was most unfortunately taken.

It has been frequently said that if an intra-Mercurial planet exist [sic], of any considerable magnitude, it ought to be visible during total eclipses of the sun. But who has not remarked the difficulty of finding a small or faint object when we know not where to look for it, and how easily it may be found when its position has been once pointed out? Mitchel's detection of the companion of Antares and Clark's discovery of that of Sirius are cases in point. Fortunately, however, neither argument nor explanation is any longer necessary. The new planet was undoubtedly seen during the total eclipse of July 29, 1878, by two astronomers, Prof. James C. Watson, director of the Ann Arbor Observatory, and Mr. Lewis Swift, of Rochester, New York. The former is the discoverer of more than twenty asteroids; the latter is an amateur, who has detected several new comets. Prof. Watson was stationed at Separation, Wyoming Territory. The planet was not found by him till half the time of totality was past. It was about 2½° southwest of the sun, and appeared about as bright as a 4½ magnitude star. Mr. Swift, who selected a position near Denver, Colorado, took with him his excellent comet-seeker for the special purpose of searching for intra-Mercurial planets. Two stars were seen by him at the estimated distance of 3° southwest of the sun. They were of the same magnitude—about the fifth— and at a distance apart of six or seven minutes. A straight line drawn through them pointed very nearly to the sun's centre. Mr. Swift supposed one of the stars to be Theta Cancri. The other was doubtless the planet observed by Prof. Watson, although the estimated distance from the sun was somewhat greater. Both observers describe it as a *red* star. According to Prof. Watson, "it shone with an intensely ruddy light, and it certainly had a disk larger than the spurious disk of a star." Its appearance in the telescope indicated that it was approaching its superior conjunction, or, in other words, was situated beyond the sun.

The distance of Vulcan from the centre of the system, though still uncertain, is supposed to be about one-seventh that of the earth. If this estimate be nearly correct, the solar light and heat at its surface must be about fifty times greater than at the surface of the earth. The corresponding period is nearly twenty days. In other words, Vulcan's year is believed to be less than three weeks in length. The sun is twenty-five days in completing its axial rotation; so that in the new planet we have probably another instance in which, as in the case of the inner satellite of Mars, a planetary body performs its orbital revolution in less time than is occupied by the central orb in completing its rotation. Again, as seen from the sun's surface, all the old planets rise in the east and set in the west. But this is reversed in the case of Vulcan. It rises in the west, and, after having been fifty-seven days above the horizon of any point in which the plane of its orbit intersects the sun's surface, must set in the east.

But it is useless to speculate in regard to the elements of this planet's orbit, its magnitude, physical constitution, etc. It ought certainly to be found near its greatest elongation by some of the powerful telescopes now in use. When so detected a few observations will furnish data for the complete determination of its period and distance, together with the form and inclination of its orbit.

The interesting observations of Prof. Watson and Mr. Swift will not only stimulate astronomers to renewed search for the planet so fortunately detected, but must lead also to a more thorough examination of the space within Mercury's orbit. It is not improbable that the detection of Vulcan may be merely the first in a series of similar discoveries. The solar disk will doubtless be closely watched about February 11th–17th, March 19th–27th, and October 1st–14th, as it has been claimed that at these epochs small round spots have been seen passing across the sun. In short, the prospect of planetary discoveries in this part of the system is at present more hopeful than in the space beyond the orbit of Neptune.

THE SUPPOSED PLANET VULCAN
Elger, T. G. E.; *Astronomical Register*, 7:164, 1869

In the second volume of Petit's *"Traité d'Astronomie pour les gens du Monde."* I find a notice of Coumbary's observation, of which the following is a translation:—

"In a letter from Constantinople addressed to M. Leverrier and communicated by him to the Academy of Sciences of Paris on the 29th May 1865, M. Aristide Coumbary states, *'that on the 8th May 1865 he saw a small black speck detach itself from a group of spots situated near the eastern edge and towards the top of the solar disc, and disappear 48 minutes later, at the western edge of the disc.'*

"M. Coumbary adds, *'that at the moment of egress the little black body seemed to assume an oval shape, and to be separated in the middle, as if it consisted of two bodies very near to each other. He cannot, however, be sure that this appearance was not an illusion attributable to fatigued eye-sight."*

Other observations of supposed intra-Mercurial bodies are also referred to by M. Petit:

"Two small spots were seen on the sun, *round, black, and unequal in size,* by Gruithuisen on the 26th June 1819, and by Pastorff on the following dates—23rd October 1822, 24th and 25th July 1823, six times during the year 1834 (no dates given), 18th October 1836, 1st Nov.

1836, 16th Feb. 1837. In 1834 these spots were 3″ and 1″.25 in diameter, the smaller preceding and sometimes following the larger one, at an angular distance which did not exceed 1′.16. In 1836 and 1837, arcs of 12, 6, and 14 minutes were passed over in 52, 54, and 30 minutes of time."

As I have not seen any account of M. Coumbary's observations elsewhere, I think the above extract will not be without interest to some of your readers.

AN INTRA-MERCURIAL PLANET
Russell, F. A. R.; *Nature,* 14:505, October 5, 1876

The discussion as to the existence of a planet within the orbit of Mercury leads me to communicate an observation made many years ago, which I believe nothing but the existence of an unknown planet between us and the sun can explain. On Sunday, January 29, 1860, the sun rose in a fog in London, so that he could be steadily looked at as if through a dark glass. Soon after eight o'clock a perfectly round black object was seen by four persons, including myself, clearly defined upon the lower half, according to my recollection, of the sun's disc. It passed slowly across his face and made its egress at about half-past nine a.m. In apparent size it was equal to the representations I have seen of Mercury in transit.

THE SUPPOSED PLANET VULCAN
Covington, Richard; *Scientific American,* 35:340–341, November 25, 1876

Please to add my testimony to that of others regarding the intra-mercurial planet. Unfortunately, when I saw the planet, supposing it to be known to astronomers, I did not attach such importance to the subject as to induce me to make memoranda, and at this distance of time can only think that it was about the year 1860. I was residing then in Washington Territory, and was superintending some work on a prairie, a few miles from Fort Vancouver, on the Columbia River. A range of mountains was in the distance, from behind which the sun had reached an altitude of about 30° above the horizon, when a small boy asked me what was the matter with the sun. On looking at it I saw a planet, not as your correspondent saw it, but as a perfectly rounded, well defined dark spot, having with the disk a smaller relative proportion than that you have illustrated, and situated nearer the disk's diameter. I watched its progress till its completion without a telescope, merely glancing with partially closed eyes, at very short intervals. It was in the height of summer, and the hour was so early that no one but our party, that I have heard of, saw it. I am sorry I can give so few data regarding an event of which I am as certain as of my own existence. The clear but peculiar skies of that region in summer may account for the distinctness of the view.

BRILLIANT OBJECT SEEN NEAR THE SUN
Brooks, William R.; *Popular Astronomy,* 23:449, 1915

[The following describes an enigmatic object, which because of its nearness to the sun might have been an intramercurial planet.]

Last evening about ten minutes after sunset, and just over the sunset point at an elevation of about five degrees, my daughter, Miss Anna Caroline Brooks, detected a brilliant object equaling Venus. It remained visible about two minutes, when it was covered by a cloud. Three of her companions also saw the object upon their attention being called thereto. It was not seen this evening although carefully looked for by both my daughter and myself.

I am inclined to think that this object was the nucleus of a bright comet, the tail being invisible from the overpowering light of the sky. In view of future developments I am therefore placing this observation upon record.

A TENTH PLANET?
Anonymous; *Chemistry,* 44:23–24, December 1971

Another possibility is that a tenth planet might travel in an orbit between Mercury and the sun. This was first proposed over 100 years ago by French astronomer Urbain Jean Joseph Leverrier, who predicted the discovery of Neptune. He based his prediction of the tenth planet on irregularities in Mercury's orbit and named the unknown planet Vulcan after the Roman god of fire because of its nearness to the sun.

From time to time, astronomers sighted objects thought to be Vulcan but sightings were never confirmed and, after 1910 when Einstein accounted for Mercury's irregular orbit with his general theory of relativity, most astronomers abandoned the search for Vulcan. Recently, however, the Vulcan theory was revived, partially on reports made by Henry C. Courten, Dowling College, and Grumman Aerospace Corp., Long Island, N. Y. On photographs made in Mexico during the 1970 eclipse of the sun, Courten and associates detected a number of mysterious particles which appear to be in orbits very close to the Sun (*Miami Herald,* June 15, 1970).

All the objects are very faint, and there is always the danger of detecting artifacts in the photographic plate. However, Courten feels that at least seven of the objects are real. His conclusion is based on a sensitive computer analysis to crosscheck the positions of the objects on separate plates. Also, some of the objects were confirmed by another observer in North Carolina, and one was confirmed also by a third observer in Virginia.

Courten is not sure what the objects are, but three possibilities exist: They could be comets, small planetoids, or galactic debris which is being constantly swept up by the sun as it travels through the galaxy and which gradually spirals into the sun.

VULCAN?

Anonymous; *Nature,* 246–451, December 21/28, 1973

Instruments aboard Skylab may detect an object moving in an orbit closer to the Sun than the planet Mercury, according to Henry Courten of Dowling College at Oakdale, New York. Courten has photographed the regions around the Sun regularly at total eclipses since 1966. During the 1970 eclipse in North America, one object was photographed near the Sun from three widely spaced observing sites. These images could be of a previously unknown member of the Solar System orbiting close to the Sun.

Courten believes a planetesimal "between 80 and 500 miles in diameter" moves in an orbit about 0.1 AU from the Sun. On his photographs, this appears as a star-like object between magnitude +7 and +9. Other images on Courten's plates indicate that a complete asteroid belt may exist between Mercury and the Sun.

8

TLPs: Transient Lunar Phenomena

The moon has turned out to be anything but a dead sphere "where nothing ever happens." The moonquakes detected by instruments left behind by the Apollo astronauts do not surprise us because even an old, deserted house creaks a bit as it settles. But the TLPs are something different. They are bright, starlike points of light, flashes of light, red glowing areas, and peculiar obscurations which veil lunar surface features temporarily. Literally thousands of TLPs have been recorded down the centuries; a few of the more interesting accounts are reproduced below.

Early astronomers had no doubt that the red glows were lunar volcanoes in action; the flashes of light were merely sunlight reflected from snowcapped lunar peaks. From this earthlike conception of the moon turn-of-the-century scientists turned 180 degrees to a dead-moon dictum. TLPs, of course, had no business occurring on a sterile, meteor-blasted hulk, but they kept right on happening.

A notoriously active spot on the moon is the crater Aristarchus. Glows and lights appear there frequently. Yet closeup photos from spacecraft show no active volcanoes or anything resembling fresh lava flows. Whatever causes TLPs leaves little evidence behind. Conceivably a TLP could be a sudden venting of gases from the lunar interior. This cloud of gases might become luminous due to the interaction with solar wind or possibly chemical and/or electrical activity. The fact that TLPs tend to be more frequent when the moon is closest to earth (moonquakes also peak at perigee) reinforces the gas-venting theory.

Not all of the TLPs are susceptible to the gas-venting hypothesis. Flashes resembling lightning have been observed. Some surface features carefully mapped by earlier astronomers have disappeared completely. The respected American astronomer William H. Pickering saw dark patches moving across the lunar surface which he suggested were caused by dense swarms of insects. Now if these were fireflies, several kinds of TLPs could be explained in a single hypothesis.

REMARKABLE PHENOMENA IN AN ECLIPSE OF THE MOON

Herschel, William; *Philosophical Transactions,* 82:127–128, 1792

Oct. 22, 1790, when the moon was totally eclipsed, Dr. H. viewed the disk of it with a 20-feet reflector carrying a magnifying power of 360. In several parts of it he perceived many bright, red, luminous points. Most of them were small and round. They were very numerous; as he supposed that he saw at least 150 of them. Their light did not much exceed that of Mons Porphyrites Hevelii.

OF AN APPEARANCE OF LIGHT, LIKE A STAR, SEEN IN THE DARK PART OF THE MOON, ON FRIDAY THE 7TH OF MARCH, 1794

Wilkins, Wm.; *Philosophical Transactions,* 84:450, 1794

When I saw the light speck, as shown in the sketch [not reproduced], a few minutes before 8 in the evening, I was very much surprized; for at the instant of discovery I believed a star was passing over the moon, which on the next moment's consideration I knew to be impossible. I remembered having seen, at some periods of the moon, detached lights from the serrated edge of light, through a telescope; but this spot was considerably too far distant from the enlightened part of the moon; besides, this was seen with the naked eye. I was, as it were, rivetted to the spot where I stood, during the time it continued, and took every method I could imagine to convince myself that it was not an error of sight; and 2 persons, strangers, passed me at the same time, whom I requested to look, and they said it was a star. I am confident I saw it 5 minutes at least; but as the time is only conjectural, it might not possibly be so long. The spot appeared rather brighter than any other enlightened part of the moon. It was there when I first looked. The whole time I saw it, it was a fixed, steady light, except the moment before it disappeared, when its brightness increased; but that appearance was instantaneous.

LUNAR VOLCANOES
Anonymous; *American Journal of Science,* 1:5:176–177, 1822

Dr. Olbers observed on the 5th of last February, the phenomenon which some philosophers have attributed to volcanoes in the moon. He declared that he never perceived it more distinctly. The spot called Aristarchus, threw out a very vivid light, and appeared like a star of the 6th magnitude, placed on the north-east of the moon. The evening of the 6th unhappily was not so fine as that of the preceding day, and Dr. O. could not pursue his observations, but the English journals announce that Capt. Kater had made on the 7th of Feb. a report to the Royal Society of London in which he affirms that he had seen a lunar volcano in actual eruption. Dr. Olbers thinks that the observations of Capt. K. coincide exactly with his own, but he differs from him with respect to the cause. He does not admit the existence of a volcano in the moon; he thinks that the phenomenon which Capt. K. regards as such, is produced by the reflection of the light cast by the earth on the open immense rocks of a smooth surface, situated on the part of the moon called *Aristarchus.* Should these rocks, says Dr. O. send back only a tenth part of the light which they receive from the earth, (our mirrors return one half of the incident light) the effect would be equal to a star of the sixth magnitude. It is in this way that Dr. Olbers accounts for our always seeing those spots in the same place, and also why they do not show themselves at each lunation. On the 6th of March, Dr. Olbers could distinctly see all the spots of the moon; Grimaldi, Copernicus, Kepler, Manidius, &c. Aristarchus, was particularly remarkable, but it was not so splendid as on the 5th of February.

The hypothesis of volcanoes in the moon is not modern, and at present it is almost rejected, and the explanation of Dr. Olbers is generally admitted. The spot *Aristarchus,* is plainly to be seen when the moon is illuminated by the sun, and hence it is natural that it should appear more luminous than the rest of the disc, when it is enlightened only by the earth. As to the variation of extent which is remarked commonly in the spots at the beginning of a lunation, the phenomena of refraction, produced by the position of the moon near the horizon, are sufficient to explain it without having recourse to lunar volcanoes.

OF THREE VOLCANOES IN THE MOON

Herschel, Wm.; *A Popular Display of the Wonders of Nature* ... Clarke, C. C., W. Tweedie, London, 1837, pp. 486–487

April 19, 1787, I perceive three volcanoes in different places of the dark part of the new moon. Two of them are either already nearly extinct, or otherwise in a state of approaching eruption; which, perhaps, may be decided next lunation. The third shows an actual eruption of fire, or luminous matter.

April 29, 1787, the volcano burns with greater violence than last night. I believe its diameter cannot be less than 3″, by comparing it with that of the Georgian planet; as Jupiter was near at hand, I turned the telescope to his third satellite, and estimated the diameter of the burning part of the volcano to be equal to at least twice that of the satellite. Hence we may compute that the shining or burning matter must be above three miles in diameter. It is of an irregular round figure, and very sharply defined on the edges. The other two volcanoes are much farther towards the centre of the moon, and resemble large, pretty faint nebulae, that are gradually much brighter in the middle; but no well defined luminous spot can be discerned in them. These three spots are plainly to be distinguished from the rest of the marks on the moon; for the reflection of the sun's rays from the earth is, in its present situation, sufficiently bright, with a ten-feet reflector, to show the moon's spots, even the darkest of them: nor did I perceive any similar phenomena last lunation, though I then viewed the same places with the same instrument.

The appearance of what I have called the actual fire or eruption of a volcano exactly resembled a small piece of burning charcoal, when it is covered by a very thin coat of white ashes, which frequently adhere to it when it has been some time ignited; and it had a degree of brightness, about as strong as that with which such a coal would be seen to glow in faint daylight. All the adjacent parts of the volcanic mountain seemed to be faintly illuminated by the eruption, and were gradually more obscure as they lay at a greater distance from the crater.

REPORT ON THE DISCUSSION OF OBSERVATIONS OF SPOTS ON THE SURFACE OF THE LUNAR CRATER PLATO
Birt, W. R.; *Reports of the British Association, 1871,* pp. 60–97

Although on that night we were only able to turn the telescope 150 palms long, on the moon we detected, in the lunar spot named Plato, a phenomenon not previously observed. The moon was at the time a little past its first quadrature with the sun, which it had attained on the previous day, and the spot Plato fell on the periphery of solar illumination, where is the boundary of light and darkness in the lunar hemisphere exposed to the sun. The whole of the very elevated margin, which on all sides surrounds the spot like a deep pit, appeared bathed in the white rays of the sun. The bottom of the spot, on the other hand, was still in darkness, the solar light not yet reaching it; but a track of ruddy light, like a beam, crossed the middle of the obscure area, stretching straight across it from one extremity to the other, with much the same appearance as in winter in a closed chamber the sun's rays admitted through a window are wont to present, or as they are seen in the distance when cast through openings in the clouds, or like comets' tails at night in a clear sky stretched out at length in space, as we remember to have seen in the one which in the years 1680 and 1681 was so conspicuous to all Europe. This appearance, never before seen by me in this or any other lunar spot, is represented in the figure which I give below.

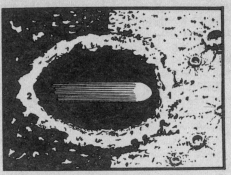

Luminous phenomenon in the crater Plato.

1, 2. The lunar spot named Plato, and the ruddy ray of the sun thrown across its dark floor from the margin of a spot 1, white and turned towards the sun. It was thus observed at Rome on the Palatine Mount, Aug. 16, 1725, at 1½ hours after sunset, with the 150-palm telescope of J. Campini.

NEW LIGHT ON A LUNAR MYSTERY
Serviss, Garrett P.; *Popular Science Monthly,* 34:158–161, December 1888

Every possessor of a telescope knows that among the mountains of the moon there are some to which the name of "shining mountains" seems peculiarly applicable. The most celebrated of these is the huge extinct volcano Aristarchus, the slopes of whose crater possess such extraordinary reflective power that it is visible on the night-side of the moon by virtue of the comparatively faint light received from the earth. Another famous bright mountain on the moon is Proclus, which rears its crest high above the eastern shore of the so-called Crisian Sea. With a telescope I have seen Proclus glittering above the brownish plains surrounding it, in the middle of a summer afternoon, when, to the naked eye, the moon appeared as a faint silvery disk, half blended with the blue of the sky. There are other natural features of the moon's surface which shine with extraordinary brightness, the most conspicuous being the systems of long "rays," radiating from such crater-rings as Tycho and Copernicus.

But in addition to these long-known and easily recognized objects, there have occasionally been seen upon the moon certain bright points, which are even more curious and mysterious than the shining mountains. The earliest observation of this kind appears to have been made by Herschel in 1783. It was repeated by him in 1787, when he did not hesitate to report, in a communication to the Royal Society, that he had discovered three lunar volcanoes in a state of eruption. Astronomers have been considerably puzzled ever since to account for Herschel's statement. Nobody could question the accuracy of his observation, so far as the power of his telescope enabled him to carry it. At the same time, few if any, especially in recent times, were willing to admit that that prince of telescopists had really seen volcanoes in action upon the moon. The complete absence of any evidence that volcanic activity did not cease upon our satellite ages upon ages ago militated too strongly against Herschel's assertion. The general conclusion finally was, that Herschel had been misled by the extraordinary brightness of some of the shining mountains which I have just described. It remained almost the only serious blot upon Herschel's record as an observer. He had described the appearance of the supposed eruption too carefully to admit any question as to his meaning. And yet, it seemed, a mere tyro in astronomical observation could hardly be deceived in such a manner, much less the most famous astronomer of his time.

But just now new light has been thrown upon the mystery, and it comes from that center of astronomical interest, the Lick Observatory. Prof. Holden believes that he has discovered, if not one of the same objects described by Herschel, a phenomenon of the same kind. It is hardly necessary to say that Prof. Holden has not discovered a lunar volcano in action, but the extraordinary appearance that he has seen sufficiently accounts for Herschel's mistake. It will be best to quote the Lick Observatory director's own words from his letter on the subject to "The Observatory," an English astronomical journal:

"I have never been able to understand how Herschel, the keenest of observers, could have been deceived in this observation until the night of July 15th of this year, when I was looking at the moon with the great telescope. At the southern extremity of the Alps, in the dark portion of the disk, not far from the terminator, I saw an illumination of the crest of a high peak which was extraordinarily and incredibly bright . . . No part of this illumination seemed less bright than a first-magnitude star, and, taken altogether, it was the brightest object I have ever seen in the sky. It was apparently ten times as bright as neighboring portions of the moon's surface. Its yellow light was tinged in places with the purple due to the secondary spectrum of the objective; and, viewed as a whole, it presented the appearance of a vast conflagration—something quite foreign to the brilliant white of the rest of the moon's surface.

"It would have required no stretch of the imagination to have supposed it to be a tremendous eruption of a range of lunar volcanoes . . . Observations on this and the succeeding nights showed that it was in fact due to a specially brilliant and favorable illumination of a mountain-ridge near the southern termination of the lunar Alps.

"I have now no doubt that the observation of Sir William Herschel referred to similar appearances."

Prof. Holden then refers to a similar, though less brilliant, display that was witnessed in 1843 by Dr. Gerling, of Marburg, apparently at the same spot on the moon.

I may add that there are at least two other recorded apparitions of this sort which were seen in that neighborhood, but evidently not in exactly the same place. The first was observed by Schroeter, the German selenographer, in 1788. He saw in the shadow of the great range of the lunar Alps, at the eastern foot of the mountains, a bright point, as brilliant as a fifth-magnitude star, which disappeared after he had watched it for fifteen minutes. Subsequently, when the region where this light appeared had become fully illuminated by the rising sun, Schroeter perceived, where the light had been, a round shadow on the surface of the moon, which was sometimes gray and sometimes black. Nothing more was ever seen of the light, so far as any record informs us, until 1865, when Grover, an English observer, caught sight of it again, under circumstances similar to those of its first apparition, and watched it for half an hour, when it once more disappeared. It should be said that, in the case of Dr. Gerling's observation, referred to by Prof. Holden, a "small, round, isolated, conical mountain" was found in the place where the light had been, on the evening following its appearance. It is altogether probable that the gray or black spot perceived by Schroeter was the shadow of a similar mountain, for it is well known that some of the lunar mountains and hills are hardly visible at all except when lateral illumination indicates their position and form by means of the shadows.

Herschel thought he had seen three active volcanoes. If Prof. Holden's discovery accounts for one of these, it is possible that the observations I have just described may give a clew to the others. The phenomenon seen by Schroeter and Grover was located fifty or sixty miles north of the point where Prof. Holden beheld the extraordinary blaze of light last July, and at a point where the mountains, drawing around a culminating peak, confront with tremendous buttresses the broad level of the Mare Imbrium.

The objection has been made by Messrs. Elger and Williams, two competent English observers, that Herschel's volcanoes can not be identical with the glittering peaks seen by either Holden or Gerling, because the latter were observed close to the line of sunrise, where the morning rays touched them, while the phenomena that attracted Herschel's attention were situated far within that part of the disk where the only light came from the earth. But Prof. Holden does not say that the illumination he witnessed was identical in *place* with those recorded by Herschel, but simply that it was identical in *kind*. Besides, it must be remembered that, if these luminous appearances are due to peculiar angles of reflection, a similar effect must be produced whether the reflecting surfaces are presented to the sunlight or only to the earth-shine. The difference would be simply in the degree of brightness of the phenomena.

But while the discovery with the Lick telescope may

account for Herschel's mistake, it does not clear up the mystery of the cause of these extraordinary lights. In every case quoted above, the illumination was evidently very much greater than that of Aristarchus, the most brilliant of the shining mountains. Proctor estimated that the reflective power of Aristarchus must be equal to that of newfallen snow. But the mountain-crest observed by Prof. Holden blazed with a dazzling brilliancy that it would be difficult to account for except upon the theory that nearly all of the sunlight falling upon it was reflected to the observer's eye. Reflection at a particular angle from vast sheets of ice, as smooth as glass, might be suggested as the cause of such a display, but how could ice be there without water or atmosphere? The suggestion that has been offered to account for the brightness of Aristarchus and the "ray" systems, namely, that they are composed of metallic dikes and masses which, for various reasons, have escaped oxidation, is recalled by the phenomenon in question. Upon that view we might have to assume that these luminous points indicated the existence of tremendous crystallized masses, with polished surfaces, throwing back the glare of the sunshine like mirrors. But then we should not be far from the view set forth in Richard Adams Locke's celebrated "Moon Hoax," that some of the glittering eminences on the moon are nothing less than enormous quartz-crystals, whose dimensions are measured by miles instead of inches!

The fact that the apparitions of extraordinary luminosity are confined to comparatively very small areas, and are visible only for a short time and at long intervals, must be taken as an indication that the reflecting surfaces to which they are due must be of such a nature, and so disposed, that they can reflect the sun's light to us only when presented at a particular angle to our line of sight; just as a piece of looking-glass, exposed to the sun at a distance, suddenly darts a piercing ray when the eye comes within the plane of reflection. That these surfaces are the flanks of mountains is in the highest degree probable, and this but serves to heighten the impression of their extraordinary nature.

The rapid appearances and disappearances, and the long periods of invisibility, are readily accounted for by the various librations of the moon, whereby it presents its disk to us at a continually varying angle, as it swims along in its "squirming orbit," under the conflicting attractions of the sun and the earth.

LIGHTNING-LIKE PHENOMENA ON THE MOON
Giddings, N. J.; *Science,* 104:146, August 9, 1946

The following observations were made some time ago and seem to me to be worthy of recording in *Science.* During the evening of 17 June 1931, I was working in the yard near our house at Riverside, California, and happened to glance at the moon. It was an unusually fine, clearly outlined new moon, and as I stood looking at it, suddenly some flashes of light streaked across the dark surface but definitely within the limits of the moon's outline. Since this was a phenomenon which I had never seen before, I continued to watch it and saw similar flashes streak across the moon again in a moment or two. Without mentioning what I had seen, I called my wife's attention to the new moon. She admired it. When I asked her to watch it closely to see if she noticed anything strange, she said: "Oh, yes, I see lightning on the moon," adding that this appeared to be confined to the moon. We watched it for some 20 or 30 minutes during which the phenomenon must have occurred at least six or seven times. The facts were recorded in my notebook as of approximately 7:40 p.m. 17 June 1931. At the time, I was inclined to attribute the phenomenon to some sort of sunlight reflection from mountain peaks on the moon or possibly some sort of electrical activity. I wrote the Mount Wilson Observatory regarding the phenomenon, and the reply very courteously discounted my observations. The observations were carefully made and carefully verified, and at the time I assumed that the phenomenon was probably something with which astronomers were familiar.

9

Mars: Is Anyone There?

We could detect the existence of intelligent Martians by decoding the signals they would obviously send in our direction, being naturally communicative as they are. Or we could admire their stupendous engineering achievements as seen through our telescopes. The history of human excursions in both of these areas is not only fascinating but of great import in our understanding of natural anomalies.

The Martian canals cannot be ignored as a terrestrial and possibly as a Martian phenomenon. These lines or streaks are well described by Schiaparelli in the first selection below. Schiaparelli was the first to see and map canals in large numbers. That canals are seen on Mars cannot be denied. Some observers have seen a great geometrical network of lines when the earth's atmosphere holds still for a moment; others, just as capable, see only a few wisps and fuzzy streaks. The phenomenon at hand, however, is not the canals themselves but rather human perception and interpretation of unusual features of the natural world. One extreme position was that of Percival Lowell, who drew meticulous maps of the canals and worried that the Martians were fighting a losing battle to survive on a dying planet.

The great variety and variability of the markings on the Martian surface have led to claims that the Martians were trying to signal us. At one time plans were suggested for planting midwestern crops in patterns by way of acknowledging the communication. Here again there is that tendency to add psycho-

logically satisfying meanings to interpretations of
natural phenomena.

Martian markings and "signals" seem to have that
same elusiveness and changeability that characterize
some terrestrial phenomena, such as ball lightning
and the Barisal guns—that will-o'-the-wisp, ghostlike
quality. Are all the frontiers of human knowledge
and experience plagued by such fuzziness and in-
determinacy? And if so, how strongly do our pre-
conceptions of the cosmos determine the image that
finally swims into focus?

SCHIAPARELLI ON MARS
Anonymous; *Nature,* 51:87–90, November 22, 1894

[Schiaparelli's work, especially his detailed maps of
Mars, first drew popular attention to the Martian canals.
Here are his views regarding them—a period piece by a
great astronomer about a problem still not fully solved.]

The Canals or Channels. All the vast extent of the continents is furrowed upon every side by a network of
numerous lines or fine stripes of a more or less pronounced dark colour, whose aspect is very variable. These
traverse the planet for long distances in regular lines, that
do not at all resemble the winding courses of our streams,
some of the shorter ones do not reach 500 kilometres (300
miles), others on the other hand extend for many thousands, occupying a quarter or sometimes even a third of a
circumference of the planet. Some of these are very easy to
see, especially that one which is near the extreme left-
hand limit of our map, and is designated by the name of
Nilosyrtis. Others in turn are extremely difficult, and resemble the finest thread of spider's web drawn across the
disc. They are subject also to great variations in their
breadth, which may reach 200 or even 300 kilometres (120
to 180 miles) for the Nilosyrtis, whilst some are scarcely
30 kilometres (18 miles) broad.

These lines or stripes are the famous canals of Mars, of
which so much has been said. As far as we have been able
to observe them hitherto, they are certainly fixed con-
figurations upon the planet. The Nilosyrtis has been seen
in that place for nearly one hundred years, and some of
the others for at least thirty years. Their length and ar-

rangement are constant, or vary only between very narrow limits. Each of them always begins and ends between the same regions. But their appearance and their degree of visibility vary greatly, for all of them, from one opposition to another, and even from one week to another, and these variations do not take place simultaneously and according to the same laws for all, but in most cases happen apparently capriciously, or at least according to laws not sufficiently simple for us to be able to unravel. Often one or more become indistinct, or even wholly invisible, whilst others in their vicinity increase to the point of becoming conspicuous even in telescopes of moderate power.

Every canal (for now we shall so call them) opens at its ends, either into a sea, or into a lake, or into another canal, or else into the intersection of several other canals. None of them have yet been seen cut off in the middle of the continent, remaining without beginning or without end. This fact is of the highest importance. The canals may intersect among themselves at all possible angles, but by preference they converge towards the small spots to which we have given the name of lakes. For example, seven are seen to converge in Lacus Phoenicis, eight in Trivium Charontis, six in Lunae Lacus, and six in Ismenius Lacus.

The normal appearance of a canal is that of a nearly uniform stripe, black, or at least of a dark colour, similar to that of the seas, in which the regularity of its general course does not exclude small variations in its breadth, and small sinuosities in its two sides. Often it happens that such a dark line opening out upon the sea is enlarged into the form of a trumpet, forming a huge bay, similar to the estuaries of certain terrestrial streams. The Margaritifer Sinus, the Aonius Sinus, the Aurorae Sinus, and the two horns of the Sabaeus Sinus are thus formed, at the mouths of one or more canals, opening into the Mare Erythraeum or into the Mare Australe. The largest example of such a gulf is the Syrtis Major, formed by the vast mouth of the Nilosyrtis, so called. This gulf is not less than 1800 kilometres (1100 miles) in breadth, and attains nearly the same depth in a longitudinal direction. Its surface is little less than that of the Bay of Bengal. In this case we see clearly the dark surface of the sea continued without apparent interruption into that of the canal. Inasmuch as the surfaces called seas are truly a liquid expanse, we can-

not doubt that the canals are a simple prolongation of
them, crossing the yellow areas or continents.

Of the remainder, that the lines called canals are truly
great furrows or depressions in the surface of the planet,
destined for the passage of the liquid mass, and constituting
for it a true hydrographic system, is demonstrated by the
phenomena which are observed during the melting of the
northern snows. We have already remarked that at the
time of melting they appeared surrounded by a dark zone,
forming a species of temporary sea. At that time the canals
of the surrounding region become blacker and wider, increasing to the point of converting, at a certain time, all
of the yellow region comprised between the edge of the
snow and the parallel of 60° north latitude, into numerous
islands of small extent. Such a state of things does not
cease, until the snow, reduced to its minimum area, ceases
to melt. Then the breadth of the canals diminishes, the
temporary sea disappears, and the yellow region again re-
turns to its former area. The different phases of these vast
phenomena are renewed at each return of the seasons, and
we have been able to observe them in all their particulars
very easily during the oppositions of 1882, 1884, and
1886, when the planet presented its northern pole to terrestrial spectators. The most natural and the most simple
interpretation is that to which we have referred, of a
great inundation produced by the melting of the snows—
it is entirely logical, and is sustained by evident analogy
with terrestrial phenomena. We conclude, therefore, that
the canals are such in fact, and not only in name. The
network formed by these was probably determined in its
origin in the geological state of the planet, and has come
to be slowly elaborated in the course of centuries. It is
not necessary to suppose them the work of intelligent beings, and notwithstanding the almost geometrical appearance of all of their system, we are now inclined to believe
them to be produced by the evolution of the planet, just
as on the Earth we have the English Channel and the Channel of Mozambique.

The Gemination of the Canals. The most surprising
phenomenon pertaining to the canals of Mars is their
gemination, which seems to be produced principally in the
months which precede, and in those which follow the
great northern inundation, at about the times of the

equinoxes. In consequence of a rapid process, which certainly lasts at most a few days, or even perhaps only a few hours, and of which it has not yet been possible to determine the particulars with certainty, a given canal changes its appearance, and is found transformed through all its length, into two lines or uniform stripes, more or less parallel to one another, and which run straight and equal with the exact geometrical precision of the two rails of a railroad. But this exact course is the only point of resemblance with the rails, because in dimensions there is no comparison possible, as it is easy to imagine. The two lines follow very nearly the direction of the original canal, and end in the place where it ended. One of these is often superposed as exactly as possible upon the former line, the other being drawn anew, but in this case the original line loses all the small irregularities and curvature that it may have originally possessed. But it also happens that both the lines may occupy opposite sides of the former canal, and be located upon entirely new ground. The distance between the two lines differs in different geminations, and varies from 600 kilometres (360 miles) and more, down to the smallest limit at which two lines may appear separated in large visual telescopes—less than an interval of 50 kilometres (30 miles). The breadth of the stripes themselves may range from the limit of visibility, which we may suppose to be 30 kilometres (18 miles), up to more than 100 kilometres (60 miles). The colour of the two lines varies from black to a light red, which can hardly be distinguished from the general yellow background of the continental surface. The space between is for the most part yellow, but in many cases appear whitish. The gemination is not necessarily confined only to the canals, but tends to be produced also in the lakes. Often one of these is seen transformed into two short, broad, dark lines parallel to one another, and traversed by a yellow line. In these cases the gemination is naturally short, and does not exceed the limits of the original lake.

The gemination is not shown by all at the same time, but when the season is at hand, it begins to be produced here and there, in an isolated, irregular manner, or at least without any easily recognisable order. In many canals (such as the Nilosyrtis for example) the gemination is lacking entirely, or is scarcely visible. After having lasted for some months, the markings fade out gradually and disappear until another season equally favourable for their formation. Thus it happens that in certain other seasons (especially near the southern solstice of the planet) that few are seen, or even none at all. In different oppositions the gemination of the same canal may present different appearances as to width, intensity and arrangement of the two stripes, also in some cases the direction of the lines may vary, although by the smallest quantity, but still deviating by a small amount from the canal with which they are directly associated. From this important fact it is immediately understood that the gemination cannot be a fixed formation upon the surface of Mars, and of a geographical character like the canals.

The observation of the geminations is one of the greatest difficulty, and can only be made by an eye well practised in such work, added to a telescope of accurate construction and of great power. This explains why it is that it was not seen before 1882. In the ten years that have transpired since that time, it has been seen and described at eight or ten observatories. Nevertheless, some still deny that these phenomena are real, and tax with illusion (or even imposture) those who declare that they have observed it.

Explanations of the Gemination of Canals. Having regard then to the principle that in the explanation of natural phenomena, it is universally agreed to begin with the simplest suppositions, the first hypotheses on the nature and cause of the geminations have for the most part put in operation only the laws of inorganic nature. Thus the gemination is supposed to be due either to the effects of light in the atmosphere of Mars, or to optical illusions produced by vapours in various manners, or to glacial phenomena of a perpetual winter, to which it is known all the planets will be condemned, or to double cracks in its surface, or to single cracks of which the images are doubled by the effect of smoke issuing in long lines and blown laterally by the wind. The examination of these ingenious suppositions leads us to conclude that none of them seem to correspond entirely with the observed facts, either in whole or in part. Some of these hypotheses would not have been proposed had their authors been able to examine the geminations with their own eyes.

It is far easier to explain the gemination if we are willing to introduce the forces pertaining to organic nature. Here the field of plausible supposition is immense, being capable of making an infinite number of combinations capable of satisfying the appearances even with the smallest and simplest means. Changes of vegetation over a vast area, and the production of animals, also very small, but in enormous multitudes, may well be rendered visible at such a distance. An observer placed in the moon would be able to see such an appearance at the times in which agricultural operations are carried out upon one vast plain—the seed time and the gathering of the harvest. In such a manner also would the flowers of the plants of the great steppes of Europe and Asia be rendered visible at the distance of Mars—by a variety of colouring. A similar system of operations produced in that planet may thus certainly be rendered visible to us. But how difficult for the Lunarians and Areans to be able to imagine the true causes of such changes of appearance, without having first at least some superficial knowledge of terrestrial nature! So also for us, who know so little of the physical state of Mars, and nothing of its organic world, the great liberty of possible supposition renders arbitrary all explanations of thus sort, and constitutes the gravest obstacle to the acquisition of well-founded notions. All that we may hope is that with time the uncertainty of the problem will gradually diminish, demonstrating, if not what the geminations are, at least what they cannot be. We may also confide a little in what Galileo called "the courtesy of nature," thanks to which, sometimes from an unexpected source, a ray of light will illuminate an investigation at first believed inaccessible to our speculations, and of which we have a beautiful example in celestial chemistry. Let us therefore hope and study.

PHOTOGRAPHS OF THE MARTIAN CANALS
Anonymous; *Nature,* 72:302–303, July 27, 1905

Since the opposition of Mars in 1901, persistent efforts have been made at the Lowell Observatory to secure photographs of the planet on which the canals could be seen definitely. After making a number of exposures with a camera in which the film was continuous, so that a large

number of short exposures—as in the bioscope—could be
made on the one film, Mr. Lampland succeeded in obtaining negatives which demonstrate indubitably the actual
existence of the "canals" Nilosyrtis, Pyramus, Casius,
Protonilus, Astaboras S., and Thoth. In addition to these,
the "regions" Syrtis Major, Mare Erythraeum, Mare Icarium, Hellas and the north polar cap, and the "oasis" Lucus
Ismenius are plainly discernible. A photographic print
from a negative secured on May 11 at 19h. 44m.–48m.
(G.M.T.) on which these features are visible is affixed in
the *Lowell Observatory Bulletin,* No. 21, accompanied by a
drawing made by Mr. Lowell immediately before the exposure was made. Other photographs secured show other
canals, and Mr. Lampland is to be congratulated, in
company with Mr. Lowell, upon thus securing unquestionable evidence of the actual existence of these features.

THE NEW CANALS OF MARS
Lowell, Percival; *Nature,* 82:489–491, February 24, 1910

[Percival Lowell founded Lowell Observatory specifically for the study of Mars. After observing the planet and
its canals for many years, he concluded that Mars was inhabited and was crisscrossed by a network of artificial
waterways. The variability of the canals naturally presented a problem to anyone of his persuasion. In this selection he explains the "new" canals.]

The word "new" when applied to a celestial phenomenon may be used in either of two senses. It may mean
new to earthly observation, i.e. one which has never been
seen by human beings before, or, secondly, new in itself,
that is, one which has had no previous existence. New canals on Mars in the first sense, though always interesting,
and at times highly important, are no novelty at this observatory, inasmuch as some four hundred have been
discovered here in the last fifteen years. When Schiaparelli
left his great work, he had mapped about 120 canals; with
those detected here since, the number has now risen to
between five and six hundred. Each of the four hundred
thus added to the list, however rich an acquisition at the
time it first came to be noticed, was not necessarily otherwise remarkable.

To observe, however, a canal new in the second meaning of the word, one, that is, that had never existed anteriorly, and to prove the fact, is an astronomical detection of far-reaching significance for the bearing it has upon the whole Martian question.

On September 30, 1909, when the region of the Syrtis Major came round again into view, after its periodic hiding of six weeks due to the unequal rotation periods of the earth and Mars, two striking canals were at once evident to the east of the Syrtis in places where no canals had ever previously been seen. Not only was their appearance unprecedented, but the canals themselves were the most conspicuous ones on that part of the disc. They ran one from the bottom of the Syrtis (lat. 20°N., long. 285°), the other from a point part way up its eastern side (lat. 17°N., long. 284°), and, curving slightly to the left as they proceeded south, converged to an oasis, itself new, on the Cocytus (lat. 5°N., long. 265°), about two-thirds of the distance to where that canal meets the Amenthes. The Amenthes itself was not visible, except possibly as a suspicion. With the two main canals were associated several smaller ones, and at least two oases which had never been seen before, and from the interconnection of all of them these clearly made part of the new piece of Martian triangulation.

The phenomena were recorded in many independent drawings by Mr. E. C. Slipher and the director, and in the course of the next few days were photographed, appearing on the plates to the eye as the most conspicuous canals in the presentment of the planet. It is opportune that detailed photography of Mars in Mr. Lampland's skilful hands should have been so perfected as to make this possible; for the photographs taken by both Mr. E. C. Slipher and the director record these canals so that anyone may see them. There are thirty images, more or less, on each plate, and the canals appear on every image; on some more distinctly than on others, owing to the state of our air at the time, but recognisably on all; for each image had a pose of about two seconds and a half, and its definition varied according to the seeing at the time. Owing to the grain of the plate being much coarser than that of the eye, the two canals appear merged in one in the photographic images as a single line, its linear character, however, being quite distinct to one of good eyesight.

The photographs of this region taken in 1907 show no such feature.

No remembrance of ever having seen them before could be recalled by either observer, both being familiar with the planet, except that Mr. Slipher turned out to have drawn one of them the evening previous.

The record books were then examined, when it appeared that not a trace of them was to be found in the drawings of August, July, June, or May when this part of the planet was depicted. That they had not been observed in previous years was then conclusively ascertained by examination of the records of those years. The record of canals seen here is registered after each opposition in a fresh map of the planet's surface. This has been done since the beginning of the critical study of Mars at this observatory in 1894. Now, when these maps came to be scrutinised for the canals, each of them failed to show any such features. Nor had any observer previous to 1894 recorded them, as the observatory library of the subject bore witness. Schiaparelli had never seen them, nor had his predecessors or successors. This determined definitely that no human eye had ever looked upon them before. But, stirring as it is to know that one is the first to see a new geographical feature on another planet, akin to the thrill of finding unknown land in our own Antarctic regions, a much deeper scientific interest attaches to the question whether a phenomenon previously undiscovered was also previously non-existent. For in that case one has seen something come into being, with all that such origination implies.

It might seem to persons not versed in the subject that its absence on the charts was proof that a canal was itself new in the second sense because it was so in the first; but study of Mars has shown that this cannot be taken off-hand for granted. Several points must each be carefully considered. In the first place, one must be sure that the phenomenon could have been seen before, yet was not. It must be of a size which could not have escaped detection previously. Now, the great majority of canals discovered here were beyond the hope of detection elsewhere, owing to the character of the air, the improvement in instrumental means, and the long acquired knowledge of the observers. That they were not seen by Schiaparelli, therefore, by no means implies that they did not exist in his day—or even in the earlier days of observation here. We see to-day vastly more than we did in 1894, because of the experience acquired since. In the present case, however, this possibility of error was excluded by the size of the canals in question. They were not difficult detail of the order here mentioned, but, as I have said, the most conspicuous on the disc, canals which no observer of any standing whatever in good air could possibly pass by. They would strike any skilled observer of such matters the moment he looked at the planet. So far as this point went, then, they could not have existed before.

ON THE SUGGESTED MOVEMENT OF THE CANALS OF MARS
Lowell, Percival; *Popular Astronomy*, 23:478, 1915

The suggestion that the canals of Mars move over the face of the planet seems to call for a word of comment. In the first place we must carefully distinguish between observation and interpretation. Now as to what was observed the phenomenon is not new, having been detected and recorded nineteen years ago at the Lowell Observatory. As to its interpretation further study of the planet there under the site's exceptional conditions revealed the cause of it, which was not movement at all but something quite different, to wit: the existence of many more canals than had till then been discovered and the varying individual visibility of each. The showing of some of these canals at one time and their apparent obliteration at a subsequent date, combined with the self-assertion of others, would result in just the apparent shift observed. This deduction was clinched by the eventual detection of both sets simultaneously. The reader will readily appreciate this by turning to the photographs of one of the Flagstaff globes of Mars and noting the canals in various regions, especially those in the neighborhood of the Solis Lacus. For such investigation the best of drawings are necessary, which is why the observatory was founded where it is.

MARKINGS OF MARS

Worthington, James H.; *Nature,* 85:40, November 10, 1910

[Many astronomers besides Lowell saw canals on Mars. Expert testimony is recorded here which again confirms their subjective existence. The testimony of the waxing and waning of canals, however, resembles to some degree the UFO evidence, and one is tempted to wonder about the psychic content of such observations.]

I have recently returned by way of Tasmania from a series of visits to the chief observatories in the United States, which included a month's stay at the Lowell Observatory during the past opposition of Mars. This visit was made with the express object of testing by my own observation the reality of the data on which Dr. Lowell has based his speculations.

I find on my return that so much scepticism has been raised by the observations and arguments of M. Antoniadi and others that a record of my own experience may be of some value.

When I first looked at Mars at Flagstaff (September 27, 1909) I saw with great difficulty three streaks, presumably canals. The seeing was bad, and the general faintness of the planet's markings at that time is admitted by all. I continued to observe Mars on every possible night (which was nearly every night) until October 25, and as my eye became accustomed to the work I saw more and more. The canals were seen repeatedly better—this with the 24-inch refractor generally stopped down to about 18 inches. I found that with more than 20 inches the air was nearly always too unsteady, and with less than 15 inches too much separating power was lost. The canals were seen best with a power of 390 diameters.

Clearer they became each night until, on October 25, the seeing being the best I ever experienced, the canals came out with amazing clearness and steadiness, sharp and clean, like telegraph wires against the sky, the oases also being exquisitely defined. Whereas on previous nights the canals could be held only by short glimpses of perhaps half a second at a time, they were now steadily visible for three or four seconds together, when a short flicker would sweep over them; during the lucid intervals the limb also of the planet was perfectly steady, as I have never seen it before or since. Of the objective existence of these markings in the image at the focus of the telescope there could be no manner of doubt, and Lowell's representations of them are nearer the actual appearance than any I have seen, though even in his drawings the lines seem hardly fine enough. The effect produced on my mind by this remarkable definition, which lasted for upwards of one and a half hours (from about 8:30 until after 10 p. m.), was staggering and ineffaceable. Soon after ten the definition went to pieces.

It may be relevant to mention that a few evenings previously I had obtained a fair and convincing view of the canals with the 40-inch reflector (full aperture and a power of about 700), when they had appeared hazy and broader, but the image had been very unsteady, and only obtained in very short flashes; but nothing that I had hitherto seen had prepared me for the astonishing steadiness and *fineness* of the details visible on this superb night.

There is in my mind no sort of doubt that the revelation of this night was due both to the perfection of the instrument (which its maker long ago pronounced to be the best that the firm of Alvan Clark ever turned out) and the atmospheric conditions which are found at Flagstaff. With respect to these I would mention, as pointing to the freedom from water vapour, that I have seen the thermometer fall from more than 70°F. at 3 p. m. to below the freezing point at 3 a. m. without a trace of hoarfrost, and the general clearness of the air was such that I could see Uranus with the naked eye within 5° of the horizon, and could nearly every night count nine stars in the Pleiades and separate ε and ζ Lyrae.

The telescope also afforded on other nights ample evidence of the extraordinary clearness of the air. On many occasions both satellites of Mars, when not very near the limb, could be seen, without screening the planet, with 18 inches of aperture; and on one occasion with this aperture I picked up one of them unawares while looking for canals with a *yellow screen.* (N. B.—The importance of colour screens in rendering the canals visible does not seem to be sufficiently appreciated.)

In the face of all this positive evidence, and in the absence of any evidence that the observing conditions at

Meudon, just outside Paris, ever approach these best conditions at Flagstaff, I find it impossible myself to attach any serious weight to the ingenious and plausible contentions of M. Antoniadi, which seem to have been much too hastily accepted in this country.

As to the deductions which Dr. Lowell has drawn from his observations I have nothing to say except that the startlingly artificial and geometrical appearance of the markings did *force* itself upon me.

CURIOUS GEOMETRICAL FIGURES APPEARING UPON MARS

Pickering, William H.; *Scientific American,* 134:57–58, January 1926

It is a rather curious coincidence that at each of the recent very near approaches of the earth to Mars, strikingly regular, although only temporary geometrical figures should have appeared upon its surface. The well-known cross, centered in the approximate circle of Hellas, appeared to Schiaparelli in 1879. It may have appeared in the unusually close apparition of 1877, but in that year he saw only the circle and the single vertical canal. The diameter of the circle is 900 miles. The cross has of late years been replaced by an irregular curved structure.

The next very close approach of our planet occurred in 1892. In that year a regular pentagon with central radiating canals was seen in Arequipa. One of the canals was missing, but it may have been too delicate for our 13-inch telescope, or it may have been covered by a temporary Martian cloud when we made our drawing. The center of the pentagon was located at Ascracus Lake, as it is now called, although then unnamed, and the diameter of the figure was 800 miles.

In the year 1909 no very complicated figure seems to have been seen. The Lowell Observatory published no special report on that apparition, as they had done for some of the earlier years. M. Jarry-Deloges on September 26 drew [a figure], which is perhaps more interesting than striking, because large four-sided figures are most unusual upon Mars. The central meridianal canal is Laestrigon, the two lower ones Tartarus and Cerberus. The horizontal one, Aesculapius, has become more prominent of late years than formerly, while the two upper ones are rarely seen, but both have been confirmed by later observers. The length of Laestrigon is 1,200 miles. (*Observations des Surfaces Planetaires, 2, Plate 9.*)

At the apparition of 1924 the earth passed closer to Mars than had been the case for over a century, and closer than will be the case again for a century more. This year an unusually large and complicated figure appeared. Again it was pentagonal, apparently a favorite figure with the supposed Martians, but in a still different place. The pentagon of Elysium, which later changed into a circle, is of course well known to all students of the planet. It measures 800 miles in diameter, but this one is much larger, measuring approximately double the size. Moreover it is not a true pentagon, although of that nature, but a five-pointed star with symmetrical appendages attached.

•   •   •   •   •   •   •   •   •   •   •   •   •   •   •   •   •

It is indeed curious that these complicated figures should occur on Mars, and still more curious that they should all be only temporary, and should appear only at the very close apparitions of the planet, while at other apparitions the numerous other canals should present no symmetrical structures. There is of course a definite system to their customary arrangement that we are now gradually beginning to understand, and as above noted, the avoidance of large four-sided figures among them is of itself curious. Some people will doubtless believe that these designs are not due to mere accident, but are artificial, and constructed for our especial edification, and as an announcement of the existence of intelligent life on their planet. If so, we wish the Martians would plant them out, or otherwise construct them, more frequently than once in every fifteen and a half years. If not due in the past to chance, we wonder very much what figure will appear at the next close opposition in 1939. However we must not expect too much of the Martians, and if they have been doing this sort of thing for the last 10,000 years or more, we must consider them to be far more persevering in their endeavors to communicate, than the inhabitants of our own self-satisfied, and very unresponsive planet.

SIGNALS FROM MARS
Anonymous; *Nature,* 66:18, May 1, 1902

[Flashes of light seen on Mars have been interpreted as signals, but as this item demonstrates, most are merely TMPs (transient Martian phenomena).]

In the *Proceedings* of the American Philosophical Society for December 1901 (vol. xl. No. 167), Mr. Percival Lowell refers at some length to the observations that led to the announcement in the Press that Mars had been signalling to the earth on a night in December 1900. It may be mentioned that the *original* despatch read as follows: —"Projection observed last night over Icarium Mare, lasting seventy minutes." (Signed) "Douglas." In the present paper Mr. Lowell describes in detail some of the individual observations, and points out how the Flagstaff observations of 1894 showed that on general principles the Martian projections were most probably not due to the existence of mountain peaks. A close study of the surface markings led both Messrs. Lowell and Douglas to the result that these several projections were not caused by such permanent surface markings as mountains, but were the effect of clouds floating in the planet's atmosphere. At the opposition of 1894 more than 400 projections were seen in the course of nine months, and since that time other observations have helped to show that the non-reappearances of these projections at such favourable times when, if they were mountains, they should have been seen, have proved their non-permanent character. In fact, permanences like mountains were found to do violence to the observations, and the alternative explanation chosen was something floating in the planet's atmosphere and capable of reflecting light, or, in other words, clouds. Mr. Lowell, in his concluding remarks, says that the surface marking, Icarium Mare, is undoubtedly a great tract of vegetation, and the observation of December is completely explained if it be assumed that a cloud was formed over this region and rose to a height of thirteen miles, and then, travelling east by north at about twenty-seven miles an hour, passed over the desert of Aeria and there was dissipated after an existence of three or four days. The Flagstaff observations thus tell us that mountains on Mars, if there be any, have still to be discovered.

10

The Satellite of Venus

Any astronomy book will tell you that Venus has no moon, but then textbooks rarely mention Vulcan either. Neith, as the temporary moon of Venus was called, was almost as well established as Vulcan, the intramercurial planet, in the middle 19th century. It too had been seen by several reputable observers. Most convincing was the fact that Neith was seen in the same phase or crescent shape as Venus. This tended to prove that those who saw it were not observing a nearby star. Once again, though, the apparently sound observational foundation eroded away. Today Neith resides with Vulcan and the Martian canals in the astronomical trash heap. To compensate for such losses and preserve some symmetry in the universe, we now have two unexpected moons circling Mars, the planet Pluto, and a host of minor planets. These phenomena will be dealt with later.

The discovery and loss of Neith did not have the emotional impact on astronomers that Vulcan did. Satellites can come and go but planets seem to have some deeper significance. In any case Neith did not perform for expectant observers in the late 19th century, either as a bright companion to Venus or as an accompanying spot during transits of the sun. The old observations were written off as telescopic ghosts or misidentifications of known stars. The possibility that a satellite might have been captured temporarily by Venus was not considered likely because this would challenge the belief that the solar system has been and will be stable for millions of years.

THE SATELLITE OF VENUS
Webb, T. W.; *Nature,* 14:193–195, June 29, 1876

That something strongly resembling a satellite has been
occasionally seen near Venus, especially about the middle
of the last century, is beyond a doubt. It is equally certain, and familiar to all experienced observers, that reflected images, or technically "ghosts," may, under certain
circumstances, be formed in the eye-piece of the telescope,
and might be the means of causing deception: and the
whole matter is reduced to the simple inquiry, whether all
the recorded instances admit of his easy explanation;
though, if they do not, it must be remembered that the
existence of a satellite would not necessarily follow.

•   •   •   •   •   •   •   •   •   •   •   •   •   •   •   •

The name of Cassini at the head of them [the observers
of the satellite] at once commands attention, but there is
nothing in his two observations in 1672 and 1686 that
does not lend itself to Father Hell's hypothesis, excepting
the care and experience of such an observer, who must
have been familiar with every telescopic defect. The observation of Meier, which seems to have lain unnoticed
in the *Astron. Jahrbuch,* 1788, till brought forward by
Schorr, is on that account worthy of being cited in full.
"1759, May 20, about 8h. 45m. 50s., I saw above Venus
a little globe of far inferior brightness, about 1½ diam. of
Venus from herself. Future observations will show whether
this little globe was an optical appearance or the satellite
of Venus. The observation was made with a Gregorian
telescope of thirty inches focus. It continued for half an
hour, and the position of the little globe with regard to
Venus remained the same, although the direction of the
telescope had been changed." During so lengthened an
observation it seems natural to suppose that the eye must
have been repeatedly removed and replaced, which could
not have occurred without the detection of an optical illusion.

In 1761, when the expected transit drew attention to
Venus, Montaigne, at Limoges, was persuaded to undertake the inquiry, though he had little faith in the existence

of the satellite, and was not greatly disposed to enter upon
an examination in which so many great men had failed.
However, on May 3 he saw a small crescent 20′ from
Venus; it is expressly stated that the observation was repeated several times, and that after all he was not certain
if it was not a small star; which, with a power of between
forty and fifty, was not surprising. The next evening and on
the 7th and 11th it was again seen, rather more distant,
and each time in an altered position, but with the same
phase as its primary; and on the 7th it was seen, and even
much more distinctly, when Venus was not in the field.
The improbability is obvious of such persistency in an illusion so readily detected. The cause may indeed have lain
in the object-glass; such telescopes have been known. War-
gentin, at Stockholm in the same year, found that his instrument produced a deception from this cause; and the
6-inch Cauchoix achromatic at Rome showed minute
comites to bright stars a little too frequently for the credit
of those who trusted it. Montaigne's changed position angles may be thought to indicate this cause of error, as his
9-ft. refractor probably admitted of rotation in its bear-
ings, but it is a singular coincidence that these changes
should all have been in the direction of orbital revolution,
and still more, in such proportions as to be reconcilable
with Lambert's calculated period of about eleven days;
and it is quite unintelligible that he should not have subsequently detected the fault in his telescope, as from his esti-
mation of angles and distances he was evidently not a
novice in observation. Three years later, in 1764, Rodkier,
in Copenhagen, saw such an appearance on two evenings
with a power of thirty-eight on a 9½-ft. refractor; on the
latter occasion with a second telescope also. There is little
in this to contravene the Vienna theory, especially as this
second telescope had a coloured meniscus eye-glass, and
he failed in finding it with two other instruments; but it is
more remarkable that on two evenings a week later the
same telescope told the same tale to four different observers, one of whom was Horrebow, the Professor of Astronomy, and who, we are assured, satisfied themselves by several experiments before the second observation that it was
not a deception. That the necessary conditions for its being
such could have been maintained before so many eyes, is,

notwithstanding its admitted pale and uncertain aspect, what could not possibly have been anticipated. But we have not yet done with this temporary outbreak, so to speak, of visibility. Before this month of March was ended, Montbarron at Auxerre, far removed from all possibility of communication, and with a very different kind of telescope, a Gregorian reflector of thirty-two inches, which of course was fixed as to its optical axis, perceived on three separate evenings, at different position-angles, something which, though it had no distinguishable phasis, was evidently not a star, and which he never could find again.

There remains still the observation of the celebrated optician Short. It is indeed chronologically misplaced here, but has been intentionally deferred as affording the strongest point in the whole affirmative evidence. As his own account is an interesting one, and has seldom, if ever, been reprinted, our readers may not be displeased to see it here as it stands in Phil. Trans. vol. xli. :—

"An Observation on the Planet Venus (with regard to her having a satellite), made by Mr. James Short, F.R.S., at sunrise, October 23, 1740.—Directing a reflecting telescope of 16.5 inches focus (with an apparatus to follow the diurnal motion) towards Venus, I perceived a small star pretty nigh her; upon which I took another telescope of the same focal distance, which magnified about fifty or sixty times, and which was fitted with a micrometer in order to measure its distance from Venus, and found its distance to be about 10° 2′10″ (sic). Finding Venus very distinct, and consequently the air very clear, I put on a magnifying power of 240 times, and to my great surprise found this star put on the same phasis with Venus. I tried another magnifying power of 140 times, and even then found the star under the same phasis. Its diameter seemed about a third, or somewhat less, of the diameter of Venus; its light was not so bright or vivid, but exceedingly sharp and well defined. A line, passing through the centre of Venus and it, made an angle with the equator of about eighteen or twenty degrees. I saw it for the space of an hour several times that morning; but the light of the sun increasing, I lost it altogether about a quarter of an hour after eight. I have looked for it every clear morning since, but never had the good fortune to see it again. Cassini, in his Astronomy, mentions much such another observation. I likewise observed two darkish spots upon the body of Venus, for the air was exceeding clear and serene."

THE SATELLITE OF VENUS
A., J.; *Sky and Telescope,* 13:333, August 1954

How much confirmation do you need to place an observational discovery beyond any reasonable doubt? This is the important and disturbing question raised by the story of a satellite of Venus, which at one time was confidently accepted as a member of the solar system. No fewer than 33 observations of it by 15 different astronomers were recorded during the 17th and 18th centuries, beginning with F. Fontana at Naples on November 11, 1645. In the year 1761 alone, 18 observations of the object were made.

Some of these sightings were by well-known observers, who even today have a reputation for reliability. Thus G. D. Cassini, director of the Paris Observatory and discoverer of Cassini's division in Saturn's rings, wrote in his journal for August 28, 1686:

"At 4:15 a.m. while examining Venus with a telescope of 34 feet focal length, I saw at 3/5 of its diameter to the east an ill-defined light, which seemed to imitate the phase of Venus, but its western edge was more flattened. Its diameter was very nearly 1/4 that of Venus. I observed it with attention for a quarter of an hour, when, on quitting

Several observers saw a small bright object near Venus with the same phase relationship, suggesting the existence of a satellite.

the telescope for five minutes, I could not find it again, the dawn being too bright."

In 1773, the German astronomer Johann Lambert calculated the orbit of the satellite of Venus. He found that it revolved about its primary in 11 days five hours, at a mean distance of 66½ radii of the planet, in an orbit whose eccentricity was 0.195.

Widespread interest was aroused when Lambert announced these results to the Berlin Academy of Sciences. The king of Prussia, Frederick the Great, proposed that the satellite be named after his friend, the French astronomer-mathematician, Jean d'Alembert. The latter prudently declined the honor, explaining that his place on earth was so insignificant he had no ambition for one in the skies.

Yet nothing can be more certain than that no such sizable satellite exists. It has never been seen since 1768. Veteran observers of Venus such as Schroeter, William Herschel, and Maedler could not find it. More recently, E. E. Barnard, whose interest in satellites was marked, made many observations of Venus with telescopes up to the Yerkes 40-inch in size without finding any companion. Currently, scores of amateurs every year scrutinize Venus with telescopes more powerful than those with which the supposed satellite used to be seen, without coming upon this object.

Even in the last century, the satellite of Venus found a few champions. In 1875, a curious book, *Der Venusmond*, was published in its defense by the German, Dr. F. Schorr. He argued that the many failures to see it were due to a brightness variation, such that the satellite was normally so faint as to be invisible. Schorr's elaborate hodgepodge was more enthusiastic than critical, and soon sank into the vast abyss of forgotten semiscientific literature, without having cleared up the mystery.

What the old observers really saw was finally explained by Dr. Paul Stroobant, of the Brussels Observatory, then at the start of his career as the most distinguished Belgian astronomer of the last generation. In his memoir of 1887, Stroobant reprinted in full all the original statements of the observers of the satellite of Venus, described the earlier hypotheses to account for the observations, and subjected all this to a searching examination.

In the first place, Lambert's orbit was clearly impossible,

as it required the mass of Venus to be 10 times greater than it actually is. Next, the descriptions of the satellite were highly contradictory. Several accounts spoke of a large disk showing the same phase as Venus; some at least of these observations must refer to "ghosts" caused by reflections within the telescopes, which would be particularly noticeable for so bright an object as Venus. Other observers had described the satellite as starlike, and Stroobant, by calculating the positions of Venus at the dates in question, could identify in seven cases what star the observer had mistaken for a satellite. It is possible, though not certain, that the "satellite" seen by Roedkiaer at Copenhagen on March 5, 1761, was the planet Uranus—20 years before its recognition by Herschel.

There remained little else of the observations except some statements so vague as to inspire no confidence. So final was Stroobant's critique that the one-time belief in a satellite of Venus has been almost forgotten by now.

III

GEOPHYSICS

11

The Brocken Specter and His Kin

A wild tale has long circulated about a giant specter seen by mountain climbers on the Brocken, a German mountain. As the story goes, there was once a climber working his way along a precipice, who suddenly saw an immense human figure rise out of the mists toward him. In his fright he lost his footing and fell to his death. Doubtless just a story, but the Brocken specter does exist, not only on the Brocken but anyplace where shadows are cast upon mist and screens of water droplets.

That one's shadow can be seen, even in giant proportions, on a wall of white mist is not surprising. Some features of the phenomenon, however, are more difficult to explain. A common feature of the Brocken specter is the "glory," a set of concentric rings of color centered on the observer's line of sight or, equivalently, the shadow of his head. Sometimes several rings are seen, each with the rainbow's succession of colors. Doubtless their origin is the same as that of the rainbow; that is, the reflection of the solar spectrum by water droplets. The curious feature here concerns the visibility of the observer's shadow and his private set of colored rings to other observers in the vicinity. Some see only their own shadows; others see the shadows of everyone present. Then too, the circles of color are sometimes elliptical rather than circular. The glories are also apparently distorted by the approach of other observers. Another unusual feature comprises the dark streaks that seem to radiate from the observer's arms. There is much here that is difficult to explain in terms of conventional optics.

The Brocken specter type of phenomenon also occurs when a field of dew-laden grass is spread out before a viewer. With the sun at his back, the observer sees his shadow cast upon the field with his head surrounded by a halo. More awe-inspiring is the specter seen from atop Adam's Peak in Ceylon. When conditions are right, the shadow of the entire peak is thrown upon a wall of vapor. A viewer on the summit sees the shadow of the peak surrounded by a glory. In addition, there are dark projections that seem analogous to the streaks sometimes seen radiating from the arms of an individual's shadow in the usual Brocken specter.

THE CIRCLE OF ULLOA

Zurcher, Frederic; *Meteors, Aerolites, Storms, and Atmospheric Phenomena,* C. Scribner & Co., New York, 1876

[Antonio de Ulloa a famous Spanish scientist, gave this classic description of the Brocken specter.]

He was on Pambamarca with six companions at daybreak. The top of the mountain was entirely covered with dense clouds. As the sun rose, it dispelled these clouds, and nothing remained in their stead but some very light mists, which it was almost impossible to distinguish. Suddenly, on the side opposite that in which the sun rose, each of the travellers saw, at a dozen fathoms from where he stood, an image of himself reflected in the air, as though upon a mirror. This image appeared in the centre of three rainbows shaded with different colors, and surrounded at a certain distance by a fourth arch of a single color. The tinting farthest on the outside of each arch was flesh-colored, or red, the next shade was orange, the third was yellow, the fourth straw-color, and the last one green. All these arcs were perpendicular to the horizon; they moved about and followed the person reflected in every direction, surrounding his image like a gloria. What was most remarkable was, that, although the seven travellers stood together in a single group, each of them saw the phenomenon only in relation to himself, and was disposed to deny its existence in reference to the others. The extent of these arches increased progressively in proportion to the height of the sun. At the same time their colors faded away, the *spectra* became paler and paler and more vague, and at last the phenomenon entirely disappeared. When this display began, the shape of the arcs was oval; and, toward the last, it was perfectly circular.

Shadow of a balloon cast upon a mist with three glories, as seen by the balloonists.

SPECTRE OF THE BROCKEN AT HOME
Rogers, J. Innes; *Nature*, 22:559, October 14, 1880

[Rogers relates a case where artificial light created a Brocken specter. The circles of color are absent.]

Having occasion ten days ago to go into my garden about half past ten o'clock at night I found there was a thick white fog, through which, however, a star could be seen here and there. I had an ordinary bedroom candlestick in my hand with the candle lighted, in order to find the object I wanted. To my great surprise I found that the lighted candle projected a fantastic image of myself on the fog, the shadow being about twelve feet high, and of oddly distorted character, just as the spectre of the Brocken is said to be. It is of course usual on going into the open air to use a lantern with a solid back for any light that may be wanted, and with this, of course, such a shadow would not be seen; but in this charmingly foggy valley of the

Thames, and in these days of "Physics without Apparatus," the effect I saw can probably be seen only too often. May not the gigantic spirits of the Ossianic heroes, whose form is composed of mist, through which the stars can be seen, be derived from the fantastic images thrown upon the mountain fogs from the camp fires of the ancient Gaels? In a land where mists abound a superstitious people might very readily come to consider a mocking cloud-spectre to be supernatural, though it was really their own image magnified. If it be true that in our earlier stages of development we resemble more nearly the past forms of life and thought, I may mention in this connection that, thinking to amuse a little child of three, I threw a magnified shadow of her on the wall with a candle, and then by moving it in the usual way, made the figure suddenly small. Instead of the changing shadow giving the pleasure intended, the child was terrified, as the warriors of Morven may have been when they saw their shadows on the clouds.

THE SO-CALLED "BROCKEN SPECTRES" AND THE BOWS THAT OFTEN ACCOMPANY THEM

Sharpe, Henry; *Royal Meteorological Society, Quarterly Journal,* 13:245–272, 1887

[Three accounts are selected from this compilation.]

Mr. Claude Wilson writes: With three friends, I reached the top of Scawfell Pike at half past one o'clock on Christmas day, 1883. We mounted on the top of the cairn which marks the summit of the mountain. Our faces were turned in the direction in which the fog, which had hitherto enveloped us, was lifting, exposing in the distance a thick bank of white cloud, and we were spectators of a sight which is, I believe, rarely observed in these islands. The sun was shining brightly at our backs, and immediately before us, apparently at the distance of a quarter of a mile, there appeared a complete halo, elliptical in form and of the colours of the rainbow. In the centre of this we saw the images of our figures, exactly corresponding in shape, though gigantic in size. Every action on our part was faithfully reproduced on this atmospheric screen, and we amused ourselves for some time by testing the accuracy of this natural magic lantern. The effect was weird and beautiful in the extreme, and one could not help feeling that 50 years ago what we saw would have been ascribed to supernatural agency.

. . . .

Dr. Frederick Taylor writes: If it is not too late for the subject of circular rainbows to have any interest for the readers of the *Alpine Journal,* I should like to record that I was witness of one in Switzerland last August (1884), under circumstances similar to those described by your other correspondents. While staying at the Bel Alp, Mr. Gotch and I ascended the Grisighorn on August 13th, and were on the summit about four in the afternoon. As we sat under the shelter of the cairn facing towards the Sparrenhorn the sun was at our backs, and from time to time clouds rolled up before us from the rocks beneath. Suddenly we saw the shadow of the summit of the mountain and of ourselves thrown on the cloud, and at the same time a rainbow with the colours fully developed became apparent. As we sat, the rainbow was already more than the usual semicircle, and on mounting on the cairn I saw a complete circle of colours, with the red external, the violet internal. Of this circular rainbow my head was the centre, and my feet touched the lower limb. Mr. Gotch also saw a secondary bow. The phenomenon remained some time, varying in the brightness of the colours and the intensity of the shadow.

In reference to the question you asked me in your letter of the 7th February, as to the size of the shadow that I saw on the Grisighorn in 1884, I find I have no actual notes, and I cannot lay my hands on the few notes, &c., that I put together before making my communication to the *Alpine Journal.* I have a rough sketch that I made at the time, and from that I should infer that the figure was a little larger than life. On receiving your letter, I wrote to Mr. Gotch, who was with me on the Grisighorn; and he writes that his impression was that the shadow appeared life size at first when the cloud was thick or close—that later on the glacier became discernible below us, and then (the cloud being more distant) the shadow appeared gigantic—the difference being the result of a difference of impression as to the size, following different conceptions as to distance: and he suggests that two people at the same time might have different impressions as to the size of the shadow presented to them.

Elliptical glories with dark rays
reported by Taylor.

Dr. Taylor afterwards lent me two sketches that he had made of the phenomenon, and told me that the dark rays moved as he moved his arms.

• • • • • • • • • • • • • • •

As far as I can remember, the sketch represents exactly

Distorted and intersecting glories created when two
observers approach one another.

what we saw in Skye, the lower side of the circle merging into the shadow of the ridge on which we stood, but leaving visible about as much of the legs as the sketch shows. I do not recollect that the bow was coloured, but that it was merely a disc of light with the shadow projected on it, and also that if the arms were held out the disc became distorted. Another point that I remember is that when two of us came near each other our discs cut in upon one another thus, and that the whole thing became visible to both of us.

When forwarding this, Mr. White wrote to me: I cannot remember the distortion of the circle, but there was something peculiar when we came near each other.

THE SUNRISE SHADOW OF ADAM'S PEAK, CEYLON
Abercromby, Ralph; *Nature*, 33:532–533, April 8, 1886

Some of the phenomena of the shadow of Adam's Peak in the early morning have been remarked by almost every traveller who has visited this island. The mountain rises to a height of 7352 feet as an isolated cone projecting more than 1000 feet above the main ridge to which it belongs. The appearance which has excited so much comment is that just after sunrise the shadow of the Peak seems to rise up in front of the spectator, and then suddenly either to disappear or fall down to the earth.

Various suggestions have been made as to the source of this curious shadow; among others one, which was published in the *Phil. Mag.*, August 1876, that attributed the rise of the shadow to a kind of mirage effect, on the supposition that the air over the low country was much hotter than on the Peak top.

I determined to attempt the discovery of the true nature of this appearance, and was fortunate to see it under circumstances which left no doubt as to the real origin. Through the courtesy and hospitality of Mr. T. N. Christie, of St. Andrew's Plantation, I was able to pass the night on the summit, and to carry up a few necessary instruments.

The morning broke in a very unpromising manner. Heavy clouds lay all about, lightning flickered over a dark bank to the right of the rising sun, and at frequent intervals masses of light vapour blew up from the valley and enveloped the summit in their mist. Suddenly, at 6:30 a.m., the sun peeped through a chink in the eastern sky, and we saw a shadow of the Peak projected on the land; then a little mist drove in front of the shadow, and we saw a circular rainbow of perhaps 8° or 10° diameter surrounding the shadow of the summit, and as we waved our arms we saw the shadow of our limbs moving in the mist. Two dark lines seemed to radiate from the centre of the bow, almost in a prolongation of the slopes of the Peak, as in the figure.

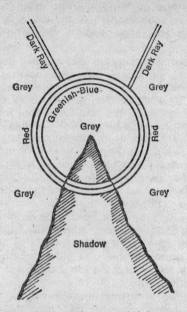

Shadow of Adam's Peak surrounded by a glory, as seen by observers on the summit. Note the peculiar dark rays.

Twice this shadow appeared and vanished as cloud obscured the sun, but the third time we saw what has apparently struck so many observers. The shadow seemed to rise up and stand in front of us in the air, with rainbow and spectral arms, and then to fall down suddenly to the earth as the bow disappeared. The cause of the whole was obvious. As a mass of vapour drove across the shadow, the condensed particles caught the shadow, and in this case were also large enough to form a bow. As the vapour blew past, the shadow fell to its natural level—the surface of the earth.

An hour later, when the sun was well up, we again saw the shadow of the Peak and ourselves, this time encircled by a double bow. Then the shadow was so far down that there was no illusion of standing up in front of us.

I believe that the formation of fog-bow and spectral figures on Adam's Peak is not so common as the simple rising up of the shadow, but one is only a development of the other. In fine weather, when the condensed vapour is thin and the component globules small, there is only enough matter in the air to reflect the Peak shadow in front of the spectator, and no figure is seen unless the arms are waved. In worse weather the globules of mist are large enough to form one or two bows, according to the intensity of the light. We were fortunate to see the lifted shadow accompanied by fog phenomena, which left no doubt as to the cause of the whole appearance.

Any idea of mirage was entirely disproved by my ther-mometric observations, which cannot be detailed here for want of space.

12

The Fata Morgana and Other Mirages

Strictly speaking, the fata morgana is the mirage of a magnificent city seen across the Straits of Messina, but the name is often applied to any spectacular mirage. And why not? The name derives from Morgan le Fay, King Arthur's enchantress sister, whose magic could just as easily make a city appear on any shore in the world, luring seafarers to a watery fate.

Most mirages are associated with the sea. Ships and landfalls are seen long before they poke above the horizon. Inverted ships and greatly distorted ships are common. Good mirages appear less frequently over land. However, the most common mirage of all is that of the sky seen in the air above a hot roadway. But let us talk of less mundane things: armies in the sky, multiple mirages, sideways mirages, and images that are not so easy to explain.

Mirages sometimes display highly magnified objects. Islands and cities hundreds or even thousands of miles away may appear on the horizon. Polar ice may seem to be a distant mountain range; a fact which led to the embarrassing "discovery" of Crockerland in the Arctic a few decades ago. Stones and hillocks become buildings and great mountains. To magnify in this fashion, the atmosphere must behave like a lens—several lenses in the case of multiple mirages. Just how magnifying air lenses are formed is not well known. Mirages frequently show distant people and objects with great clarity—something expected only from rigid, precisely ground glass lenses. Like a glass lens, the air lens focuses scenes in a very restricted area. Moving the head up or down a few feet destroys the image. Lateral or sideways mirages are also difficult to imagine because the layers of air that create the mirages are at different temperatures and should not be very stable when oriented vertically; yet sideways mirages are not unknown.

The question that no conventional physicist will admit into the discussion is whether some images seen in the sky may not be mirages at all but rather visual projections through time and/or space that are completely divorced from real objects. Are the visions of armies, unidentified cities, fair, idyllic countryside, and ghost ships all images of real things in the space-time continuum? Or do we verge here on the psychic? Some of the observations recorded below seem to indicate that we do.

THE REAL FATA MORGANA
Talman, C. Fitzhugh; *Scientific American*, 106:335, April 13, 1912

"When the rising sun shines from that point whence its incident ray forms an angle of about 45 degrees on the sea of Reggio, and the bright surface of the water in the bay is not disturbed either by the wind or the current, the spectator being placed on an eminence of the city, with his back to the sun and his face to the sea—on a sudden he sees appear in the water, as in a catoptric theater, various multiple objects, such as numberless series of pilasters, arches, castles well delineated, regular columns, lofty towers, superb palaces with balconies and windows, extended alleys of trees, delightful plains with herds and flocks, armies of men on foot and horseback, and many other strange figures, all in their natural colors and proper action, and passing rapidly in succession along the surface of the sea, during the whole short period of time that the above-mentioned causes remain. But if, in addition to the circumstances before described, the atmosphere be highly impregnated with vapor and exhalations not dispersed by the wind nor rarefied by the sun, it then happens that in this vapor, as in a curtain extended along the channel to the height of about thirty palms and nearly down to the sea, the observer will behold the scene of the same objects not only reflected from the surface of the sea, but likewise in the air, though not in so distinct and defined a manner as in the sea. And again, if the air be slightly hazy and opaque, and at the same time dewy and adapted to form the iris, then the objects will appear only at the surface of the sea, but they will be all vividly colored or fringed with red, green, blue, and the other prismatic colors."

So runs the classical description of the Fata Morgana, written in 1773 by the Dominican friar, Antonio Minasi, and since become the common property of encyclopaedists the world over.

Minasi was born not far from Reggio, and saw the Fata Morgana himself three times. His description is probably, in the main, accurate, though, as we shall presently see, he limits the time of occurrence of the phenomenon too narrowly in stating that the sun must be at an altitude of about 45 degrees. He was the first writer to point out that the Fata Morgana occurs in two distinct varieties; viz., the *marine Morgana,* which appears to lie in or beneath the water, and the *aerial Morgana,* which extends upward to a considerably greater apparent altitude. Minasi's third variety, the *iridescent Morgana,* appears not to have been observed since his time. The atmospheric refractions to which the Fata Morgana, in common with other forms of mirage, is due are not usually attended with a sensible dispersion of light (i.e., separation of the prismatic colors), but that such dispersion may sometimes occur is by no means impossible. In fact, we shall have occasion later to mention a form of mirage, seen in another part of Italy, in which iridescent coloring is stated to be a common feature.

Minasi's attempts to explain the Fata Morgana are far less happy than his descriptions. In his day little was really known about abnormal refractions in the atmosphere, though he lived upon the eve of the important discoveries of Gruber, Busch, Monge and Biot. The Straits of Messina are subject to strong tidal currents, which often run in opposite directions at a given time; that is to say, in midchannel the current sets to the north while along shore it is running south, and *vice versa*. Minasi supposed that the surface of the water thus acquired, at times, marked differences of level, so that it behaved like a mirror lying, not horizontal, but tilted at a slight angle, or at several angles in different places, and reflecting objects along the Calabrian shore (i.e., the shore of the Italian mainland, on which Reggio lies). He therefore took the Morgana to be the reflected image of Reggio and the adjoining coast— the same coast from which the phenomenon is seen. In Minasi's picture, which has been the basis of the greater number of the representations of the Fata Morgana shown in textbooks and reference books, the city in the background is Reggio, while in the foreground are shown all three of the forms of the phenomenon that he has described. It was intended to be a generalized diagram of the Fata Morgana, rather than a faithful picture of its appearance at any one time.

Minasi's explanation is of course no longer accepted, and we now know that the terrestrial objects seen in the Morgana are the refracted images of such objects on the Sicilian coast, or in some cases on parts of the Calabrian coast remote from the place of observation. Moreover, if we except the altogether unconvincing narrative of the French traveler Jean Houel, there are no cases on record in which the Morgana has been seen *from* the Sicilian side of the straits.

It is most remarkable that a phenomenon so renowned as the Fata Morgana has been the subject of extremely few accurate scientific investigations conducted on the spot. The rarity of the phenomenon, however, serves in a measure to explain this fact. Many people who have spent their whole lives in and about Reggio have never once seen the famous spectacle.

In our own time only three persons, two of whom lived for some years in Reggio and were eye-witnesses of the phenomenon, have attempted to collect and discuss all the existing information concerning it. Pernter, in his great "Meteorologische Optik," not only publishes the principal descriptions of the Morgana that had appeared up to the year 1902, but includes several that he himself gathered by diligent correspondence. In 1902 Dr. Boccara, professor of physics at the Technical Institute at Reggio, pub-

lished a memoir on the subject, in which he discussed all
the earlier observations and three made by himself. Finally, in 1903, Giovanni Costanzo published what is no doubt
the most important contribution to the descriptive side of
the subject; but postponed, as the theme of a second memoir not yet published, the theoretical discussion of the
phenomenon.

The last-named writer has collected, in a convenient table, abstracts of all available trustworthy descriptions of
the Morgana, from that of Fazello (1558) down to the
present time.

So far as we know, the Fata Morgana is not specifically
mentioned by any writer before Fazello, although the
phenomenon of mirage, in general, was well known to the
ancients; while the name "Fata Morgana" has not been
found, in this particular application, in any extant work
before that of Marc Antonio Politi (1617). In other uses
the name is, of course, much older; for Morgan le Fay,
the fairy sister of King Arthur, was a favorite theme of
mediaeval romance. The legend of this fairy, who dwelt
in a marvelous palace under the sea, appears to have been
carried to southern Italy by the Norman settlers in the
11th century. The phantoms of the Straits of Messina
were subsequently alleged to be wrought by her enchant-
ments for the purpose of luring mariners to destruction.
According to this tale, the seaman would mistake the aerial
city for a safe harbor, and would be led hopelessly astray
in endeavoring to reach it. Hence this enchantress was the
mediaeval successor of Scylla and Charybdis, who also had
their home in the Straits of Messina.

MIRAGES OR CLOUDS?
Anonymous; *Nature*, 32:541, October 1, 1885

[The mirages described in this and the following selection are truly fantastic, and conventional explanations do
not seem stretchable enough to account for them.]

On September 12, just after sunset, a remarkable mirage
was seen at Valla, in the province of Sudermania, Sweden.
It appeared first as a great cloud-bank, stretching from
south-west to north, which gradually separated, each cloud
having the appearance of a monitor. In the course of five

minutes one had changed to a great whale blowing a column of water into the air, and the other to a crocodile. From time to time the clouds took the appearance of various animals, and finally that of a small wood. Subsequently they changed to a pavilion, where people were dancing, the players being also clearly visible. Once again the spectacle changed, now into a lovely wooded island with buildings and parks. At about nine o'clock the clouds had disappeared, leaving the sky perfectly clear. The air was calm at the time of the display, the temperature being 6°C.

MIRAGES OR CLOUDS?
Anonymous; *Nature,* 32:552, October 8, 1885

On September 29, between 8 and 9 p.m., a mirage somewhat similar to that described last week [preceding selection] was again observed by many persons at Valla in Sweden. The entire lower part of the north-western horizon shone with a lurid glare, above which was a cloud-bank assuming the most remarkable forms. From time to time animals, trees, and shrubs were seen. Soon a bear changed into an elephant, and soon a dog into a horse. Later on groups of dancers were seen, men being distinguished from women. Further north the cloud formed an oak forest, in front of which was a valley, and nearer still a park with sanded paths. At about 9:30 the cloud sank into a mass, and the phenomenon disappeared.

EXTRAORDINARY MIRAGE IN THE FIRTH OF FORTH
Anonymous; *Symons's Monthly Meteorological Magazine,* 6: 98–99, 1871

For some time past the atmospheric phenomena at the mouth of the Firth of Forth have been of a remarkably vivid and interesting character, and have attracted a great deal of attention. During the past week especially, scarcely a day has passed without exhibiting extraordinary optical illusions in connection with the surrounding scenery, both at sea and on shore. As an instance of the unusual nature of these phenomena, the whole of the Broxmouth policies, mansion-house, and plantation, were one day apparently removed out to sea. One of the finest displays of mirage, however, occurred on Saturday afternoon. The early part of the day had been warm, and there was the usual dull, deceptive haze extending about half-way across the Firth, rendering the Fife coast invisible. The only object on the Fife coast, indeed, which was brought within the range of the refraction was Balconie Castle on the "East Neuk," which appeared half-way up the horizon, and in a line with the Isle of May. The most extraordinary illusions, however, were those presented by the May island, which, from a mere speck on the water, suddenly shot up in the form of a huge perpendicular wall, apparently 800 to 900 feet high, with a smooth and unbroken front to the sea. On the east side lay a long low range of rocks, apparently detached from the island at various points, and it was on these that the most fantastic exhibitions took place. Besides assuming the most diversified and fantastic shapes, the rocks were constantly changing their positions, now moving off, and again approaching each other. At one time, a beautiful columnar circle, the column seemingly from 20 to 30 feet high, appeared on the outermost rock. Presently the figure was changed to a clump of trees, whose green umbrageous foliage had a very vivid appearance. By and by the clump of trees increased to a large plantation, which gradually approached the main portion of the island, until within 300 or 400 feet, when the intervening space was spanned by a beautiful arch. Another and another arch was afterwards formed in the same way, the spans being nearly of the same width, while the whole length of the island, from east to west, seemed as flat and smooth as the top of a table. At a later period the phenomena, which were constantly changing, showed huge jagged rifts and ravines in the face of the high wall, through which the light came and went as they opened and shut, while trees and towers, columns and arches, sprang up and disappeared as if by magic. It is a singular fact, that during the four hours the mirage lasted, the lighthouse, usually the most prominent object from the south side of the Firth, was wholly invisible. The last appearance which the island assumed was that of a thin blue line half-way up the horizon, with the lighthouse as a small pivot in the centre; and the extraordinary phantasmagoria were brought to a close about seven o'clock by a drenching rain, which fell for two hours.

MIRAGE ON THE CORNISH COAST
Horton, Percy H.; *Royal Meteorological Society, Quarterly Journal,* 41:71, 1915

A most curious phenomenon was to be seen from the Cornish coast at Mawnan, a headland at the mouth of Helford River, five miles from Falmouth, from 3:45 to 4:45 in the afternoon of Saturday October 24, 1914.

In a shallow cloudbank stretching across the horizon from south-east to south gradually appeared what seemed to be a line of coast, with woods, trees, fields, hedges, and houses in their natural colours.

At first I thought it was merely a peculiar arrangement of clouds, but soon I recognised that it was a complete reflected panorama of this coast, and I gradually identified St. Keverne with its church spire, the Helford River, Mawnan Church, Rosemullion, Falmouth Harbour, and St. Anthony.

Shortly before the whole scene faded away, a reflection of Pendennis Head with the castle and the military huts, emerging like some huge ship from a fog bank, appeared most distinctly and was visible for several minutes. Every detail of the whole scene was reversed as in a looking-glass and slightly magnified, for although the panorama seemed to be some twenty miles away, everything appeared as it would to an observer from the distance of only a mile or so. The colours were a little less bright than those of the real coast at the time.

The scene as a whole was visible all the time, but the details of a small portion only were quite distinct at any one time, commencing in the south and gradually moving towards the east, the effect being that of a powerful searchlight being very slowly turned from right to left on to the opposite shore of a large lake. Nothing of it could be seen through a telescope; at least I found it impossible to get it into focus.

I presume that the reason that the reflected objects were seen reversed and not inverted, as is usual in mirages, was the fact that my point of observation was about 300 feet above sea-level, and I was therefore, as it were, looking down upon the mirage, the reflecting medium of which was between the horizon and myself, whereas in most instances mirages are the reflection *in the sky* of objects *beyond* the horizon.

A curious point I noticed was that the reflection of some of the objects was not reversed precisely to correspond with my view of the real objects. For instance, I could see St. Keverne Church itself, but its *reflection* seemed to be from an entirely different point of view. This would, I think, mean either that the cloudbank or medium of reflection was irregular in its reflecting surface and reflected different points at different angles; or that, perhaps more probably, the cloudbank acted as a large mirror from far beyond the object, and showed me the reversed view of the coast as it would appear if observed from the point of reflection; and, since most of the scenery, viz. Helford River, Rosemullion, Pendennis Castle, and the fields, etc., inland were quite out of my range of vision, and yet were all reflected, I am inclined to think that the latter theory is the correct one.

Another curious point was that although the sun was behind me and therefore the coast was in the shade, the reflection was not a silhouette, as one would have expected, but the details showed up distinctly as though a brilliant light were shining on them.

ON THE FATA MORGANA OF IRELAND

M'Farland, Mr.; *Reports of the British Association,* Part 2, 29–30, 1852

[The following curious and charming quotations evoke thoughts of the legendary sunken cities off the British Isles and France, such as Lyonnesse. What real lands are to the west of Ireland? Where are the real cities and squadrons of troops?]

These singular illusions are termed in the Irish language *Duna Feadhreagh,* or Fairy Castles. As proof that the Morgana had appeared as an island, either resting or floating on the sea prior to 1185, Mr. M'Farland read a passage from the topographical history of that country, by Giraldus Cambrensis (lib. ii. c. 12). He then referred to the *"Miranda loca,* quae vidit St. Brandanus in Oceano," to which Usher alludes in his 'De Hibernia' (p. 813), and quoted an unpublished History of Ireland, composed about 1636 (and now remaining in MS. in the Library of the Royal Irish Academy at Dublin), that speaks of an "Iland which lyeth far att sea, on the west of Connaught, and sometimes is perceived by the inhabitants of the Owles and Iris; also from St. Helen Head, beyond the haven of Calbeggs (Killibegs, Donegal). Likewise, severall seamen have discovered it at sea as they have sailed on the western coast of Ireland." Mr. M'Farland also read from the Chronographical Description of Connaught, written in 1684, by Roderick O'Flagherty, and published by the Irish Archaeological Society, in which it is recorded (p. 68), that, "From the Isles of Arran and the West continent, often appears visible that enchanted island, called O'Branil, and in Irish Beg-ara, or the Sessen Arran, set down in cards of navigation. . . . There is, westward of Arran, in sight of the next continent, Skerde, a wild island of huge rocks; these sometimes appear to be a great city far off, full of houses, castles, towers, and chimneys; sometimes full of blazing flames, smoke, and people running to and fro. Another day you would see nothing but a number of ships, with their sailes and riggings; then so many great stakes or reekes of corn and turf." Mr. M'Farland next cited the 'History of the Parish of Ramoan (Ballycastle),' by the Rev. Wm. Conolly (1812), in which it is stated, that the author had received a minute description of the Fata Morgana from several persons who saw it, on different summer evenings, along the shore of the Giant's Causeway; shadows resembling castles, ruins and tall spires darted rapidly across the surface of the sea, which were instantly lengthened into considerable height; they moved to the eastern part of the horizon, and at sunset totally disappeared. This work makes mention of an earlier one (of 1748), by a gentleman who resided near the Causeway, and which presented a long account of an enchanted island, annually seen floating along the coast of Antrim. Reference was afterwards made to 'Plumptree's Narrative' (of 1817), as showing that, at Rathlin—a considerable island opposite to Ballycastle—a belief then prevailed, that a green island rose every seventh year, out of the sea, between it and the promontory of Bengore; the inhabitants asserting that many of them had distinctly seen it, crowded with people spinning yarn, and engaged in various other occupations common to a fair. The notes to the second book of Dr. Drummond's poem on the 'Causeway' were also glanced at, as containing an account of other cases of the Fata Morgana, by the Bushfoot Strand and Tor-point. So, a person still living (and whose name, &c. were given) conceived that he had a sight of the floating isle off Fair-Head; that it seemed to be well-wooded; and that he could distinguish upon it the forms of buildings, and a woman laying out clothes, Mr. M'Farland then mentioned that, in June 1833, he himself and a party of friends, when standing on a rock at Portbalintrea, perceived a small roundish island as if in the act of emerging from the deep, at a distance of a mile from the shore; at first it appeared but as a green field, afterwards it became fringed with red, yellow and blue; whilst the forms of trees, men and cattle rose upon it slowly and successively; and these continued for about a quarter of an hour, distinct in their outlines, shape and colour; the figures, too, seemed to walk across it, or wandered among the trees, the ocean bathed it around, the sun shone upon it from above; and all was fresh, fair, and beautiful, till the sward assumed a shadowy form, and its various objects, mingling into one confused whole, passed away as strangely as they came. Further, Morgana had occasionally assumed the semblance of a beautiful bridge that spanned the Sound between the Skerry rocks and the strand at Portrush and having people passing and repassing over it. A particular instance of this was stated, as well as of the appearance of the sea, at Ballintoy, of what resembled a city with its streets, houses, spires, &c. Two occasions were then specified, in which the Fata had been seen in the sky—the one in the summer of 1847, over the Ferry at Lough Foyle, and the other on the 14th of December 1850, near to the Bannmouth; and in the course of which the images of troops, ships, &c. were reflected on the clouds. Four other cases of the Aerial Morgana were adduced, as witnessed about the town and coast of Waterford in 1644, and at the close of the last and commencement of the present centuries, and taken from the 'Voyages and Observations' of M. le Gown, Brewer's 'Beauties of Ireland' (vol. ii. p. 307, n.), and the 13th volume of the Phil. Mag., Old Series. Mr. M'Farland considered that these various exhibitions of the Fata Morgana might all be accounted for by applying to those parts of the coast on which they had been displayed, the theories of Minasi and M. Honel, as advanced by them in explanation of similar phaenomena seen on and about the Strait of Messina. The Northern Channel of Ireland presents, to a very great degree, the same data as regards shape, indentations, currents, and bitumen, as that strait does, and on which their theories rest; and he believed that, to some extent at least, so did the sea in the neighbourhood of the isles of Arran and town of Waterford. Where the Marine Morgana was found, the Aerial might be expected, and the Prismatic was a mere corollary to the first.

UNEXPLAINED SHIP'S IMAGE
Johnston, R.; *Marine Observer,* 32:183, 1962

M.v. *Glengyle.* Captain R. Johnston. London to Port Said. Observer, Mr. A. J. Child, Extra 3rd Officer. 2nd December 1961. Between 1440 and 1445 GMT the unusual refraction effects shown in the sketch were observed. A Blue Funnel ship was seen on the horizon towards the south at 1440, with the funnel much enlarged due to refraction: simultaneously a 'watery looking' image of the same vessel was seen on the horizon in the WNW. At 1443 the sun was obscured by hills some 63 miles distant and

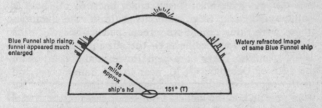

A peculiar sideways mirage, inexplicable in terms of conventional mirage theory.

3,000–7,000 ft. high. The vessel and its image now looked larger than they did 3 min. previously. The image disappeared at 1445, which was, by calculation, the time of sunset. Air temp. 77°F, sea 78°. Wind ESE'ly, force 2.

Small amounts of C_M8 present. Occasional lightning seen from 1800–2200.

Position of ship: 24°36′N, 35°05′E.

Note. We cannot explain this observation, except by suggesting that the 'watery looking' image was that of another ship well below the horizon (i.e., images of two similar ships were observed).

A DOUBLE VERTICAL-REFLECTION MIRAGE AT CAPE WRATH

Brunt, D.; *Nature,* 111:222–223, February 17, 1923

[Double mirages, such as the one described below, require two sets of nearly identical, colocated meteorological conditions. Such coincidences must be very rare indeed.]

On the morning of December 5, 1922, about 10:30 a.m. G.M.T., Mr. John Anderson, lightkeeper at the Cape Wrath Lighthouse, Durness, observed a mirage of an unusual character. Mr. Anderson focussed his telescope on a sheep which was grazing on top of a conical hill (height about 200 feet) about a quarter of a mile away, and immediately noticed an unusual appearance in the atmosphere around. On swinging the telescope slightly upward, he observed that a belt of the atmosphere appeared to be land and sea, giving a perfect representation of the whole of the coast line from Cape Wrath to Dunnet Head.

The appearance in the mirage was an exact replica of what would have been seen from a distance of about 10 miles out at sea. In a direction south of the lighthouse there were three repetitions of the mirage one above the other, with sea separating each pair. The entrance to Loch Eriboll and the other bays could be seen and easily recog-

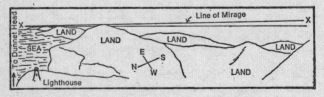

Land forms at the site of a double mirage.

nised in the main mirage, though Cape Wrath itself was rather indistinct.

.   .   .   .

The mirage was practically invisible to the naked eye, and was only visible from a very restricted area. Mr. Anderson states that it was not visible at a distance of 20 yards either way from his original position, but was still visible 4 or 5 yards from that point. Mr. Anderson estimates the apparent height of the image above the ground as about 1000 feet, in a southerly direction, while the distance from Cape Wrath of the triple image shown on the map is about 12 miles.

The phenomenon was observed for about thirty minutes, when it was blotted out by heavy, dark clouds from the south-west. Within a short time the sky was darkly overcast and rain began to fall, lightly at first, accompanied by slight fog; later rain fell very heavily, the rain-gauge giving a total of 1.97 inches for the afternoon.

The mirage was seen by practically all the residents at the station.

13

Fish and Frog Falls

"Of course a waterspout or whirlwind deposited them" is the common response to news of a fish fall. No one can deny the possibility, even likelihood, of such a meteorological explanation after seeing *The Wizard of Oz*. But the venerable waterspout must possess some unusual refinements if it is to account for all of the facts concerning fish falls.

To begin, there exist many well-documented fish and frog falls—no one seriously denies that they do take place. The stranger aspects of these falls appear only after reviewing many reports. First, the transporting mechanism (whatever it may be) prefers to select only a single species of fish or frog or whatever animal is on the menu for the day. Second, size selection is also carefully controlled in many instances. Third, no debris, such as sand or plant material, is dropped along with the animals. Fourth, even though saltwater species are dropped there are no records of the accompanying rainfall being salty. All in all, the mechanism involved is rather fastidious in what it transports. The waterspout theory is easiest to swallow when the fish that fall commonly shoal on the surface in large numbers in nearby waters. It is much harder to fit the facts to the theory when the fish are from deep waters, when the fish are dead and dry (sometimes headless), and when frogs fall in immense numbers without frog-pond debris accompanying them.

A final feature of animal falls hints ever so slightly that some falls may even come from outer space!

This feature is the "footprint" or pattern of the fall, which is usually rather small (a few hundred feet long) and highly elliptical. Bunched objects in orbit around the earth that enter the atmosphere would land in this kind of pattern. The speculation is a wild one, but it is within the realm of possibility that past terrestrial cataclysms (an oceanic meteor impact, for example) have ejected part of the biosphere into orbit. Although rarer than fish and frog falls, sedimentary rocks, flesh, huge ice chunks, and petroleum have been reported as falling to earth. But these falls are clearly "impossible" because they do not fit the accepted conception of the universe.

SHOWERS OF ORGANIC MATTER
McAtee, Waldo L.; *Monthly Weather Review*, 45:217–224, May 1917

[McAtee's survey is extensive, covering invertebrates, insects, "blood," etc. Only the sections on fish and frogs are included here.]

The fall of vertebrate animals from the skies like rain is, of course, the most interesting of all the showers of organic matter, and—it must be admitted—the hardest to believe. Yet there cannot be the slightest doubt that there are genuine phenomena of this character, though perhaps not so numerous as the recorded instances. These occurrences, if observed by man, naturally make profound impressions and in the olden times especially, the tales of showers of fishes and the like were improved by each teller, so that soon they reached the state of the unbelievable.

Frogs, toads.—I quote only one of the older writers, Athenaeus, who flourished about 200 A.D. He is the author of a polyhistorical work called the "Deipnosophists," in which he quotes about 800 authors, whose works he consulted at the Alexandrian Library, 700 of whom would have been unknown, except for the fortunate preservation of Athenaeus' work. In a chapter entitled "De pluvius piscium," he says:

"I know also that it has very often rained fishes. At all events Phenias, in the second book of his Eresian Magistrates, says that in the Chersonesus it once rained fish uninterruptedly for three days; and Phylarchus in his fourth book, says that people had often seen it raining fish, and often also raining wheat, and that the same thing had happened with respect to frogs." At all events Heraclides Lembus, in the 21st book of his history, says: "In Paeonia and Dardinia, it has, they say, before now rained frogs; and so great has been the number of these frogs that the houses and the roads have been full with them; and at first for some days the inhabitants, endeavoring to kill them, and shutting up their houses endured the pest; but when they did no good, but found that all their vessels were filled with them, and the frogs were found to be boiled up and roasted with everything they ate, and when besides all this they could not make use of any water, nor put their feet on the ground for the heaps of frogs that were' everywhere, and were annoyed also by the smell of those that died, they fled the country." [*The Deipnosophists or Banquet of the Learned,* Book XV, pt. 2, pp. 526–527]

For numbers of frogs and the far reaching effects of their fall this tale can scarcely be surpassed, but it will be well to recount some later instances, especially some of the more circumstantial ones. Holinshed informs us that in Great Britain—Frogs fell in Angueshire during the time of Agricola. Frogs were reported to have descended, during the summer of 1846 over the Humber, upon the decks of vessels in the river and on the coast near Killinghome lights. [Thompson, David P.; *Introduction to Meteorology,* pp. 164–165. 1849]

A later account recites that—

"During the storm that raged with considerable fury in Birmingham (England) on Wednesday morning, June 30 [1892], a shower of frogs fell in the suburb of Moseley. They were found scattered about several gardens. Almost white in color, they had evidently been absorbed in a small waterspout that was driven over Birmingham by the tempest." [*Symon's Meteorological Magazine,* 32:107]

Several notices have from time to time been brought before the French Academy of showers of frogs having fallen in different parts of France. M. Duparque states in a letter that—

"In August, 1814, after several weeks of drouth and heat, a storm broke one Sunday about 3:30 p.m., upon the village of Fremon, a quarter league from Amiens. This storm was preceded by bursts of wind so violent that they shook the church and frightened the congregation. While traversing the space separating the church from presbytery, we were soaked, but what surprised me was to be struck on my person and my clothing by small frogs. . . . A large number of these small animals hopped about on the ground. On arriving at the presbytery, we found the floor of one of the rooms in which a window facing the storm had been left open covered with water and frogs." [*L'Institut*, 2:354]

Showers of toads seem to be more common in some regions than those of frogs. I have seen accounts of 13 different occurrences of the kind in France. A French scientist M. Mauduy, curator of natural history at Poitiers, had personal experience with two such showers, which he narrates briefly as follows:

"On the 23rd of June, 1809, during a hot spell, I was caught in a rain storm in which with the very large drops were mixed little bodies the size of hazelnuts, which in a moment, covered the ground, and which I recognized as little toads. The second occasion, occurred in August, 1822, during a stormy and very hot period. I was again surprised by a heavy shower of large drops mixed, as was the other, with little toads, some of which fell on my hat. This time the animals were the size of walnuts. I found that I was more than a league distant from any brook, river, or marsh." [*L'Institut*, 2:409]

A considerable discussion of the subject of rains of toads was carried on in 1834 in the French scientific magazine from which I have quoted. I cite two more bits of testimony by eye witnesses, one of which has been widely reproduced.

M. Heard, writes:

"In June, 1833, I was at Jouy near Versaille. I saw toads falling from the sky; they struck my umbrella; I saw them hopping on the pavement, during about 10 minutes in which time the drops of water were not more numerous than the toads. The space upon which I saw the multitude of these animals was about 200 fathoms." [*L'Institut*, 2:353]

M. Peltier in his oft-copied statement says:

"In support of the communication of Col. Marmier, I cite an incident I observed in my youth; a storm advanced upon the little village of Ham, Department of the Somme,

where I lived, and I observed its menacing march, when
suddenly rain fell in torrents. I saw the village square
covered everywhere with little toads. Astonished by this
sight, I held out my hand and was struck by several of
the reptiles. The dooryard also was covered; I saw them
fall upon the slate roof and rebound to the pavement. . . .
Whatever the difficulty of explaining the transport of the
reptiles, I affirm, without doubt the fact which made such a
profound impression upon my memory." [*L'Institut*, 2:
346–347]

The most remarkable account of a shower of toads, that
I have seen, so far, is the following:

"In the summer of 1794 M. Gayet was quartered in the
village of Lalain, Department du Nord . . . near the territory which the Austrians, then masters of Valenciennes,
had flooded with water from the Scarpe. It was very hot.
Suddenly, at about 3 o'clock in the afternoon, there fell
such an abundance of rain that 150 men of the grand
guard, in order not to be submerged, were obliged to leave
a large depression in which they were hidden. But what
was their surprise when there began to fall on the ground
all about a considerable number of toads, the size of hazelnuts, which began to jump about in every direction. M.
Gayet, who could not believe that these myriads of reptiles fell with the rain, stretched out his handkerchief at
the height of a man, his comrades holding the corners;
they caught a considerable number of toads, most of which
had the posterior part elongated into a tail, that is to say,
in the tadpole state. During this rain storm, which lasted
about half an hour, the men of the grand guard felt very
distinctly on their hats and on their clothing the blows
struck by the falling toads. As a final proof of the reality
of this phenomenon, M. Gayet reports that after the storm
the three-cornered hats of the men of the guard held in
their folds some of the reptiles." [*L'Institut*, 2:354]

Fish.—For reports of the falling of frogs and toads
from the skies, we have been far afield, for the very good
reason that I have not found any cases reported from the
United States. But for fishes, there are several reports.
Before giving these accounts, allow me to introduce a few
statements that tend to show how fishes get started on the
aerial journeys that terminate in fish rains.

To show the tremendous power of waterspouts, we may

quote M. Oersted's declaration that "At Christiansoe a waterspout emptied the harbour to such an extent that the greater part of the bottom was uncovered." Naturally under such circumstances fishes and any other organisms in the water may change their habitat very abruptly. Waterspouts have been observed to accomplish the comparatively insignificant tasks of emptying fish ponds and scattering their occupants.

A prodigy of this kind is recorded to have occurred in France, at a town some distance from Paris, during a violent storm. When morning dawned, the streets were found strewed with fish of various sizes. The mystery was soon solved, for a fish pond in the vicinity had been blown dry, and only the large fish left behind. [Reess' *Cyclopedia*]

So, during a storm on December 28, 1845, at Bassenthwaite, England, fish were blown from the lake to dry land.

Proceeding now to the United States records, Mr. Thomas R. Baker states that—

"During a recent thunderstorm at Winter Park, Fla., a number of fish fell with the rain. They were sunfish from 2 to 4 inches long. It is supposed that they were taken up by a waterspout from Lake Virginia, and carried westward by the strong wind that was blowing at the time. The distance from the lake to the place where they fell is about a mile." [*Science*, 21:335]

In the *Monthly Weather Review* for June, 1901 (p. 263), is the note "Mr. J. W. Gardner, voluntary observer at Tillers Ferry, S. C., reports that during a heavy local shower about June 27 [1901] there fell hundreds of little fish (cat, perch, trout, etc.) that were afterwards found swimming in the pools between the cotton row."

In all, I am acquainted with four records of falls of fishes in the United States, two in South America, eight in Great Britain, two in France, and six in India and neighboring countries. These are all well vouched for, or fairly modern and circumstantially related instances. The older, chiefly traditional, records would make a long list.

One of the most ancient records of fish having fallen from the atmosphere in Great Britain is the following: "About Easter, 1666, in the parish of Stanstead, which is a considerable distance from the sea, or any branch of it, and a place where there are no fish ponds and rather scarcity of water, a pasture field was scattered all over with small fish, in quantity about a bushel, supposed to have been rained down from a cloud, there having been at the time a great tempest of thunder, rain, and wind. The fish were about the size of a man's little finger. Some were like small whitings, others like sprats, and some smaller, like smelts. Several of these fish were sold publicly at Maidstone and Dartford. A shower of herrings is recorded to have taken place near to Loch Leven, in Kinross-shire, about the year 1825; the wind blew from the Firth of Forth at the time, and doubtless the fish had been thereby carried from the sea across Fifeshire to the place where they were found. In 1828, similar fish fell in the county of Ross, 3 miles distant from the Frith of Dingwall. On the 9th of March, 1830, in the Isle of Ula, in Argyleshire, after a heavy rain, numbers of small herrings were found scattered over the fields; they were perfectly fresh, and some not quite dead. On the 30th of June, 1841, a fish measuring 10 inches in length, with others of smaller size, fell at Boston; and during a thunderstorm, on the 8th of July, in the same year, fish and ice fell together at Derby." [Thompson, D. P.; *Introduction of Meteorology,* p. 103, 1849]

A convincing statement of personal experience with a rain of fishes is that of John Lewis, of Abderdare, who says that while working, February 9:

"I was startled by something falling all over me—down my neck, on my head, and on my back. On putting my hand down my neck I was surprised to find they were little fish. By this time I saw the whole ground covered with them. I took off my hat, the brim of which was full of them. . . . They covered the ground in a long strip about 80 yards by 12 yards, as we measured afterwards. . . . We gathered a great many of them . . . and threw them into the rain pool, where some of them now are. . . . It was not blowing very hard, but uncommon wet. . . . The person who took this testimony adds that he secured about 20 of the little fish, some of which were 4 and 5 inches long. A number of these fishes were exhibited for several weeks in the aquaria house of the Zoological Society in the Regent's Park, London." [Tomlinson, Charles; *The Rain-Cloud and the Snow-Storm,* pp. 193–194]

The accounts of rains of fishes in South America are by

Alexander von Humboldt, whose language relating to them is as follows:

"When the earthquakes, which precede every eruption in the chain of the Andes, shake with mighty force the entire mass of the volcanoes, the subterranean vaults are opened and emit at the same time water, fishes, and tufamud. This is the singular phenomenon that furnishes the fish *Pimelodes cyclopum,* which the inhabitants of the highlands of Quito call 'Prefiadilla,' and which was described by me soon after my return. When the summit of the mountain Carguairazo to the north of Chimborazo and 18,000 feet high, fell, in the night between the 19th and 20th of June, 1698, the surrounding fields, to the extent of about 43 English square miles, were covered with mud and fishes. The fever which raged in the town of Ibarra seven years before had been ascribed to a similar eruption of fishes from the volcano Imbaburu." [*Annals of Philosophy,* 22:130]

There are several well authenticated reports of falls of fish in India, and this has given rise to the belief that the phenomenon is more frequent there than elsewhere. This may be true on account of the favoring circumstances of extensive river flood plains, numerous shallow water tanks, a fish fauna rich in shoal water forms, and a hot whirlwind-breeding climate. Certainly the description of fish rains in that part of the world are numerous, specific, and astonishing as to the magnitude of the phenomena.

One of the oldest reports, brief but with a humerous touch, I quote first. It is by Lieut. John Harriott, who says:

"In a heavy shower of rain, while our army was on the march a short distance from Pondicherry, a quantity of small fish fell with the rain to the astonishment of all. Many of them lodged on the men's hats. . . . They were not *flying fish,* they were dead and falling from the well-known effect of gravity; but how they ascended or where they existed I do not pretend to account. I merely relate the simple fact." [*Struggles Through Life,* pp. 141-142, 1809]

A very valuable account of a shower of fishes is that by J. Prinsep, editor of the Journal of the Asiatic Society of Bengal. He writes:

"The phenomenon of fish falling from the sky in the

rainy season, however incredible it may appear, has been attested by such circumstantial evidence that no reasonable doubt can be entertained of the fact. I was as incredulous as my neighbors until I once found a small fish in the brass funnel of my pluviometer at Banares. I have now before me a note of a similar phenomenon, on a considerable scale which happened at the Nokulhatty factory, Zillah Dacca Jedalpur, in 1830.

"Mr. Cameron, who communicated the fact, took the precaution of having a regular deposition of the evidence of several natives who had witnessed the fall made in Bengalee and attested before the magistrate; the statement is well worthy of preservation in a journal of science. . . . The shower of fish took place on the 19th of February, 1830, in the neighborhood of the Surbundy factory, Feridper (p. 650)." [*Journal of the Asiatic Society of Bengal,* 3:650–652]

There are depositions of nine eye witnesses, of which I quote two:

Shekh Chaudari Ahmed, son of Mutiullah, inhabitant of Nagdi, relates in his deposition: "I had been doing my work at a meadow, when I perceived at the hour of 12 o'clock the sky gather clouds, and began to rain slightly, then a large fish touching my back by its head fell on the ground. Being surprised I looked about, and behold a number of fish likewise fell from heaven. They were saul, sale, guzal, mirgal, and bodul. I took 10 or 11 fish in number, and I saw many other persons take many."

Shekh Suduruddin, inhabitant of Nagdi, was called in and declared in his deposition saying: "On Friday, at 12 o'clock p.m., in the month of Phalgun . . . when I was at work in a field, I perceived the sky darkened by clouds, began to rain a little and a large fish fell from the sky. I was confounded at the sight, and soon entered my cottage, which I had there, but I came out again as soon as the rain had ceased and found every part of my hut scattered with fish; they were boduli, mirgal, and nouchi, and amounted to 25 in number." [*Journal of the Asiatic Society of Bengal,* 3:650–652]

The large number of fishes that may rain down is illustrated by another Indian instance which was reported as follows:

"On the 16th or 17th of May last a fall of fish happened

in monon Sonare, pergunna Dhata Ekdullah, Zillah Fut-
teppur. The zemindzry of the village have furnished the
following particulars which are confirmed by other accounts. About noon, the wind being from the west, and a
few distant clouds visible, a blast of high wind, accompanied with much dust, which changed the atmosphere to a
reddish yellow hue came on; the blast appeared to extend
in breadth about 400 yards. . . . When the storm had
passed over, they found the ground south of the village to
the extent of two bigahs strewed with fish, in number not
less than three or four thousand. The fish were all of the
Chalwa species (*Clupea cultrata*), a span or less in length,
and from 1½ to ½ seer in weight; when found they were
all dead and dry. Chalwa fish are found in the tanks and
rivers of the neighborhood . . . the nearest water is about
half a mile south of the village." [*Journal of the Asiátic
Society of Bengal,* 3:367]

For the number of fishes that fell this account is not
surpassed, but for all-around interest, and credulity in-
spired by the name of its distinguished author, the testimony of Francis de Castelnau is supreme. The note is
entitled "Shower of Fishes; earthquake at Singapore," and
was published in 1861.

"We experienced here an earthquake at 7:34 p.m.,
February 16, that lasted about two minutes; it was followed by hard rains, which on the 20th, 21st, and 22d
became veritable torrents. The last day at 9 a.m. the rain
redoubled in fury, and in a half hour our inclosed plot
became a sea of water. . . .

"At 10 o'clock the sun lifted and from my window I
saw a large number of Malays and Chinese filling baskets
with fishes which they picked up in the pools of water
which covered the ground. On being asked where the fishes
came from, the natives replied that they had fallen from
the sky. Three days afterwards, when the pools had dried
up, we found many dead fishes.

"Having examined the animals, I recognized them as
Clarias batrachi, Cuvier and Valenciennes, a species of cat-
fish which is very abundant in fresh water in Singapore,
and the nearer Malayan Islands, in Siam, Borneo, etc.
They were from 25 to 30 centimeters long, and therefore
adult.

"These siluroids, the same as Ophicephalus, etc., are

able to live a long time out of water, and to progress some distance on land, and I thought at once that they had come from some small streams near by; but the yard of the house I inhabited is inclosed in a wall that would prevent them entering in this manner. An old Malay has since told me that in his youth he had seen a similar phenomenon." [*Comptes Rendus,* 52:880–881)

A SHOWER OF FROGS
Hale, C. P.; *Notes and Queries,* 8:7:437, June 1, 1895

A shower of frogs in London! To the inhabitants of the metropolis it may come as a surprise to know that such a thing has been experienced. Looking through the pages of an old volume of that once popular miscellany the *Mirror,* I found, under the heading 'A Shower of Frogs,' the following item:—

"A correspondent of the *Sun,* who hails from 7, Sackville Street, states that, as he was walking up Tower Street on Monday afternoon, July 30, 1838, he saw some dozens of young frogs hopping on the foot and carriage pavements; which he conjectures had been precipitated to the earth in a heavy shower that had fallen about an hour before, as they were scattered to a considerable distance. He describes the largest of the frogs as not exceeding half an inch in length, while some were extremely minute, but all exceedingly lively."—*Mirror,* Aug. 4, 1838.

This, if not unique, must be a very rare phenomenon in London.

In the 'British Apollo," vol. i. p. 410, an instance of the phenomenon is brought to the notice of the authors of that production by a correspondent, who mentions that on riding "out in a warm evening, when near the Town's End, he saw a vast number of small frogs on the road, not larger than bees, which some people affirm'd came down in a shower of rain, which fell just before."

In these days it may be interesting to read the reply with which the narrator of the above incident was favoured in explanation of its occurrence. Says the learned writer, to whom the task of dispelling this "vulgar error" (sic) was accorded:—

"That opinion of young frogs coming down in a shower

of rain certainly deserves not the least rank among vulgar errors; we may almost as well imagine, that any other animal, terrestrial or aquatick should drop from the clouds. Do not we see plainly that their spawn lies together in the water in a cluster, which being of a glutinous substance is not very apt to be dispers'd and carried up into the air to be hatched there. If then after a shower of rain, especially in warm weather, they are sometimes found in great numbers upon the ground, it is only because by that pleasant rain they are invited abroad from those holes where they lay lurking before."

FALL OF FISHES FROM THE ATMOSPHERE IN INDIA
Prinsep, M.; *American Journal of Science*, 1:32:199–200, 1837

[This fall of rotten and even headless fish casts doubt on the waterspout theory, for where do headless fish occur in nature?]

As for myself, my credulity is compelled to yield to the discovery I made one day of a small fish, in my pluviometer, which was situated on an isolated pile of stones about five feet high, in my garden at Benares. A note from M. Cameron informs me that a rain of fishes occurred on the 19th of February, 1830, near Feridpoor. This fact was asserted before a magistrate, by many ocular witnesses, and it was their concurring testimony that towards noon of the above mentioned day, the sky was obscured, the rain commenced to fall, and shortly after, fishes of various sizes fell from the atmosphere. A large number were collected by several witnesses; some were found destitute of a head, and had commenced to putrefy; others were entire and fresh, but no one dared to eat them.

SHOWER OF FISH IN NEW SOUTH WALES, JANUARY 24TH, 1887
Anonymous; *Royal Meteorological Society, Quarterly Journal*, 13:314–315, 1887

Mr. H. C. Russell, F. R. S., Government Astronomer for New South Wales, has forwarded to the Society some correspondence which he has received respecting a shower of fish. The following extracts from the letters by Mr. G. S.

Hay, Telegraph Station, Walgett, to Mr. Russell, will be of interest.

"January 28th.—I have the honour to report for your information that the mailman running between Walgett and Goodooga, via the Comborah Springs, north-west from here, brought into town a small fish having the appearance of a small bream, about 3 inches long, which he states he found in the wheel track on a sand ridge about 25 miles this side of the Narran river. The place was alive with them. He says that on Monday night, January 24th, there was a terrific storm of rain and wind, and that these fish fell in the shower. The Narran lake is some 20 or more miles from the spot. I may add that the keeper of the Bunghill Tank, a Government watering place on this route, on hearing of the presence of the fish proceeded with a tub and collected a number of them which he intended placing in the Tank to stock it."

"February 10th.—Re shower of fish reported by me for your information, I have seen the keeper of the Bunghill Tank, who states that he collected over 100 fish and placed them in the Tank. They were all alike so far as he observed, and much about the same size. When the rain water had subsided they were lying dead in thousands. There is a *warrambool* or lagoon two miles south-west of the road, and is known to contain fish; and as the storm travelled from that direction, it is supposed the fish must have been lifted from the *warrambool* and carried along till the storm burst in crossing the track, which is cleared through some thick timber and on an elevated ridge of sand and gravel. There were great atmospheric disturbances along here at the time, twisting winds and thunderstorms from all directions, but principally from south-west to north-east or north, and during the week over 8 ins. of rain fell."

14

Pwdre Ser or the "Rot of the Stars"

"Star jelly" is still another name for pwdre ser, but nothing can be as descriptive as "rot of the stars." The basic phenomenon has been the same since written history began. A meteor is seen to land nearby, investigation reveals a jellylike mass in the approximate location, thus we have star jelly or, more scientifically, a "gelatinous meteor." The incongruity is that common meteorites are hard lumps of rock and metal well suited to surviving the fiery plunge through the earth's atmosphere from outer space. Gelatin would be consumed in a few seconds. Thus the co-location of meteor impact and gelatinous mass *must* be coincidental.

Actually, several of the accounts that follow indicate little doubt that the observer did perceive gelatinous masses to fall and that there was also a luminous display of some kind. In addition, the testimony of legends and folklore is overwhelmingly in favor of the reality of gelatinous meteors, as the first selection by Hughes proves. Obviously, this does not mean that all gelatinous masses found in meadow and field fell from the sky, but neither can we deny the possibility of gelatinous meteors just because terrestrial nature happens to produce lumps of gelatin.

Scientists who have tried to explain pwdre ser always opt for the terrestrial interpretation; that is, some form of plant or animal life or possibly some half-digested matter disgorged by an animal. It seems that common characteristics of pwdre ser are its smell and general rottenness. But if rotten fish can fall from the sky (chapter 13), why not malodorous gelatin? Pwdre ser has one other interesting feature: it seems to evaporate rapidly, removing all evidence of the unusual phenomenon. Genuine animal matter is not so fleeting and ephemeral.

Then what is pwdre ser? No one knows for sure; that is why it is included in this book.

PWDRE SER
Hughes, T. McKenny; *Nature,* 83:492–494, June 23, 1910

[This is one of the classic accounts of star jelly, or gelatinous meteors.]

In my boyhood I often lived on the coast of Pembrokeshire. Wandering about with my gun I was familiar with most natural objects which occurred there. One, however, which I often came across there, and have seen elsewhere since, greatly roused my curiosity, but I have not yet met with a satisfactory explanation of it.

On the short, close grass of the hilly ground, I frequently saw a mass of white, translucent jelly lying on the turf, as if it had been dropped there. These masses were about as large as a man's fist. It was very like a mass of frog's spawn without the eggs in it. I thought it might have been the gelatinous portion of the food disgorged by the great fish-eating birds, of which there were plenty about, as kingfishers eject pellets made up of the bones of the fish they eat, or that possibly there might be some pathological explanation connecting it with the sheep, large flocks of which grazed the short herbage. But the shepherds and owners of the sheep would have known if such an explanation were admissible. They called it "pwdre ser," the rot of the stars.

Years afterwards I was in Westmorland, on the Geological Survey, and again not unfrequently saw the "pwdre ser." But I now got an addition to my story. Isaac Hindson, of Kirkby Lonsdale, a man whose scientific knowledge and genial personality made him a welcome companion to those who had to carry on geological research in his district, told me that he had once seen a luminous body fall, and, on going up to the place, found only a mass of white jelly. He did not say that it was luminous. I have never seen it luminous, but that may be because when it was light enough to see the lump of jelly, it would probably be too light to detect luminosity in it.

Then, in my novel reading, I found that the same thing was known in Scotland, and the same origin assigned to it, for Walter Scott, in "The Talisman," puts these words in the mouth of the hermit:—"Seek a fallen star and thou shalt only light on some foul jelly, which in shooting through the horizon, has assumed for a moment an appearance of splendour." I think that I remember seeing it used elsewhere as an illustration of disappointed hopes, which were "as when a man seeing a meteor fall, runs up and finds but a mass of putrid jelly," but I have lost the reference to this passage.

Thus it appeared that in Wales, in the Lake District, and in Scotland, there existed a belief that something which fell from the sky as a luminous body lay on the ground as a lump of white jelly.

I asked Huxley what it could be, and he said that the only thing like it that he knew was a nostoc. I turned to Sachs for the description of a nostoc, and found that it "consists, when mature, of a large number of moniliform threads interwoven among one another and imbedded in a glutinous jelly, and thus united into colonies of a specifically defined form . . . The gelatinous envelope of the new filament is developed, and the originally microscopic substance attains or even exceeds the size of a walnut by continuous increase of the jelly and divisions of the cells."

All the nostocs, however, that I have had pointed out to me have been of a green or purplish or brown-green colour, whereas the "pwdre ser" was always white, translucent in the upper part, and transparent in the lower part, which appeared to occur among the roots of the grass, as if it grew there. Moreover, the mass was much larger than a walnut, in fact, would generally about fill a half-pint mug.

The only reference I can find from which it would appear that the writer was describing a nostoc is the passage in Drdyen and Lee (1678).

"The shooting stars end all in purple jellies." In the following note, appended to this passage, it is clear that the writer thought that the jelly-like matter found where shooting-stars had seemed to fall, was white.

Note.—"It is a common idea that falling stars, as they are called, are converted into a sort of jelly. Among the rest, I had often the opportunity to see the seeming shooting of the stars from place to place, and sometimes they appeared as if falling to the ground, where I once or twice found a white jelly-like matter among the grass, which I imagined to be distilled from them; and thence foolishly conjectured that the stars themselves must certainly consist of a like substance."

Poets and divines carry the record of this curious belief far back into the seventeenth century.

Suckling (1541) says:—

> "As he whose quicker eye doth trace
> A false star shot to mark't place
>   Do's run apace,
> And, thinking it to catch,
> A jelly up do snatch."

Jeremy Taylor (1649):—

"It is weaknesse of the organ that makes us hold our hand between the sun and us, and yet stand staring upon a meteor or an inflamed gelly."

Henry More (1656):—
"That the Starres eat . . . that those falling Starres, as some call them, which are found on the earth in the form of a trembling gelly, are their excrement."

Dryden (1679):—
"When I had taken up what I supposed a fallen star I found I had been cozened with a jelly."

William Somerville (1740):—

> "Swift as the Shooting Star that gilds the night
> With rapid transient Blaze, she runs, she flies;
> Sudden she stops nor longer can endure
> The painful course, but drooping sinks away,
> And like that falling Meteor, there she lyes
> A jelly cold on earth."

Several old writers, however, while agreeing as to the mode of occurrence of the "pwdre ser," and recognising the widespread belief that it was something which fell from the sky and was somehow connected with falling stars, have tried to find some more commonplace and probable explanation of the phenomenon, and most of them refer it to the stuff disgorged by birds that had fed on frogs or worms.

* * * * * * * * * * * * * * * * *

The Rev. John Morton, of Emmanuel College (1712), is, however, the only one who, so far as I can ascertain, ever tried any experiments with the view of finding out what it really was. He set some of it on the fire, and when he had driven off all the watery part, there was left a film like isinglass, and something like the skins and vessels of animal bodies. He records many observations as to its time and mode of occurrence; for instance, he says that "in 1699–1700 there was no star-gelly to be found about Oxenden till a wet week in the end of February, when the shepherds brought me above thirty several lumps." This and other observations suggest that it is a growth dependent upon the weather, &c. On the other hand, he says that he saw a wounded gull disgorge a heap of half-digested earthworms much resembling star-jelly, and that Sir William Craven saw a bittern do the same in similar circumstances.

The Hon. Robert Boyle, 1744, explaining how clammy and viscous bodies, such as white of egg, are reduced to a thin and fluid substance, says:—

"And I remember, I have seen a good quantity of that jelly, that is sometimes found on the ground, and by the vulgar called a star-shoot, as if it remained upon the extinction of a falling star, which being brought to an eminent physician of my acquaintance, he lightly digested it in a well-stopt glass for a long time, and by that alone resolved it into a permanent liquor, which he extols as a specifick to be outwardly applied against Wens."

Pennant seems to have supposed that its origin was that suggested by Morton, for in his description of the winter mew he says:—"This kind (i.e. the Coddy Moddy or Winter Mew) frequents, during winter, the moist meadows in the inland parts of England remote from the Sea. The gelatinous substance, known by the name of star shot, or star gelly, owes its origin to this bird or some of the kind, being nothing but the half digested remains of earth-worms, on which these birds feed and often discharge from their stomachs."

I have found it commonly near the sea, but have never seen any trace of earth-worms or other similar food in it.

Here, then, we have a well-known substance which may be of different origin in different cases, respecting the general appearance of which, however, almost all accounts agree. The variety of names under which it is known point to its common and widespread occurrence, e.g. powdre ser, star-slough, star shoot, star shot, star-gelly or jelly, star-fall'n.

We have in every name, and in every notice in literature, a recognition of the universal belief that it has something to do with meteors, yet there does not appear to be any evidence that anybody ever saw any luminosity in the jelly. Nor has anybody seen it disgorged by birds, except in the case of those two wounded birds where some half-digested gelatinous mass was thrown up. Nor has anyone watched its growth like nostoc from the ground.

In 1908 I was with my wife and one of my boys on Ingelborough, where we found the "powdre ser" lying on the short grass, close to the stream a little way above Gaping Ghyl Hole. For the first time I felt grateful to the inconsiderate tourist who left broken bottles about, for I was able to pack the jelly in the bottom of one, tie a cover on, and carry it down from the fell. I sent it, with the sod on which it appeared to have grown, to my colleague, Mr. E. A. Newell Arber, with a brief sketch of my story and the reason why I thought it of interest. Mr. Arber reported that it was no nostoc, and said that he had sent it over to Mr. Brookes, in the Botany School, who reported that it was a mass of bacteria.

That is the end of my story, but I confess I am not satisfied. The jelly seemed to me to grow out from among the roots of the grass, and the part still tangled in the grass was not only translucent but quite transparent.

What is it, and what is the cause of its having a meteoric origin assigned to it? Has anyone ever seen it luminous?

Should anyone come upon it I should be very grateful if they would send it, and the sod on which it is found, to the Botany School at Cambridge, with a label indicating what the parcel contains, so that it may be attended to before decay has perhaps obscured important features.

A CATALOGUE OF METEORITES AND FIREBALLS
Gregg, R. P.; *Reports to the British Association*, 62–63, 1860

January 21, 1803, Silesia. A shooting star, got larger and larger until it fell to earth. Between Barsdorf and Freiburg. Seemed to pass close to ground; a whizzing noise heard, then it seemed to lie burning on the ground; next day a jelly-like mass found on the snow. Curious, if true.

ACCOUNT OF AN EXTRAORDINARY METEORIC PHENOMENON
Acharius, E.; *North American Review*, 3:320–322, September 1816

[From the Transactions of the Swedish Academy of Sciences, for 1808, page 215. Translated by Mr. J. C. Hauff.]

Having received intelligence from several persons, although differently and variously related, of an extraordinary and probably hitherto unseen Phenomenon, which was observed in the air last month, at and about the village of Biskopsberga, near the Town of Skeninge, which accounts not being testified to me by eye-witnesses, nor agreeing as to facts and circumstances, I resolved to proceed to the place myself for obtaining an exact and detailed account thereof; and as I find so many singular circumstances attending this Meteor, which deserve to be known, I have thought it my duty to communicate them to the Royal Academy, and thereby to save so remarkable an occurrence from oblivion, which, although difficult to explain, still affords an additional proof of those many wonderful operations of Nature, which take place in our Atmosphere.

On the 16th of last May, being a very warm day, and during a gale of wind from south-west, and a cloudless sky, at about 4 o'clock, p.m. the sun became dim, and lost his brightness to that degree, that he could be looked at without inconvenience to the naked eye, being of a dark-red, or almost brick colour, without brilliancy. At the same time there appeared at the western horizon, from where the wind blew, to arise gradually, and in quick succession, a great number of balls, or spherical bodies, to the naked eye of a size of the crown of a hat, and of a dark brown colour. The nearer these bodies, which occupied a considerable though irregular breadth of the visible heaven, approached towards the sun, the darker they appeared, and in the vicinity of the sun, became entirely black. At this elevation their course seemed to lessen, and a great many of them remained, as it were, stationary; but they soon resumed their former, and an accelerated motion, and passed in the same direction with great velocity and almost horizontally. During this course some disappeared, others fell down, but the most part of them continued their progress almost in a straight line, till they were lost sight of at the eastern horizon. The phe-

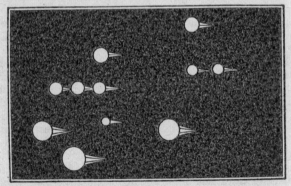

Strange parade of gelatinous globes with "tails" seen in Sweden circa 1807. Reportedly the size of a hat crown, these bodies were seen in immense numbers.

nomenon lasted uninterruptedly, upwards of two hours, during which time millions of similar bodies continually rose in the west, one after the other irregularly, and continued their career exactly in the same manner. No report, noise, nor any whistling or buzzing in the air was perceived. As these balls slackened their course on passing by the sun, several were linked together, three, six, or eight of them in a line, joined like chain-shot by a thin and straight bar; but on continuing again a more rapid course, they separated, and each having a tail after it, apparently of three or four fathoms length, wider at its base where it adhered to the ball, and gradually decreasing, till it terminated in a fine point. During the course, these tails which had the same black colour as the balls, disappeared by degrees.

It fortunately happened, that some of these balls fell at a short distance, or but a few feet from Mr. Secretary K. G. Wettermark, who had then for a long while been attentively looking at the phenomenon, in the aforesaid village. On the descent of these bodies, the black colour seemed gradually to disappear the nearer they approached the earth, and they vanished almost entirely till within a few fathoms distance from the ground, when they again were visible with several changing colours, and in this particular exactly resembling those air-bubbles, which children use to produce from soapsuds by means of a reed. When the spot, where such a ball had fallen, was immediately after examined, nothing was to be seen; but a scarcely perceptible film or pellicle, as thin and fine as a cobweb, which was still changing colours, but soon entirely dried up and vanished. As somewhat singular, it may be observed, that the size of these balls, to the sight, underwent no particular change; for they appeared of the same dimension, at their rise from the western horizon, as well as on their passing by the sun, and during the whole of their course to the eastern part of the heavens, where they disappeared.

Such have been the real circumstances attending this phenomenon, to which all the people in the village can testify. I have drawn up this report from the accounts of none but eye witnesses, and have compared them one with the other; and I cannot doubt the truth of the incidents, having been related to me in a manner agreeing in particulars and details. The labourers of Peter Manson, a farmer, being at work in the field, were the first who observed the phenomenon, and as it continued so long, all the people in the village were gradually observing it; it therefore could not be an illusion, possibly affecting one or other individual.

I leave it to the genius of more skilful and able men, to unfold the causes of this occurrence; but as an hypothesis may be hazarded, without being censured, it may be supposed, that perhaps a strong gust of wind, (coup de vent) from some mountainous or woody tracts, or regions at a distance, had loosened, collected and carried along with it, some probably vegetable substances of a jelly-like nature, which, in passing through the air, having incorporated some additional matter by a chemical union therewith, formed themselves into thin globular masses, or by the effect of the air and wind, were formed into bubbles, which became perceptible to the eye by the sun's light. But, why did the sun lose his brightness? and how could this innumerable quantity of such a soapy and jellied substance, be generated or produced in one place?

OBSERVATIONS ON THE METEORS OF NOVEMBER 13TH, 1833

Olmsted, Denison; *American Journal of Science*, 1:25:363–411, 1834, pp. 393 and 408–409

[In his lengthy analysis of the great meteor shower of 1833, Professor Olmsted reported several falls of gelatinous matter.]

Matter supposed to come from the Meteors.—In several instances, material substances were supposed by the observers to fall upon the earth; and in a number of cases, matter was found which was supposed to have proceeded from the meteors.

We have received a communication from Mr. H. H. Garland, of Nelson Co., who states, that on hearing a large drop of water fall on the roof of a coop, he immediately looked, and discovered a substance of about the circumference of a twenty five cent piece, of the consistence and appearance of the white of an egg made hot, or perhaps, animal jelly broken into fragments would be a better comparison. (Richmond Enquirer.)

Persons in this town saw particles of "fiery rain" strike the ground, and on examination, discovered *lumps of jelly*, as they term them. (Rahway, New Jersey Advocate.)

After sun-rise, a mass of gelatinous matter was found, which, from its singular texture, is supposed to have formed one of the large meteors. Its appearance resembled soft soap. It possessed little elasticity, and on the application of heat, evaporated as readily as water. The manner in which this substance fell on the ground, indicated that it had fallen with prodigious force. (Newark, N. J. paper.)

A woman at this place (West Point,) who was milking about sunrise, on the 13th, saw something come down "with a sposh" before her. On looking she saw a round flattened mass, about a tea cup or coffee cup full, looking like boiled starch, so clear that she could see the ground through it. At 10 o'clock, she went out to show it to some persons, and no vestige of it remained. A boy observed some minute white particles on the spot, as large as small shot, or pin's heads, or irregular shape, and falling to powder, and disappearing when he went to take them up. I went to the spot with the woman and boy, and concluded that if I heard of any analogous facts from other quarters, I would consider this as entitled to notice, but not otherwise. (Mr. Alexander C. Twining to Prof. Olmsted.)

15

Ball Lightning

Ball lightning cannot be ignored. It exists. Thousands of people have seen it, and hundreds of scientists have written about it. Nevertheless, it remains as inscrutable as ever.

One reason ball lightning resists explanation is that it is so variable. It may be no larger than a pea or it may rival a house in size. It may be violet, red, yellow, or change colors during the few seconds it exists. The shape of ball lightning is usually spherical, but rods, dumbbells, spiked balls, and other shapes have been reported. The phenomenon may glide silently around a room and quietly dematerialize. Most ball lightning, though, seems to explode violently; or it might be better to say that its disappearance is accompanied by an explosion. One has to hedge because the actual explosions often seem to occur elsewhere—outside the house in which the ball has appeared, for example. This fact plus the frequent materialization of ball lightning in closed rooms suggests that electrical induction may be involved. In other words, electrical forces from a surrounding storm may create a glowing ball of plasma in the air after the fashion of St. Elmo's fire. When the electrical forces are relieved (with a detonation), the ball lightning disappears. Observers, however, have no doubt that something palpable has visited them because the room is usually filled with a sulfurous stench and considerable material damage.

Strangely, ball lightning rarely hurts people even though it may follow and hover about them. Ordinary lightning, in contrast, kills many. The listing of ball lightning's peculiar attributes could fill many more pages. It is better to let the observers tell what they saw. Many were shocked that such a weird apparition exists, and scared, too, because of the uncanniness of the phenomenon.

No reasonable scientific explanation exists for ball lightning. Electromagnetic plasmas, chemical reactions in the air, antimatter meteorites, nuclear reactions, and many other ideas have been tendered and found wanting. It is even possible that intense electrical forces may somehow distort our space-time continuum and provide a fleeting window onto some unknown cosmos.

VIOLET BALL SURROUNDED WITH RAYS
Anonymous; *Nature*, 42:458, September 4, 1890

The Caucasus papers relate an interesting case of globular lightning which was witnessed by a party of geodesists on the summit of the Bohul Mountain, 12,000 feet above the sea. About 3 p.m., dense clouds of a dark violent colour began to rise from the gorges beneath. At 8 p.m., there was rain, which was soon followed by hail and lightning. An extremely bright violet ball, surrounded with rays which were, the party says, about two yards long, struck the top of the peak. A second and a third followed, and the whole summit of the peak was soon covered with an electric light which lasted no less than four hours. The party, with one exception, crawled down the slope of the peak to a better sheltered place, situated a few yards beneath. The one who remained was M. Tatosoff. He was considered dead, but proved to have been only injured by the first stroke of lightning, which had pierced his sheepskin coat and shirt, and burned the skin on his chest, sides, and back. At midnight the second camp was struck by globular lightning of the same character, and two persons slightly felt its effects.

GLOBULAR LIGHTNING
Anonymous; *Royal Meteorological Society, Quarterly Journal,* 23:307, 1897

According to the *Zeitschrift für Elektrotechnik,* August, 15, this unusual and interesting phenomenon was observed at the watering-place, Szliacs, on May 25. About noon on that day a violent thunderstorm broke over Szliacs. At 2:45 a ball of lightning about the size of a man's head was seen to descend, and float about 6 feet above the ground. It whizzed past the stair railings of the "Villa Buda," throwing a workman, who was standing near, against the pillars which support the steps. It then passed through an open window into a room on the ground floor, passed within a few paces of the bath superintendent sitting at a table, and close by a porter standing in the room, then out into the open again through a closed window, in which it cut a hole about the size of a fist. When outside, the lightning ball struck a poplar standing 15 paces in front of the building. From this it tore off the bark and wood to a depth of 2 cm., a breadth of 20 cm., up to a height of 10 metres, whence it descended on the other side to the earth, leaving behind it a narrow channel. The detonation which accompanied the lightning was not louder than the report of a gun. Nobody was injured. Another case is reported from Nioheim, in Prussia. A lightning discharge, accompanied by crashing thunder resembling the discharge of a mass of broken glass on the pavement, struck a farmhouse near the station. The following peculiarities in the appearance of the lightning were noted by six eye-witnesses. It descended from the cloud to the outside of the chimney in the form of a ball, about the size of a cannon ball. After the ball was an interval of 1 to 1½ metres, then a discharge in the form of a bundle of rays, so large that a man could scarcely have encompassed it with his arms, of 1 to 2 m. in length. The ball appeared to be accompanied by a short sharp report, while the crashing thunder appeared to be due to the discharge.

GLOBULAR LIGHTNING
Gilmore, G.; *Nature,* 103:284, June 12, 1919

[The protuberances on the ball are particularly interesting here, as is the fact the explosion did not seem to come from the ball, indicating that ball lightning may be an electrical induction effect.]

On the night of May 14 a thunderstorm took place over Dublin. A shower of rain fell after 9 p.m., but between about 9:25 and 9:40 there was practically no rain, only a few drops falling. At about 9:50 I went outside, and when I had gone about two steps from the door I suddenly saw a luminous ball apparently lying in the middle of the street. It remained stationary for a very brief interval—perhaps a second—and then vanished, a loud peal of thunder occurring at the same time. The ball appeared to be about 18 in. in diameter, and was of a blue colour, with two protuberances of a yellow colour projecting from the upper quadrants. It left no trace on the roadway. The street is about eight yards wide from footpath to footpath, with houses on both sides, the total distance across the street between the houses being about twenty yards. There are no tramlines on the street. When I observed the ball its distance from me was about ten yards. The thunder was heard just at the disappearance of the ball, but the sound seemed to come from overhead rather than from the place where the ball was. This was the first peal of thunder that I heard, and there was no more thunder or lightning until after 10:15. From 10:40 onwards the thunderstorm was rather violent and the rain heavy. The rain ceased about 12 midnight, but sheet lightning continued to play over the sky. I was looking towards the north at about 12:15, where the sky was fairly clear, with small white clouds scattered over it, when I saw a yellow-coloured ball which appeared to travel a short distance and then disappear. This ball was high up in the sky, and appeared smaller than the first ball described above.

AN OCCURRENCE OF "BALL LIGHTNING"
Falkner, M. F.; *Meteorological Magazine*, 93:95, March 1964

On the evening of Wednesday, 6 November 1963, at approximately 11:05 p.m., my father saw in his bedroom, in the centre of the room, a small, egg-shaped ball of brilliant light. Within the space of a few seconds, this small ball of light spread itself to form a sheet of darkish green light as wide as the room itself (approximately 12 feet). This curtain of light then moved towards my father and turned greyish colour. The whole sight then vanished as suddenly as it appeared, with a very loud bang, similar to the report from a rifle. The light was witnessed only by my father but the bang was heard by both my brother, from a neighbouring bedroom and my mother, who was downstairs in the kitchen. The bedroom light was on and it was raining at the time. We would not believe that this phenomenon had occurred if it were not for the fact that the very loud bang was heard by three people who were each in different rooms at the time.

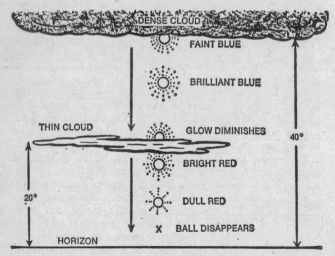

In one observation, ball lightning descending through a cloud changed color.

BALL LIGHTNING
Sheldon, G. S.; *Marine Observer*, 37:59, 1967

17th April 1966. When about 80 miles west of Cape Otway at about 0230 LMT a faint blue glow emerged from the underside of a layer of cloud whose base was at an elevation of 40° above the horizon. It was seen on a bearing of 320° from the ship. The glow brightened rapidly, becoming a ball of brilliant blue light as it fell. It dimmed as it passed behind a band of thin cloud but on reappearing it was seen as a ball of bright red light. The intensity of the colour diminished as the object fell and it disappeared when about 5° above the horizon. It was visible for 7 sec from first to last sighting. The sequence of events is shown in the diagram.

ON GLOBULAR LIGHTNING
Mendenhall, T. C.; *American Meteorological Journal*, 6:437–447, 1890

[Only two of the cases cited by Mendenhall are given here, but these are significant because of the rolling action and sounds noted.]

As a curious description of a still more curious phenomenon, the following account by the Rev. A. Vievar is given in nearly the words of the original:

On Sunday the 12th of March, 1731 or 1732 (the exact year seems to be uncertain) while walking in his garden between one and two o'clock in the afternoon he heard as it were a loud clap of thunder from the northeast. While looking into the air the noise was repeated very loud, but seemed more like the violent fall of a house, so that he expected every moment an outcry from the town; but he was soon undeceived when it began again, and he found it made towards him, with a different noise from the former, being like the grinding of flint stones, but very loud. The object seemed to be about three feet wide. He found it sink in the air and as it seemed to point directly at his head, he laid himself down on a grass slope to let it pass over. However, at the upper end of the walk it fell to the ground and came rolling down the grass walk and he can compare it to nothing better than to that of a violent grinding of flint stones, or a coach and six at full speed on a causeway of loose stones. He lay attentive, expecting to see something, and saw a piece of wood come running before it. When the phenomenon came to the water side it twisted up a large stake that stood in its way and tossed it towards him with much violence, and immediately fell into the water, with the violence and noise of a red-hot mill-stone.

He had seen the seas break against a rock in a storm but never saw a greater ferment caused by the boiling of the waters. It staid about a quarter of a minute in the water, and then mounted again into the air, and went rattling away but with much less violence. He heard it for about a quarter of a mile and lost it. It came against the wind and not faster than a man may walk. The froth and foam of the water remained thirty hours afterwards.

•   •   •   •   •   •   •   •   •   •   •   •   •   •   •

On November 4, 1749, the captain of the ship *Lizard* was taking observations, when he was asked by an under officer to look to the windward which he did and observed a large ball of blue fire rolling on the surface of the water at about three miles distance. It came on them very fast and rising out of the water at the ship's side "it went off with an explosion as if hundreds of cannon had been fired at once." The ship was filled with a sulphurous smell and the masts were much injured; several men were injured by the shock. The ball appeared to be as large as a mill-stone when it struck the ship.

SOME COMMENTS ON BALL LIGHTNING

Uman, M. A.; *Journal of Atmospheric and Terrestrial Physics,* 30:1245–1246, June 1968

What follows is an exact transcription of a letter received from the pilot of a KC-97 USAF tanker aircraft.

"Dear Sirs:

"Was reading an account in June 16 *Nashville Tennessean* re Kugelblitz studies.

"I had an interesting experience in 1960 which I will

describe to you on the premise that it may be of some interest to you.

"I was at the controls of a KC-97 USAF tanker aircraft, heavily loaded with JP-4 fuel for offload to B-47 bombers. En route to the refueling rendezvous (Elko, Nevada vicinity) we were in the clouds at 18,000′. There was light precipitation, temp. was above freezing and there was no turbulence.

"I recall that St. Elmo's fire was dancing around the edges of the aircraft front windows. (This is a not too uncommon occurrence but may have some significance to you.) The crew was experienced in all phases of all-weather operation and not concerned or apprehensive about any portion of the mission to be accomplished.

"As I was concentrating on the instruments on the panel (no outside visual references were visible) a ball of yellow-white color approximately 18″ in diameter emerged through the windshield center panels and passed at a rate about that of a fast run between my left seat and the co-pilot's right seat, down the cabin passageway past the Navigator and Engineer. I had been struck by lightning 2 times through the years in previous flights and recall waiting for the explosion of the ball of light! I was unable to turn around and watch the progress of the ball as it proceeded to the rear of the Aircraft, as I was expecting the explosion with a full load of JP-4 fuel aboard and concentrated on flying the aircraft. After approximately 3 seconds of amazingly quiet reaction by the 4 crew members in the flight compartment, the Boom operator sitting in the rear of the aircraft called on the interphone in an excited voice describing a ball of fire that came rolling through the aft cargo compartment abeam the wings, then danced out over the right wing and rolling off into the night and clouds! No noise accompanied the arrival or departure of the phenomenon."

BALL LIGHTNING
Jennison, R. C.; *Nature,* 224:895, November 29, 1969

I was seated near the front of the passenger cabin of an all-metal airliner (Eastern Airlines Flight EA 539) on a late night flight from New York to Washington. The aircraft encountered an electrical storm during which it was enveloped in a sudden bright and loud electrical discharge (0005 h EST, March 19, 1963). Some seconds after this a glowing sphere a little more than 20 cm in diameter emerged from the pilot's cabin and passed down the aisle of the aircraft approximately 50 cm from me, maintaining the same height and course for the whole distance over which it could be observed.

The observation was remarkable for the following reasons. (i) The appearance of the phenomenon in an almost totally screened environment; (ii) the relative velocity of the ball to that of the containing aircraft was $1.5\pm0.5\text{ms}^{-1}$, typical of most ground observations; (iii) the object seemed perfectly symmetrical in all three dimensions and had no polar or toroidal structure; (iv) it was slightly limb darkened having an almost solid appearance and indicating that it was optically thick; (v) the object did not seem to radiate heat; (vi) the optical output could be assessed as approximately 5 to 10 W and its colour was blue-white; (vii) the diameter was 22 ± 2 cm, assessed by eye relative to the surroundings; (viii) the height above the floor was approximately 75 cm; (ix) the course was straight down the whole central aisle of the aircraft; (x) the object seemed to be in perfect equilibrium; (xi) the symmetry of the object was such that it was not possible to assess whether or not it was spinning.

A TRULY REMARKABLE FLY: BALL LIGHTNING
Mohr, Frederick B.; *Science*, 151:634+, February 11, 1966

On 25 August 1965, I was editing an article entitled "Soviet research of ball lightning" prepared by Ansen Iwanovsky of this division for publication in the September issue of the *Foreign Science Bulletin*. We discussed at some length the unusual behavior of ball lightning and the fact that the relatively few eyewitness reports available contained conflicting statements.

On the same day my uncle and aunt, Mr. and Mrs. Robert B. Greenlee, were relaxing on their fiberglass-screened, roofed patio in Dunnellon, Florida. The temperature was in the 90's, the sky was overcast, and there was a slight drizzle; the Greenlees had heard thunder some distance to the west of their immediate vicinity. Mrs. Greenlee and a neighbor, Mrs. Riggs, were seated a few feet apart in aluminum chairs, and Mr. Greenlee was standing about three feet from Mrs. Greenlee. Mrs. Greenlee had just swatted a fly when a ball of lightning the size of a basketball appeared immediately in front of her. The ball was later described as being of a color and brightness comparable to the flash seen in arc welding, with a fuzzy appearance round the edges. Mrs. Riggs did not see the ball itself, but saw the flyswatter "edged in fire" dropped on the floor. The movement of the ball to the floor was accompanied by a report "like a shotgun blast." The entire incident was over in seconds.

None of the witnesses felt any heat from the ball, and Mrs. Greenlee showed no signs of external injuries, although she complained of pain in the back of her neck and has had occasional headaches since. The explosion was heard by a neighbor about 150 feet away, and it was subsequently learned that another neighbor's electric range had been shorted out at the same time. There was no damage of any sort at the Greenlees, nor were there any marks on the patio floor where the flyswatter had fallen.

With regard to the fly, Mrs. Riggs commented, "You sure got him that time."

CURIOUS PHENOMENON IN VENEZUELA
Cowgill, Warner; *Scientific American,* 55:389, December 18, 1886

[Cowgill was attached to the U.S. consulate at Maracaibo. This apparition has many attributes of ball lightning but the physiological effects are unusual. It sounds almost as if radioactivity were involved.]

During the night of the 24th of October last, which was rainy and tempestuous, a family of nine persons, sleeping in a hut a few leagues from Maracaibo, were awakened by a loud humming noise and a vivid, dazzling light, which brilliantly illuminated the interior of the house.

The occupants, completely terror stricken, and believing, as they relate, that the end of the world had come, threw themselves on their knees and commenced to pray, but their devotions were almost immediately interrupted by violent vomitings, and extensive swellings commenced to appear in the upper part of their bodies, this being particularly noticeable about the face and lips.

It is to be noted that the brilliant light was not accompanied by a sensation of heat, although there was a smoky appearance and a peculiar smell.

The next morning the swellings had subsided, leaving upon the face and body large black blotches. No special pain was felt until the ninth day, when the skin peeled off, and these blotches were transformed into virulent raw sores.

The hair of the head fell off upon the side which happened to be underneath when the phenomenon occurred, the same side of the body being, in all nine cases, the more seriously injured.

The remarkable part of the occurrence is that the house was uninjured, all doors and windows being closed at the time.

No trace of lightning could afterward be observed in any part of the building, and all the sufferers unite in saying that there was no detonation, but only the loud humming already mentioned.

Another curious attendant circumstance is that the trees around the house showed no signs of injury until the ninth day, when they suddenly withered, almost simultaneously with the development of the sores upon the bodies of the occupants of the house.

This is perhaps a mere coincidence, but it is remarkable that the same susceptibility to electrical effects, with the same lapse of time, should be observed in both animal and vegetable organisms.

I have visited the sufferers, who are now in one of the hospitals of this city; and although their appearance is truly horrible, yet it is hoped that in no case will the injuries prove fatal.

16

Earthquake Lights

The earth shakes and the sky lights up, fireballs are seen, and searchlight beams punctuate the horizon. This has happened for thousands of years according to written records. The collective testimony affirming the existence of earthquake lights has generally been ignored. Why? The primary reason is the same one that hinders the serious investigation of many anomalous phenomena: there is no obvious cause-and-effect relationship between earthquakes and earthquake lights. Indeed, earthquake lights have long been written off as misidentification of common phenomena or just plain illusions seen in stressful situations.

This condescending attitude is changing, though. So many luminous phenomena were seen during the great Japanese quakes in the twenties and thirties that earthquake lights can no longer be ignored. Derr's survey at the end of this chapter confirms that earthquake lights are now on the list of "acceptable phenomena."

Earthquake lights, like ball lightning, are highly variable. Often they overlap other phenomena, such as ball lightning, ordinary lightning, and the so-called mountaintop glow, which are apparently electric discharges of some sort. Oddities also abound: flames issuing from the ground, great sparks, waves of light sweeping close to the ground, and perhaps even the wheels of light described in chapter 17. The list of varieties is so long that it may be impossible to find a single cause.

Many theories of earthquake lights depend upon

electricity, piezoelectricity in particular. Piezoelectricity is generated in solids when there are pressure changes. Seemingly piezoelectricity is made to order to explain earthquake lights. Quake pressure waves squeeze rocks, the piezoelectric effect generates electricity, which in turn causes luminous electrical discharges. Piezoelectricity may be *one* cause of earthquake lights, but it cannot operate at sea where earthquake lights are also seen. There must be more to the story, and the field is wide open to the theorists who now have a scientifically acceptable, still very mysterious phenomenon to explain.

EARTHQUAKES AND THEIR CAUSES
Lake, John J.; *English Mechanic*, 21:51–52, April 2, 1875

[Lake firmly believed in the electrical nature of earthquakes and quoted the following observations to prove his point.]

The earthquakes of 1692, in Jamaica, and 1693 in Sicily, present very strong evidences of general electric disturbance in the globe at those times. One evening in February, 1692, at Alari in Sicily, the village seemed to the country people to be in flames. The fire, as they imagined, began little by little and increased for about a quarter of an hour, when all the houses in the place appeared to be enveloped in one flame which lasted about six minutes and then began to decay, as from want of more fuel. Many who ran to render assistance, observed this increase as they passed along the road, but on entering the village found all to be a delusion. Such appearances of fire and light occur in other localities subject to earthquake, e.g., at Cowrie, Perthshire, one morning before daybreak, in 1842, the light is stated to have been so brilliant that birds were distinguished on the trees. Again in Sicily, about the 15th of May, following the incident at Alari, two hours before sunset, the atmosphere being very clear, the heavens appeared on a sudden all on fire, without any flashes of lightning or the least noise of thunder. This lasted at Syracuse about a quarter of an hour, when there appeared in the air over the city two bows, the colours extremely bright, after the usual manner, and a third with the extremities inverted, and, as not a single cloud was visible in any part of the sky, the abnormal state of the atmosphere is clear. It was also during this summer that the unusually severe thunderstorm occurred at Geneva that so materially affected the future career of the celebrated Robert Boyle. The earthquake at Jamaica began on the 17th June, and their greatest violence seems to have been spent in the mountains. Terrific noises were heard amongst them at Port Royal during the last shock, and they were so torn and rent as to present a very shattered appearance and quite new forms. In this month Etna emitted extraordinarily loud noises for three days together. A singular circumstance during this catastrophe at Jamaica was the derangement of the wind. The land-breeze often failed, and the sea-breeze blew all night, whereas the land-breeze should blow all night, and the sea-breeze all day. There was an earthquake on the 8th September, 1692, in Europe, but I have not yet been able to find out the locality.

᠙ • • • • • • ᠙ • • ᠙ • • • • • ᠙

The earthquake of London, 1749, also exhibited strong symptoms of electric action. The year abounded with thunder and lightning, coruscations frequently appeared in the air, and the aurora removed to the south, showing upon two occasions unusual colors. Dr. Stephen Hales heard a rushing in his house which ended in an explosion in the air as from a small cannon, and attributed it to the escape of the fluid by the steeple of the church of St. Martin's-in-the-Fields, adjoining. The Rev. J. H. Murray refers to the electrical disturbances on the east coast of South America, contemporaneous with the great earthquakes on the west coast in 1868, and considers them related. He describes one storm, just at the time of the earthquake, as giving "an idea of what the bombardment of Sebastopol must have been like."

The phenomena of seaquake are of a similar character. We have ourselves seen electric clouds thrown into auroral forms contemporaneously with the disturbance of the sea at another locality. Examples might be extensively multiplied, but the above would seem sufficient to show that a leading cause of earthquake is electric action, and that volcanoes sometimes produce the same by direct convulsion, and at others by disturbing the electric equilibrium of a locality.

LUMINOUS PHENOMENON ACCOMPANYING THE CYPRUS EARTHQUAKE, JANUARY 20, 1941
Aziz, Abdulazim; *Nature,* 149:640, June 6, 1942

A bright flash associated with the earthquake was seen from the eastern and central parts of the island. A Nicosia Hodja who was on the minaret for morning prayer, in describing the event, said that he first heard a deafening noise suggesting the impact of a gigantic projectile on the surface of the earth with a simultaneous rocking motion so severe that he feared the minaret would collapse. Afterwards he saw a brilliant reddish object like a huge globular lightning moving slowly towards the east. The tremors then changed into horizontal waves and gradually vanished. There is strong evidence that direction of the flash was pointing to the epicentral area.

ELECTRICAL PHENOMENON
Watt, J. B. A.; *Nature,* 32:316–317, August 6, 1885

[The phenomenon described by Watt was so close to the earth that it may have had a seismic origin.]

About ten o'clock in the evening of July 23 a party of four of us were standing at the head of the avenue leading to this house [Midlothian, England], when we saw a feebly-luminous flash appear on the ground at a distance of some thirty yards down the avenue. It rushed towards us with a wave-like motion, at a rate which I estimate at thirty miles an hour, and seemed to envelop us for an instant. My left hand, which was hanging by my side, experienced precisely the same sensation as I have felt in receiving a shock from a weak galvanic battery. About three minutes afterwards we heard a peal of thunder, but, though we waited for some time, we neither saw nor heard anything further.

The gardener, who was one of the four, thus describes

what he saw:—I thought it was a cloud of dust blowing up the avenue, and before I could think how that could be when there was not a breath of wind, I saw you three gentlemen covered for a second in a bright light, and that was all. Another of the party says that he observed what seemed to be a luminous cloud running up the avenue with a wavy motion. When it reached the party it rose off the ground and passed over the bodies of two of them, casting a sort of flash on their shoulders. The distance traversed was about twenty yards, and the time occupied between two and three seconds. (My own estimate of distance and velocity makes the time occupied almost exactly two seconds.) The day had been extremely hot and sultry, as also had the preceding day been, the thermometer readings being sometimes 80°F. in the shade.

On asking the gardener for further particulars, he tells me that the distance traversed by the luminous cloud was about forty yards, and that, when it had gone about half the distance, he saw a flash of lightning in the direction of it, but sideways; also that the top of the cloud seemed to be three or four feet from the ground, and it gradually rose higher as it came along. When the cloud reached the party he saw one of them distinctly by its light, the night being otherwise quite dark at the time; and, lastly, that the cloud went a few yards beyond the party into the open space in front of the house, and then disappeared.

CURIOUS LIGHTNING IN THE ANDES
Anonymous; *Scientific American*, 106:464, May 18, 1912

[The focus of this item is a phenomenon called the mountaintop glow. Since these glows seem augmented during earthquakes, they may have a common cause.]

Dr. Walter Knoche, the German director of the Chilean meteorological service, has begun an investigation of the remarkable displays of so-called "heat lightning" which are often observed along the crest of the Andes, and are sometimes visible far out at sea. (In one case Dr. Knoche saw them from Easter Island, 300 miles from the Chilean coast.)

Thunderstorms are rare in Chile, and this fact may possibly be explained on the assumption that the Andes

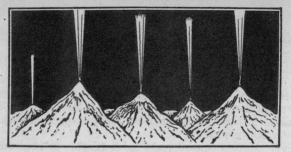

Conceptual view of searchlightlike beams seen radiating from peaks of the Andes during earthquake activity. The normal "Andes glow" seems accentuated by seismic activity.

act as a gigantic lightning-rod, between which and the clouds silent discharges take place on a vast scale. The visible discharges occur during the warm season, from late spring to autumn, and appear to come especially from certain fixed points. According to Dr. Knoche they are confined almost exclusively to the Andes proper, or Cordillera Real, as distinguished from the coast cordillera. Viewed from a favorable point near their origin there is seen to be, at times, a constant glow around the summits of the mountains, with occasional outbursts, which often simulate the beams of a great searchlight, and may be directed westward so as to extend out over the ocean. The color of the light is pale yellow, or rarely reddish.

One striking feature of these discharges is that they are especially magnificent during earthquakes. At the time of the great earthquake of August, 1906, throughout central Chile the whole sky seemed to be on fire; never before or since has the display been so brilliant. The natives regard these lights as the reflection in the sky of the glowing lava in the craters of volcanoes; but there seems to be no doubt that they are electrical discharges.

It is planned to make spectroscopic observations of this singular phenomenon, and also, if possible, measurements of the electrical state of the atmosphere in the high Andes where it appears to have its origin. Possibly the result may be to connect up "Andes lightning" with a peculiar form of aurora which has been observed by Lemstrom over mountain summits.

EARTHQUAKE LIGHTS: A REVIEW OF OBSERVATIONS AND PRESENT THEORIES
Derr, John S.; *Seismological Society of America, Bulletin,* 63: 2177–2187, December 1973

[Derr's review paper presents an admirable summary of earthquake lights. His technical section on theory is omitted in favor of his summary remarks on the present status of hypotheses.]

The problem of earthquake lights (EQL), or luminous phenomena, as noted by Byerly (1942), has always been the darkest area of seismology. Very few scientists have ever worked on the problem, and few today are willing to tackle it because most of the reports are personal observations of untrained observers, and, until recently, there were no "hard data" which could be subjected to scientific analysis. Observations, however, have been made for many years, as suggested by an old Japanese haiku, quoted by Finkelstein and Powell (1971).

> The earth speaks softly
> To the mountain
> Which trembles
> And lights the sky

Recently, popular interest in EQL has been raised by press reports and the search for methods for earthquake prediction. The data which are now available consist of pictures of luminous phenomena taken at Matsushiro, Japan, from 1965 to 1967. This paper includes descriptions of the phenomenon, and reviews several theories advanced to date as possible explanations.

The first known investigations which led to significant interpretations and conclusions were done in the early 1930's by two Japanese seismologists, Terada (1931, 1934) and Musya (1931, 1932, 1934), and were described by Davison (1936, 1937). Musya collected some 1,500 reports of EQL from the Idu Peninsula earthquake of November 26, 1930, at 4:30 a.m. "The observations were so abundant and so carefully made that we can no longer feel much doubt as to the reality of the phenomena and of their connection with the shock. In most of them, the sky was lit up as if by sheet lightning, and nearly all the observers agree in estimating the duration of a single flash as decidedly longer than that of lightning. At one place on the east side of Tokyo Bay, the light resembled auroral streamers diverging from a point on the horizon. Beams and columns of light were seen at different places, several observers comparing the beams to those of a searchlight. Others describe the lights as like that of fireballs. Some state that detached clouds were illuminated or that a ruddy glow was seen in the sky. At Hakona-Mati, close to the epicentre and to the northeast, a flash of light was seen, now in one spot, now in another, and, when the earthquake was at its height, a straight row of round masses of light appeared in the southwest. According to most of the observers, the colour of the light was a pale blue or white or like that of lightning, but a large number state that it was of a reddish or orange colour. The light is said to have been so bright in Tokyo that objects in a room could be seen. At another place, about 30 miles from the epicentre, it was brighter than that of moonlight . . .

"The lights were seen to a distance of 50 miles to the east of the epicentre, nearly 70 miles to the northeast, and more than 40 miles to the west. They were seen both before and for some time after the earthquake, but were most conspicuous during the middle of the shock. The direction in which the lights were seen point, as a rule, to the neighborhood of the epicentre, that is, to the northern part of the Idu Peninsula. The light was, however, seen in other directions, sometimes in the direction of the sea . . .

"During the year following the Idu earthquake, Mr. Musya studied the luminous phenomena attending four other Japanese earthquakes. The reports that he received were most numerous for the South Hyuga earthquake of November 2, 1931. With this earthquake, the lights were usually described as beams radiating from a point on the horizon, as like lightning or a searchlight turned to the sky, and as of a blue or bluish colour. They were seen before the earthquake by 26 observers, during it by 99, and after it by 22." (Davison, 1937).

Terada and Musya reached no conclusions as to the possible causes of earthquake lights. Terada (1931) made some calculations on potential differences in the Earth, which McDonald (1968) considers to be in error. Nevertheless, he made some perceptive comments about the quality of testimonies of witnesses under stress, which are quite relevant to the problem of collecting subjective data during an earthquake.

"With regards to all these testimonies of witnesses, it must be always kept in mind that people are naturally alive to all kinds of phenomena observed at the time of a severe earthquake and apt to regard them as something connected with the catastrophal occurrence, while they forget to consider that the same phenomena are frequently observed on many other occasions not at all connected with earthquake. On the other hand, we learn from the results of investigations by psychologists in what a ludicrous manner the testimonies of people, otherwise quite normal in mentality, may appear distorted when compared to the bare truth."

Another assessment of the problem of earthquake lights is given by Byerly (1942). In addition to his general description, he documents observations of earthquake lights observed at sea. If these lights have the same cause as those observed on land, severe restrictions are placed on the mechanism of their generation.

"Occasionally during an earthquake shock or immediately before or after, observers report luminous phenomena in the heavens. All types of lights are reported seen, although it is rarely that two observers see exactly the same. There are steady glows, red and blue, and white: there are flashes, balls of fire, and streamers.

"At the time of the earthquake off the coast of northern California in January, 1922, one observer reported a glow at sea which he at first took to be a ship on fire. At the time of earthquake of October 1926, centering in Monterey Bay, an observer reported a flash at sea which resembled 'a transformer exploding.' During the Humboldt County (California) earthquake of 1932 an observer reported, 'Several of my friends and I saw to the east what appeared to be bolts of lightning travel from the ground toward the sky. The night was clear.' It has been customary to attempt to ascribe earthquake lights to secondary phenomena, since we know of no source of such lights in the original earthquake action. True, movement on a fault would generate considerable heat, and, after the Sonora earthquake of 1897, trees overhanging the fault were scorched. Such would scarcely produce flashes in the sky, particularly over the ocean. In modern times, the prevalence of electric power lines enables one to explain away many such observations as due to probably breaks in such lines; but many may not be so dismissed. Landslides in mountains may generate great heat by friction. In the Owens Valley earthquake of 1872, fires were started in the mountains by such sources. In some cases thunderstorms may happen to accompany earthquakes, and then lightning may be called upon to explain flashes. Lights over the sea have been attributed to luminous marine organisms excited by the earthquake vibrations."

More recently, research into observations of luminous phenomena in Japan has been done by Yasui (1968, 1971, 1972), who collected and studied pictures, taken by various other observers, of earthquake lights observed during the Matsushiro earthquake swarm of 1965 to 1967. He has also studied reports of other sightings in Japan. Of the approximately 35 sightings, any pictures which might have recorded unrelated phenomena—distant lightning, meteors, twilight, zodiacal light, arcing power lines—were eliminated. At least 18 separate sightings remained unexplained. He concludes that luminescence over a mountain area lasting several tens of seconds on a clear and calm winter night is not a known phenomenon. He thinks it to be an atmospheric electrical phenomenon, but the earthquake trigger mechanism is unknown.

There are five general characteristics of the phenomenon as observed by Yasui (1968):

1. The central luminous body is a hemisphere, diameter about 20 to 200 m, contacting the surface. The body is white, but reflections from clouds may be colored.

2. The luminescence generally follows the earthquake with a duration of 10 sec to 2 min.

3. The luminescence is restricted to several areas, none of them the epicentre. Rather, they occur on mountain summits in a quartz-diorite faulted rock.

4. Sferics generally follow the luminescence and are strongest in the 10 to 20 kHz range. The lumines-

cence occurs frequently at the time of a cold frontal passage.

5. There was no indication on the magnetometers at the local observatory.

The observations are not consistent with explanations based on auroras or other ionospheric phenomena, noctilucent clouds, or rapid spark discharges. However, the observations near mountain tops and along faults are consistent with large atmospheric potential gradients and with an unusual increase of radon gas in the vicinity.

Yasui believes that ionization in the lowest atmosphere becomes unusually large at the time of an earthquake and causes the luminous phenomena at the place where the electrical potential gradient is highest. The electric field is not expected to be large, as it is under a thunderstorm, nor is the atmospheric conductivity expected to be high. Therefore, some action of the earthquake must contribute to triggering luminescence, e.g., violent atmospheric oscillation, but the process is still unknown.

An unusual report of EQL near Hollister, California, was given by Nason, personal communication (1973). In this case, the lights were seen as discrete sources against a hill, also noted by Davison (1937), rather than as the more commonly observed general sky luminosity. Mr. Reese Dooley, a poultry rancher living south of Hollister, observed the EQL in 1961. There were two earthquakes about 2½ min. apart. It was dark when he felt the first one, which was strong enough to make him want to go home to check on his family. Just as he reached his car, the second one started. As he looked west toward a hill, he saw a number of small, sequential flashes from different, random places on the hillside. Nason inspected the hillside and found no electric wiring or any other conventional explanation for the lights. Clearly, Mr. Dooley was very close to the source of the lights. This observation suggests that the extensive EQL observed in Japan which lit up most of the sky could be caused by a great number of small, random point discharges over part of the epicentral area.

Lomnitz, personal communication (1972) agrees with the author's hypothesis that a whole range of precursory phenomena including lights, sounds, and animal reactions, are probably caused by electromagnetic effects. For example, Lomnitz reports his personal observation in Mexico City of extremely unusual behavior in a dog, at least 1 min. before the August 2, 1968 earthquake near the coast of Oaxaca. He also notes that luminous effects were widely observed in Mexico City at the time of the 1957 earthquake near Acapulco. Thus, any theory of EQL would have to account for the occurrence of electromagnetic effects at distances of 3° to 4° from the epicentre of a shock of magnitude 6.5 or greater.

Most recently Yasui (1972) has commented on observations of EQL during the October 1, 1969 earthquake at Santa Rosa, California (Engdahl, 1969). The lights were seen extensively over the Santa Rosa area and described in terms of lightning or electric sparks, Saint Elmo's Fire, fireballs or meteors. Some people also heard sounds like explosions. Just how many reports are genuine EQL and how many are caused by earthquake effects on man-made objects cannot be determined. From the published description, however, the Santa Rosa observations did not include what was described by Davison (1937) as appearing to be auroral streamers diverging from a point on the horizon, a description which does fit observations, for example, in Chiba prefecture, Japan, January 5, 1968, as sketched by Yasui (1971).

Conclusions. The existence of luminous phenomena, or earthquake lights, is well established. The luminosity occurs in the air close to the ground, generally over certain areas in the epicentral region principally during, but also before and after, the earthquakes. Sightings occur both on land and at sea and have been reported from as far as 3° to 4° from the epicentre of an M 6.5 shock. Two theories have been advanced which are worthy of further investigation: (1) violent low-level air oscillation, and (2) piezoelectric effect in quartz-bearing rock. If the latter theory is correct, it may be possible to develop electrical monitoring methods for earthquake prediction. Observations of EQL at sea might be explained by air oscillation but probably not by the piezoelectric effect. On the other hand, observations 3° or 4° distant are probably more easily explained by the piezoelectric effect than by air oscillation. Hence, multiple causes may be operating in different circumstances.

17

The Light Wheels of the Indian Ocean

Ships that ply the Indian Ocean, particularly the waters leading to the oil-sodden lands around the Persian Gulf, frequently encounter dazzling phosphorescent seas. As Kipling described it, the ship's wake is "a welt of light that holds the hot sky tame." Huge globs of light also rise from the depths and explode on the surface. Wavetops sparkle; and broad corridors of bioluminescence stretch from horizon to horizon. Buckets lowered into these glowing seas prove that luminescent marine organisms are the cause of the displays.

Bursting globs and long, parallel strips of phosphorescence are mundane compared to the vast rotating wheels of light seen in these same seas. Although the wheels have been ridiculed as wild sailors' tales for centuries, there have been scores of bona fide sightings since World War II. Mariners tell of great, spokelike bands of light seeming to rotate about some distant hub. Some rotate clockwise; others counterclockwise. Occasionally, two wheels will be rotating in opposite directions around separate hubs. Crews that see these fantastic apparitions do not soon forget them, and their testimonies below betray their bewilderment.

An immediate reaction is to explain the wheels of light in terms of marine bioluminescence stimulated by natural forces that, like the passing of a ship, leave behind glowing evidence of their passage. Sound waves emanating from a submarine quake have been the most popular explanation. But what combination of seismic waves can create counterrotating spirals? Furthermore, there are a few well-attested cases where the luminescence is seen in the air above the water. This fact, the persistence of the phenomenon (half an hour), and the wheels' complex nature suggest that these apparitions may not be connected with bioluminescence.

Another possible answer is electromagnetic stimulation, perhaps something connected with terrestrial discharges to outer space, like the mountaintop glows seen along the Andes. Also, collective behavior should not be ruled out. Travelers in the tropics tell amazing accounts of synchronized flashing of huge masses of fireflies.

Before we can really understand the wheels of light, we must answer the following questions: Why are they concentrated in the Indian Ocean to the near exclusion of other seas where bioluminescence is common? Do they occur only at certain times of the year? Are they correlated with solar activity? Are they earthquake-stimulated? What are the effects of ship radar and underwater explosions? Are the wheels related to the more common "white" or "milky" seas?

A STRANGE PHENOMENON
Harris, R. E.; *Nature*, 21:409–410, February 26, 1880

The most remarkable phenomenon that I have ever seen at sea was seen by myself and officers on the 5th instant between Oyster Reef and Pigeon Island (Malabar coast). At 10 p.m. we were steaming along very comfortably; there was a perfect calm, the water was without a ripple upon it, the sky was cloudless, and, there being no moon, the stars shone brightly. The atmosphere was beautifully clear, and the night was one of great quietude. At the above-named hour I went on deck, and at once observed a streak of white matter on the horizon bearing south-south-west. I then went on the bridge and drew the third officer's attention to it. In a few minutes it had assumed the shape of a segment of a circle measur-

ing about 45° in length and several degrees in altitude
about its centre. At this time it shone with a peculiar
but beautiful milky whiteness, and resembled (only in a
huge mass, and greater luminous intensity) the nebulae
sometimes seen in the heavens. We were steaming to
the southward, and as the bank of light extended, one of
its arms crossed our path. The whole thing appeared so
foreign to anything I had ever seen, and so wonderful,
that I stopped the ship just on its outskirts, so that I might
try to form a true and just conception of what it really
was. By this time all the officers and engineers had assembled on deck to witness the scene, and were all equally
astonished and interested. Some little time before the
first body of light reached the ship I was enabled, with
my night glasses, to resolve in a measure what appeared,
to the unassisted eye, a huge mass of nebulous matter.
I distinctly saw spaces between what again appeared to be
waves of light of great lustre. These came rolling on with
ever-increasing rapidity till they reached the ship, and in a
short time the ship was completely surrounded with one
great body of undulating light, which soon extended to
the horizon on all sides. On looking into the water it
was seen to be studded with patches of faint, luminous,
inanimate matter, measuring about two feet in diameter.
Although these emitted a certain amount of light, it was
most insignificant when compared with the great waves of
light that were floating on the surface of the water, and
which were at this time converging upon the ship. The
waves stood many degrees above the water, like a highly
luminous mist, and obscured by their intensity the distant
horizon; and as wave succeeded wave in rapid succession,
one of the most grand and brilliant, yet solemn, spectacles
that one could ever think of was here witnessed. In speaking of waves of light I do not wish to convey the idea that
they were mere ripplings, which are sometimes caused by
fish passing through a phosphorescent sea, but waves of
great length and breadth, or in other words, great bodies
of light. If the sea could be converted into a huge mirror
and thousands of powerful electric lights were made to
throw their rays across it, it would convey no adequate
idea of this strange yet grand phenomenon.

As the waves of light converged upon the ship from
all sides they appeared higher than her hull, and looked as

Sketch of an Indian Ocean wheel of light.

if they were about to envelope her, and as they impinged upon her, her sides seemed to collapse and expand.

Whilst this was going on the ship was perfectly at rest, and the water was like a millpond.

After about half an hour had elapsed the brilliance of the light somewhat abated, and there was a great paucity of the faint lustrous patches which I have before referred to, but still the body of light was great, and, if emanating from these patches, was out of all proportion to their number.

This light I do not think could have been produced without the agency of electro-magnetic currents exercising their exciting influence upon some organic animal or vegetable substance; and one thing I wish to point out is, that whilst the ship was stopped and the light yet some distance away, nothing was discernible in the water, but so soon as the light reached the ship a number of luminous patches presented themselves, and as these were equally as motionless as the ship at the time, it is only natural to assume that they existed and were actually in our vicinity before the light reached us, only they were not made visible till they became the transmitting media for the electro-magnetic currents. This hypothesis is borne out by the fact that each wave of light in its passage was distinctly seen to pass over them in succession, and as the light gradually became less brilliant, they also became less distinct, and actually disappeared so soon as the waves of light ceased to exist.

LUMINOUS WHEELS PUZZLE SEAMEN
Anonymous; *New Scientist*, 33:447–448, March 9, 1967

In the Gulf of Thailand and waters to the south-east, last March, three merchant ships independently observed the rare and apparently unexplained phenomenon known as the phosphorescent wheel: bands of luminosity skimming across the surface, apparently radiating from a central bright source. One of them saw it twice, a week apart; another had come across such a luminous spiral in the same region in October, bringing the total to five sightings in a few months all along a line running roughly from Bangkok to the north-western tip of Borneo.

The Marine Observer, which provides a platform for mariners with tales to tell ("Responsibility for each observation rests with the contributor") has published the five accounts, with comments from Professor Kurt Kalle of Hamburg, formerly of the German Hydrographical Institute and now a recognized authority on phosphorescent wheels.

The typical wheels seems to be a mile or more in radius, and to consist of a number of radial or spiral arms, rotating at a surprising rate. The captain of the m. v. *Chengtu* describes waves of milky-white mist, 30 ft. wide and 30 ft. apart, perhaps 8 ft. deep, passing across the ship at the rate of two a second—implying that the arms were moving at about 100 ft. a second or more. A week later the same observer encountered two such wheel systems, reinforcing to produce five or six bright flashes every second in the region of the ship, and illuminating about 80 per cent of the sea surface—not, however, brightly enough to read by. Another observer (m.v. *Glenfalloch*) reports something looking like low banks of luminous mist being thrown out from a central patch, 50 or 100 ft. across, which itself pulsed about twice a second.

Professor Kalle, commenting that such wheels are relatively common in the Borneo Sea and the Gulf of Thailand (the last reports from there were in 1957 and 1961), wonders whether the mist is an illusion due to the darkness. Luminous wheels in the water are more reasonable, it seems. And indeed, the officers of the m.v. *Beaverbank* say that, although the arms looked to be about 2 ft. above the surface, this was probably an illusion. They describe the waves as having brilliant green leading edges, and as passing the ship at between 12 and 15 a minute. They seemed to be emitted from the central source at about 75 a minute.

The wheels can apparently rotate in either direction, or indeed both at once: from the m.v. *Glenfalloch* comes a second report, this time of two wheels one above the other rotating in opposite directions.

These wheels are put down to bioluminescence; but, while patches of phosphorescent seawater due to marine life are quite credible, structures a few miles across behaving in an organized fashion and with parts moving faster than wind, water or waves are something else again.

PHOSPHORESCENT WHEELS—PERSIAN GULF

Evans, H.; *Marine Observer*, 27:90–91, 1957

S.S. *Smoky Hill*. Captain H. Evans. Bandar Mashur to Aden. Observers, the Chief Officer, Mr. K. B. Youngs, navigating apprentice, two other apprentices and three members of the watch on deck.

The following is an abstract of the observation sent to us from the journal of Mr. Youngs, together with his replies to our questions about certain details of the phenomena.

3rd April, 1956, 1930 S.M.T. The sea was a mass of flashing patches of light, each one being of considerable size, perhaps 100 yd. across. The flashes were not abrupt and gave the impression of luminous bodies in the water rising to the surface and then sinking down again. The nearer patches often went dim without completely disappearing, the length of time that each was bright and dim being approximately equal. It was not certain whether the patches stayed in the same position, but there seemed to be little, if any, change. Over a period of about 30 sec. all phosphorescence disappeared.

Ten minutes later the display was resumed in the form of parallel bars of light travelling towards the ship from about four points on the port bow, leaving her on the starboard quarter. The bars passed the ship at regular intervals of about 3 sec. Then a brighter patch was seen ahead, and as this was approached it was seen to be an area of jumbled blotches of light, the parallel bar formation having ceased. As this area was watched the profusion settled itself out and began to resemble a slowly revolving wheel. Each "spoke" of the wheel was disjointed, consisting of several separate bars of light, the component bars decreasing in intensity of light with distance from the centre of rotation. The spokes were not straight, but curved slightly in a clockwise direction. The centre round which all revolved was a brighter spot which showed no movement. This was passed by the ship at a distance of about a mile to port. The spokes could also be seen extending far off on the starboard side, not coming to an abrupt end but fading away in the distance.

The wheel showed two types of motion, that of rotation and an outward rippling movement. In addition, each spoke flashed regularly in sections so that not all of it would be visible at once. The flashing occurred at the constant rate of one per second.

A number of other wheels were subsequently seen, for the most part separately but a few were slightly intermingled. At times wheels could be seen all around the ship. Each wheel appeared to keep a fixed position relative to the others. As each wheel passed astern it became distorted and indistinct, finally appearing as just a glow in the distance. All the wheels that were seen near the ship had the same character as the one described above, with visible centres and curved spokes.

A difference of opinion arose as to which way the first wheel was rotating. It appeared to Mr. Youngs to be turning anticlockwise, with some distant bars moving clockwise, while the Chief Officer and the other two apprentices said the direction was clockwise. Independent opinions were therefore sought from three members of the watch, each of whom gave the movement as anticlockwise.

Note. This is a well-recorded observation, presenting several points of special interest. It confirms three previous observations that the wheel may develop from a moving parallel band formation. A special feature of the present observation is the clearly observed transitional stage of confused movement before the wheel developed. Another noteworthy feature is the number of wheels in action during the period of observation, the duration of which is not given. With the flashing of the wheels, and their different distances from the ship, it would probably have been difficult to estimate the total number, but one gets the impression that this was considerably more than in most, if not all, of the previously recorded observations of this phenomenon. The interruption of the luminosity of each spoke by dark sections is an unusual feature, as also is the periodic flashing of the luminous parts and the outward rippling movement. The curvature of the spokes has been previously seen on several occasions.

Finally we come to the very interesting point that different persons saw the wheel rotating in opposite directions. One of the apprentices suggested that there was no actual rotation but that the appearance of rotation was an optical illusion caused by the continuous systematic flashing, in which case the direction might not appear the same to different persons. Once the impression is formed that the rotation is in a certain direction it would be very difficult or impossible to change the mental picture. This is an interesting theory and might well be correct as regards this particular night of observation. This does not mean that the rotation of the majority of phosphorescent wheels could be explained in this way. Normally they are not complicated by flashing, and different observers of the same wheel see the same direction of rotation. Assuming that there is in most cases a genuine appearance of rotation of the wheel, it must be clearly understood that there cannot be any actual rotation of the mass of water. The rotation must be that of some form of stimulus to the light-producing organisms, though of the nature and mode of operation of this stimulus we are at present entirely ignorant. In this connection the observation of S.S. *Canton,* published in the October 1954 number of this journal, is of very great interest. On this occasion the stimulus seemed to be acting more slowly, so that the successive lighting up and fading out of individual water areas did not blend into the appearance of a rotating wheel; with close attention the successive illumination of adjacent areas could be clearly distinguished.

18

Barisal Guns, Mistpouffers, and other Waterguns

When I first started collecting observations of curious natural phenomena, I had no thought of setting up a file on strange sounds. I was soon persuaded otherwise. Mysterious sounds are everywhere! This chapter concentrates only on explosive sounds that are apparently connected with oceans and large lakes— the so-called "waterguns." In specializing, we must ignore the Yellowstone Lake whispers, the Moodus noises, Haiti's "gouffre," and many other acoustic oddities.

In this day of sonic booms and frequent blasting, detonations heard afar are written off as man-made with good reason. Fifty or more years ago the world was quieter, and people tried to track down the causes of strange sounds. For example, E. Van den Broeck compiled several hundred pages of testimony on mistpouffers in the French scientific journal *Ciel et Terre* ("Sky and Earth") in 1895 and 1896. Mistpouffers are dull, distant explosive sounds heard around the coast of Europe all the way to Iceland. Every country has its own name for them, and it turns out that they are heard on North American and Asian coasts too. Despite the universality of unexplained detonations and despite ample proof of their existence, they are a dead issue in the scientific world.

The most famous unexplained detonations are the Barisal guns heard in the vicinity of the Ganges Delta.

Waterguns, however, are not confined to salt water. Some of New York's finger lakes have their own private waterguns. Doubtless many waterguns have never seen print in scientific journals and are thus excluded from my collection. We have to assume that they are as common on freshwater shores as salt.

What can one say about a detonation except that it is loud and sharp? In the case of the Barisal guns and, in fact, many natural detonations, triplets are common—three booms in a row. A very simple observation but confounding to a scientist. Waterguns are elusive; their sources cannot be found. Journeying toward them seems to take them farther away. Waterguns seem to be fair-weather phenomena, but this does not help us much. No one has zeroed in on them. Is their origin seismic, electrical, or are they due simply to wave action or the bursting of immense gas bubbles? No one knows.

One thing is certain, reports of Barisal guns and mistpouffers are almost nonexistent in today's scientific literature. Do they still sound out on the quiet summer seas, muffled and mysterious? They may still be there but lost in the cacophony of modern technology.

"BARISAL GUNS" AND "MIST POUFFERS"
Darwin, G. H.; *Nature,* 52:650, October 31, 1895

[This letter to *Nature* by George Darwin, son of Charles, stimulated a whole series of reports of strange detonations.]

In the delta of the Ganges, dull sounds, more or less resembling distant artillery, are often heard. These are called "Barisal guns"; but I do not know the meaning of the term. The object of this note is to draw the attention of the readers of *Nature* to this mysterious phenomenon, and to the similar "mist pouffers" of the Belgian coast.

My attention was for the first time drawn to the subject some days ago by a letter from M. van der Broeck, Conservator of the Museum of Natural History of Belgium. He writes of certain "curious aerial or subterranean detonations, which are pretty commonly heard, at least, in Belgium and in the north of France, and which are doubtless a general phenomenon, although little known, because most people wrongly imagine it to be the sound of distant artillery.

"I have constantly noticed these sounds in the plain of Limburg since 1880, and my colleague of the Geological Survey, M. Rutot, has heard them very frequently along the Belgian coast, where our sailors call them 'mist pouffers' or fog dissipators.

"The keeper of the lighthouse at Ostend has heard these noises for several years past; they are known near Boulogne, and the late M. Houzeau spoke of them to my friend M. Lancaster. More than ten of my personal acquaintances have observed the fact.

"The detonations are dull and distant, and are repeated a dozen times or more at irregular intervals. They are usually heard in the day-time when the sky is clear, and especially towards evening after a very hot day. The noise does not at all resemble artillery, blasting in mines, or the growling of distant thunder."

M. van der Broeck, after referring to the "Barisal guns," says that he was disposed to regard the noises as due to some peculiar kind of discharge of atmospheric electricity. "But my colleague M. Rutot believes the origin to be internal to the earth. He compares the noise to the shock which the internal fluid mass might give to the earth's crust."

Mr. Clement Reed has informed M. van der Broeck that he believes similar noises are heard on Dartmoor, and in some parts of Scotland. I was not previously aware of anything of the kind in these islands.

Before any systematic observations are undertaken, it will be useful to form some general idea of the frequency of these sounds and of their geographical distribution.

Will any of the numerous readers of *Nature* in various parts of the world give us an account of their experiences in this matter?

BARISAL GUNS
Cooper, W. S.; *Scientific American,* 75:123, August 1, 1896

On the evening of December 28, 1885, I was with a companion in a sailboat on the Gulf of Mexico about 20 miles S.E. of Cedar Keys, Florida. We were becalmed. The next morning the sky was cloudless. There was a light fog and no breeze. The atmosphere was bracing but not frosty. We were about ten miles out but in shallow water. Shortly after sunrise we heard reports as of a gun or distant cannon. They came at intervals of about five minutes. We were not certain as to the direction. My companion, who lived several miles further down the coast, said he had often heard the reports on still mornings.

THE "GUNS" OF LAKE SENECA, N. Y.
Anonymous; *Monthly Weather Review*, 31:336, July 1903

In the *Monthly Weather Review* for September, 1897, page 393, we have given some account of the "barisal guns," the "mistpouffers," and similar phenomena whose origin is as yet not certainly understood. The following letter describes an analogous phenomenon in Seneca Lake, N. Y., and it may well be that the barisal guns have their origin in the escape of bubbles of gas just as do the "guns" of Seneca Lake.

Mr. Wm. A. Prosser, of Dresden, Yates County, N. Y., writes as follows, under date of August 18, 1903.

So far as I am personally concerned I know of no explosions of inflammable gas, and the newspaper stories are fabrications in this respect.

The "lake guns" are evidently caused by gas escaping from the sand at the bottom.

Long Point is situated about 15 miles south of Geneva, N. Y., and about 25 miles north of Watkins, N. Y., on the west side of Seneca Lake. Directly off the Point the water is very deep. Heavy currents pass either north or south at regular intervals. A heavy wind for a few hours will change the position of the extreme end of land (which extends 1½ miles eastward) several rods. When the swell is not too heavy you can always see the gas rising in bubble form, which, as a rule, makes very little noise, but larger eructations evidently produce these "lake guns." The sand would not stay in place were it not for the water holding it there at the extreme point. Large steamers can land there with but the aid of an ordinary gang plank.

I do not know that the gas is inflammable, but I could easily ascertain if it is of any special interest to you. Natural gas is found in considerable quantity within 3 or 4 miles of the point, on the outlet of Keuka Lake, but hardly in paying quantities. However, I am told that a company has been formed that will exploit the gas along the outlet, but not at the Point.

REMARKABLE SOUNDS
Smith, W. S.; *Nature*, 53:197–198, January 2, 1896

Lough Neagh is a sheet of water covering an area of upwards of 150 square miles, with very gradually receding shores, excepting at one or two spots. For many years after my settlement as minister here from England, I heard at intervals, when near the lake, cannon-like sounds; but not being acquainted with the geography of the distant shores, or the location of towns, or possible employments carried on, I passively concluded that the reports proceeded from quarrying operations, or, on fine summer days, from festive gatherings in Co. Derry, or Co. Tyrone. In time I came to understand that it was not from the opposite shores, but from the lake itself that the sounds proceeded. After questioning many of the local residents, I extended my inquiries to the fishermen, but they could assign no cause. A strange thing about the matter is that the people generally knew nothing of the phenomenon, and that it is shrouded in mystery. I have heard the sounds during the whole year . . . I have heard the reports probably twenty times during the present year, the last being on a Sunday afternoon a month since, when I heard two explosions; but with two exceptions they have all seemed to come from many miles away, from different directions at different times. They have come apparently from Toome Bay, from the middle of the lake, and from Langford Lodge Point, about nine miles distant. A fisherman thought they must be the result of confined air that reached the lake by means of springs that are believed to rise here and there in the bottom. But the lake is shallow, seldom more than 45 feet deep. The depression now covered by the lake having been caused, it is believed, by volcanic action when the trap-rock of Co. Antrim was erupted, there may possibly be subterranean passages, though I confess their occurrence does not seem very probable; while the sounds emanate, as stated, from various parts of the lake. I have as yet spoken to no one who observed any movement of the waters when explosions took place, nor have I spoken to any one who was close to the spot at the time. Rather every one seems to have heard them only in the distance, which is strange, as fishermen are on the lake during many months in the year, at all hours of the day and night.

Last winter the whole of the lake was frozen over, for the first time since 1814. One fine afternoon, when the air was still, I was skating in the neighbourhood of Shande's Castle, when these mystical guns boomed forth their reports every five or six minutes. On the last day of the skating, when thousands of people from Belfast and elsewhere were assembled in Antrim Bay, there were two fearful boomings, that startled every one near me. They seemed to think some dreadful catastrophe had occurred, as the sounds appeared to proceed from not more than half a mile away. I never before heard them so near. The ice in Antrim Bay remained as it was, but I afterwards learned that it was then breaking up six miles away, but with no alarming sounds.

19

Famous Dark Days

A dark day is not merely the veiling of the sun by ordinary clouds—they at least let through enough light to conduct the business of the world. On a dark day the pall of darkest night descends suddenly, chickens go to roost, and men and women grope for candles and pray, although perhaps not in that order.

New England's dark day of 1780 is typical of the genre and is detailed below by a meteorologist. It is famous primarily because New England was sufficiently populated to publicize reactions to it; that is, the media were impressed. Many other dark days have transpired, as other selections below demonstrate. There have also been yellow days and smoky days, but let us concern ourselves with the extreme situations, days when the sun goes out completely.

The standard explanation for a dark day is smoke in the air from forest fires in the hinterlands. This is a reasonable answer because dark days are frequently accompanied by black rains that are thick with ashes and soot. Wind drives these heavy clouds across the affected region, obscuring the sun more completely than ordinary rain clouds. But sometimes the darkness seems more irrational, descending suddenly without the approach of ominous black clouds. And where did the supposed forest fires rage? They were out west somewhere, set by Indians. In 1780, of course, "out west" was devoid of newspaper stringers and the forests of an entire state could be consumed without New Englanders knowing of it.

We will have to admit that of all the phenomena

described in this book, dark days have the most acceptable explanations. Nevertheless, may not some dark days owe their origins to some concentrations of cosmic matter passing between the earth and sun or something a bit more mysterious than soot-laden clouds?

NEW ENGLAND'S DARK DAY: 19 MAY 1780
Ludlum, David M:; *Weatherwise,* 25:113–118, June 1972

[This famous dark day was well observed. Ludlum's article is reproduced in its entirety except for the final section on "Causation," which was generally conceived to be smoke and ashes.]

Holyoke's records. An easterly circulation prevailed on the 17th and 18th and the entry "serene" indicated the prevalance of anticyclonic conditions such as often occur for a spell in mid-May. Barometers at Cambridge and Bradford also had been above the seasonal normal and fairly steady to confirm this. Several observers on these days commented on the smoky aspect of the sky with the sun rising red and remaining so for some time in its ascent. Similar conditions prevailed again at sundown.

The morning of the 19th was cloudy and cool at Salem with the temperature at 43°. Prof. Samuel Williams' thermometer at Bradford stood at 39° at 0600. His barometer read 29.82"/1009.8mb. It fell fairly steadily reaching 29.68"/1005.1mb by 1020. A southwest wind prevailed. All signs indicated the approach of a low pressure trough from the west; the rain showers and light thundery conditions occurring at various points in eastern New England during the forenoon confirmed this weather map analysis. Prior to the commencement of the darkness, several observed dark clouds approaching from the southwest and believed these brought on the obscuration. Barometers fell steadily all morning, but leveled out by noon and remained close to the low point all afternoon and evening. Cloudiness continued throughout.

Extent. Great was the curiosity of many observers to know whether their communities had been singled out and were experiencing a local phenomenon, or whether the "very uncommon darkness" might be universal. Without any rapid means of communication, they had to wait anxiously for the arrival of the mails carrying out-of-town newspapers and letters from friends at a distance in order to determine its geographic limits. Prof. Williams, then Hollis Professor of Mathematics and Natural Philosophy in Harvard College, sought to gather all pertinent information about the event. His survey contained reports from as far northward as Portland in the District of Maine, from Rupert in Vermont near the Champlain Valley, from Fort Edward in the upper Hudson Valley, and from Nine Partners in southeast New York. General George Washington entered a description of the spectacle in his weather diary when at Morristown in northern New Jersey, and captured New Englanders on prison ships in New York Bay saw and wondered at the untoward happenings in the sky. None of the weather observers around Philadelphia made note of the affair, and nothing has been found in the war-filled columns of the Pennsylvania press concerning any unusual local sky conditions. The darkness reached all along the southern coast of New England, though with less intensity than farther north; there were reports of a brightness on the southwest horizon from coastal points. The longest and most obscure blackouts occurred in northeastern Massachusetts, southern New Hampshire, and southwestern Maine, according to Prof. Williams.

Timing. In the northwestern fringe of colonial settlement at Rupert on the present New York-Vermont border, the sun rose obscured and continued so until about 1000 in the morning. At Barnstable on Cape Cod, the most easterly checkpoint, the darkness prevailed from 1400 to 1700, reaching its greatest obscurity about 1530 in the afternoon. Thus, it took approximately 7.5 hours to traverse the 180 miles separating the two points, or at a rate of approximately 25 mph. It was unlikely that the upper-airflow carried in a straight line from northwest to southeast, or that the rate of progress of the obscuring aerosol matter was uniform throughout the day. Most reports showed a definite improvement in solar illumination as the afternoon progressed, but in eastern Massachusetts a return to obscure conditions came soon after sundown and the pre-midnight darkness was considered the blackest ever known.

Intensity. Many witnesses attempted to describe the degree of darkness. In central Connecticut, at Middletown and Durham, the sun's disc was visible for most of the time "as seen through clouds of hazy air." At New Haven, Prof. Daggett thought the darkness "at least equal to what is commonly called candle-lighting in the evening." But farther northward and eastward there was an almost total obscuration during late forenoon and early afternoon. It was necessary to light candles at Providence to transact business and to serve the noontime meal. This condition prevailed generally over eastern Massachusetts. At Westborough, Rev. Ebenezer Parkham recalled: "by 12, I could not read anywhere in the house—we were forced to dine by candle light. It was awful and surprising." At Ipswich candles were required for a two o'clock meal and despite open windows one could see shadow profiles from candlelight on the walls of the room just as one did ordinarily at night. At Barnstable on Cape Cod an observer thought it "as dark or rather darker than halfway between sunlight and daylightdown."

Samuel Williams summarized this aspect of the phenomenon from his observation post in northeastern Massachusetts: "In most parts of the country it was so great, that people were unable to read common print—determine the time of the day by their clocks or watches—dine or manage their domestic business, without the light of candles. In some places, the darkness was so great, that persons could not see to read common print in the open air, for several hours together: but I believe this was not generally the case."

Coloration. The most impressive aspect of the obscuration lay in the transformed shading of all objects. It was "a kind of yellow look, the strangest day that I ever saw in my life," recalled James Parker of Shirley, Mass. To a Worcester observer, "a sickly melancholy gloom overcast the face of Nature."

The lower clouds took on "a strange yellowish and sometimes reddish appearance" according to the thickness of the filter above. At New Haven, "an unusual yellowness in the atmosphere made clean silver nearly resemble the color of brass," observed Prof. Daggett. The Harvard observing group summed up the aspect of the Cambridge sky: "the complexion of the clouds was compounded of a faint red, yellow, and brown." Objects which were normally a distinct white were highly tinged with yellow. A report from Newport, R. I., described "the yellow duskiness which overshadowed us, transfusing a yellow hue over all visible Nature."

The effect on grass and foliage impressed all. "An uncommonly lively verdure" took on "a deepest green, verging on blue," according to Williams. Natural objects had "a resplendent and beautiful tinge," wrote Dr. Samuel Tenney, "so enchanting a verdure as could not escape notice, even amidst the unusual gloom that surrounded the spectator."

Precipitation. The composition of the precipitation falling during the period of semi-darkness held the key to the causative factor of the dark day phenomenon. Williams had the scientific acumen to examine the rainfall and to determine what impurities it contained: "The water that fell was found to have an uncommon appearance, being thick dark and sooty . . . I examined a quantity of this matter; and in taste, colour and smell, it very plainly appeared to be nothing more than what the gentlemen observed at Ipswich,—the black ashes of burnt leaves, without any sulphureous, or other mixtures. (The same was observed at Concord and Dover in New Hampshire; at Berwick, and many other places in this state.)

"Being apprehensive whether there was not some uncommon matter in the air that day, I put out several sheets of clean paper in the air and rain. When they had been out four or five hours, I dried them by the fire. They were much sullied, and became dark in their colour; and felt as if they had been rubbed with oil or grease. But upon burning them, there was not any appearance of sulphureous or nitrous particles."

Psychological effect. The psychological effect of the darkening of the skies at noontime was varied. At Salem, Mass., "persons in the streets became melancholy and fear seized on all . . . Dr. Whitaker's congregation assembled at his meeting house." At New Haven, Conn., "the inhabitants were thrown into a perhaps unnecessary consternation, as if the appearance were preternatural," according to Prof. Daggett. At Newport, R. I., "a tornado or tempest, or something very unusual was expected by all . . . yet nothing tempestuous happened." Up at Stratham, N. H., the darkness "caused great terror in the minds of abundance of people." At Sutton, Mass., "people came flocking to the meeting-house" of Rev. Dr. Hall. After the period of greatest darkness, Rev. John Lathrop "found the people at the tavern nearby much agitated."

At Hartford, the Connecticut Legislature was in session. So great was the darkness that members became terrified and thought that the final day had come. A motion was consequently made to adjourn. At this, Mr. Davenport rose and said: "Mr. Speaker,—It is either the Day of Judgement, or it is not. If it is not, there is no cause for adjourning. If it is, I desire to be found doing my duty. I move that candles be brought, and that we proceed to business."

The animal kingdom proved equally susceptible to the darkness. Rev. John Lathrop noticed: "By the time of greatest darkness, some of the dunghill fowls went to roost, cocks crowed in answer to one another, woodcocks which are night birds whistled as they do only in the dark, frogs peeped; in short, there was the appearance of midnight at noonday."

THE DARK DAY IN CANADA
Anonymous; *Scientific American,* 44:329, May 21, 1881

[Montreal was the center of the darkness of 1819. Dark days are rather common, but the electrical and luminous phenomena described below are distinctly unusual.]

What was the strangest occurrence of that time, or rather the strangest thing that ever happened in the history of this country, was what has been always known as the "Phenomenon of 1819." On the morning of Sunday, November 8, 1819, the sun rose upon a cloudy sky, which assumed, as the light grew upon it, a strange greenish tint, varying in places to an inky blackness. After a short time the whole sky became terribly dark, dense black clouds filling the atmosphere, and there followed a heavy shower of rain, which appeared to be something of the nature of soapsuds, and was found to have deposited after settling a substance in all its qualities resembling soot. Late in the afternoon the sky cleared to its natural aspect, and the next day was fine and frosty. On the morning of Tuesday, the 10th, heavy clouds again covered the sky, and changed rapidly from a deep green to a pitchy black, and the sun, when occasionally seen through them, was sometimes of a dark brown or an unearthly yellow color, and again bright orange, and even blood red. The clouds constantly deepened in color and density, and later on a heavy vapor seemed to descend to the earth, and the day became almost as dark as night, the gloom increasing and diminishing most fitfully. At noon lights had to be burned in the courthouse, the banks, and public offices of the city. Everybody was more or less alarmed, and many were the conjectures as to the cause of the remarkable occurrence. The more sensible thought that immense woods or prairies were on fire somewhere to the west; others said that a great volcano must have broken out in the Province; still others asserted that our mountain was an extinct crater about to resume operations and to make of the city a second Pompeii; the superstitious quoted an old Indian prophecy that one day the Island of Montreal was to be destroyed by an earthquake, and some even cried that the world was about to come to an end.

About the middle of the afternoon a great body of clouds seemed to rush suddenly over the city, and the darkness became that of night. A pause and hush for a moment or two succeeded, and then one of the most glaring flashes of lightning ever beheld flamed over the country, accompanied by a clap of thunder which seemed to shake the city to its foundations. Another pause followed, and then came a light shower of rain of the same soapy and sooty nature as that of two days before. After that it appeared to grow brighter, but an hour later it was as dark as ever. Another rush of clouds came, and another vivid flash of lightning, which was seen to strike the spire of the old French parish church and to play curiously about the large iron cross at its summit before descending to the ground. A moment later came the climax of the day. Every bell in the city suddenly rang out the alarm of fire, and the affrighted citizens rushed out from their houses into the streets and made their way in the gloom toward the church, until Place d'Armes was crowded with people, their nerves all unstrung by the awful events of the day, gazing at, but scarcely daring to approach the strange sight before them. The sky above and around was as black as ink, but right in one spot in mid-air above them was the summit of the spire, with the lightning playing about it shining like a sun. Directly the great iron cross, together with the ball at its foot, fell to the ground with a crash, and was shivered to pieces. But the darkest hour comes just before the dawn. The glow above gradually subsided and died out, the people grew less fearful and returned to their homes, the real night came on, and when next morning dawned everything was bright and clear, and the world was as natural as before. The phenomenon was noticed in a greater or less degree from Quebec to Kingston, and far into the States, but Montreal seemed its center. It has never yet been explained.

DARKNESS AT MID-DAY
H., J.; *Notes and Queries,* 2:4:139, August 15, 1857

A total darkness at about noon which lasted for hours occurred many years back, but within the recollection of people now living, in the city of Amsterdam, the capital of Holland. As I have often been told by trustworthy people, it took place in the summer, on a fine bright day; the air was calm, and there were no indications of fog. The people in the streets, frightened at such an unusual occurrence, hastened indoors, but the darkness came on so suddenly that many of them lost their lives through walking into the different channels by which the city is divided. I never heard of a similar occurrence in any other place in Holland, nor any explanation as to the alleged cause of it.

DARK DAY IN NEW ENGLAND
Anonymous; *Nature,* 24:540, October 6, 1881

A remarkable phenomenon occurred in New England on September 6, almost exactly similar to one that occurred in the same region on May 19, 1780. The *Springfield Daily Republican* describes it as follows:—"In this city the day began with a slow gathering of fog from all the watercourses in the early hours, the thin clouds that covered the sky at midnight seemed to crowd together and descend upon the earth, and by sunrise the atmosphere was dense with vapour, which limited vision to very short distances, and made those distances illusory; and as the sun rose invisibly behind, the vapours became a thick, brassy canopy, through which a strange yellow light pervaded the air and produced the most peculiar effects on the surface of the earth. This colour and darkness lasted until about three o'clock in the afternoon, once in a while lightening, and then again deepening, so that during a large part of the time nothing could be done conveniently indoors without artificial light. The unusual complexion of the air wearied and pained the eyes. The grass assumed a singular bluish brightness, as if every blade were tipped with light. Yellow blossoms turned pale and gray; a row of sunflowers looked ghastly; orange nasturtiums lightened; pink roses flamed; lilac-hued phlox grew pink; and blue flowers were transformed into red. Luxuriant morning-glories that have been blossoming in deep blue during the season now were dressed in splendid magenta; rich blue clematis donned an equally rich maroon; fringed gentians were crimson in the fields. There was a singular luminousness on every fence and roof-ridge, and the trees seemed to be ready to fly into fire. The light was mysteriously devoid of refraction. One sitting with his back to a window could not read the newspaper if his shadow fell upon it—he was obliged to turn the paper aside to the light. Gas was lighted all over the city, and it burned with a sparkling pallor, like the electric light. The electric lights themselves burned blue, and were perfectly useless, giving a more unearthly look to everything around. The darkness was not at all like that of night, nor were animals affected by it to any remarkable extent. The birds kept still, it is true, the pigeons roosting on ridgepoles instead of flying about, but generally the chickens were abroad. A singular uncertainty of distance prevailed, and commonly the distances seemed shorter than in reality. When in the afternoon the sun began to be visible through the strange mists, it was like a pink ball amidst yellow cushions—just the colour of one of those mysterious balls of rouge which we see at the drug-stores, and which no woman ever buys. It was not till between five and six o'clock that the sun had sufficiently dissipated the mists to resume its usual clear gold, and the earth returned to its everyday aspect; the grass resigning its

unnatural brilliancy and the purple daisies no longer faint-
ing into pink. The temperature throughout the day was
very close and oppressive, and the physical effect was
one of heaviness and depression. What was observed here
was the experience of all New England, so far as heard
from, of Albany and New York city, and also in Central
and Northern New York. In reference to this phenomenon
the New York *Nation* suggests that it may be worth the
while of weather-observers to note the approximate coincidence between the interval separating the two dark days
in New England (May 19, 1780, and September 6, 1881)
and nine times the sun-spot cycle of eleven years."

THE MID-DAY DARKNESS OF SUNDAY, JANUARY 22
Herschel, J.; *Nature*, 25:289, January 26, 1882

It is to be hoped that you will receive many and good
accounts of the wonderful, perhaps unprecedented darkness which obscured London for some three hours on Sunday last, in order that its range may be localized.

It appears to have commenced about 10½ a.m., though
I cannot vouch for it, as I had been up till near dawn, and
was not roused till near noon. Then truly it was hard to believe the clock! To all practical intents and purposes it
was night; only the street lamps remained unlit. This however enabled one to realize more fully the wonderful absence of all ordinary daylight in the streets. After the first
surprise, it occurred to me to note such facts as would
hereafter constitute evidence. In the first place I sought to
establish that the phenomenon was not an ordinary thick
London fog; secondly, to find some striking measure of the
darkness, in one's immediate vicinity. A third observation
offered itself in corroboration of both. These I will give
in detail.

Looking out of a first-floor window, eastwards, I had
on the right towards the south the sharp tall spire of Lang-
ham Church, clearly visible (at a distance of 65 yards)
against the darkly lurid background afforded by the distant fog behind, which must have been the sun, then near
the meridian and at about the proper elevation, but of
course quite invisible. The clearness of the outline showed
how slight was the fog—at any rate below the level of its

apex. Next, looking across the street, fourteen yards from wall to wall, the gas-lit interiors opposite were all plainly visible—blinds not being down, nor curtains drawn, in London, during the daytime, even if the gas is lit. It was *obvious* that there was no fog to speak of. Next, as to the darkness: I say that the street lamps were not lit; consequently this observation was easy. I remarked that though one could *hear* the passers-by on the opposite pavement, they were *quite invisible*. I could only see the lower limbs as they crossed the dim lights in the opposite basement windows. Lastly, looking northwards, where a turn of the street brings a line of four-storied houses across the line of sight, at forty-five yards distance, many of the windows where the occupants were not at church, being lighted from within, were easily seen; but there was *not the faintest sky-line*: the sky, or rather background of foggy air, was utterly devoid of illumination. The windows alone stood in evidence that there were houses there, *not* obscured by fog.

Finally, so strong was the impression of *mere darkness* that, having sat down to write, I started up and went again to the window, with the ejaculation—"Why, one ought to see the stars!" and I should hardly have been otherwise than satisfied if I had seen some.

ATMOSPHERIC PHENOMENON
Anonymous; *Monthly Weather Review,* 14:79, 1886

The following is taken from the La Crosse, Wisconsin, "Daily Republican," of March 20, 1886:

Oshkosh, Wisconsin, March 19th.—A most remarkable atmospheric phenomenon occurred here at 3 p.m. The day was light, though cloudy, when suddenly darkness commenced settling down, and in five minutes it was as dark as midnight. General consternation prevailed; people on the streets rushed to and fro; teams dashed along, and women and children ran into cellars; all business operations ceased until lights could be lighted. Not a breath of air was stirring on the surface of the earth. The darkness lasted from eight to ten minutes, when it passed off, seemingly from west to east, and brightness followed. News from cities to the west say the same phenomenon was observed there in advance of its appearance here, showing that the wave of darkness passed from west to east. Nothing could be seen to indicate any air currents overhead. It seemed to be a wave of total darkness passing along without wind.

20

Curious Tornado Effects

The weaving, snakelike tornado seems a thing alive. It is deadly, too. The many tornado deaths and extensive physical damage result from the extremely violent winds (several hundred miles per hour), which are the best-known characteristic of the tornado. Many accounts on record also tell of peculiar lights, electrical activity, the burning and dehydration of vegetation, and sulfurous odor in the paths of some tornadoes. These things are over and above the rapid lightning and occasional ball lightning accompanying most intense tornadoes.

Scientists of the last century, such as the famous François Arago, were convinced that electricity was the force that created tornadoes, waterspouts, and similar rotary storms. For most of this century the electrical nature of rotary storms has been downplayed; but now there is a resurgence of interest in the subject. Photographs of nocturnal tornadoes have revealed columns of light near the funnel that are not unlike electrical glow discharges. Likewise, the rare but real burning and dehydration effects of some tornadoes are being reassessed. Modern instruments prove that tornadoes are intense sources of radio energy and also the cause of strong electrical currents in the ground near them. Something electrical transpires within the tornado, but it is highly controversial whether the electrical phenomena are merely the products of extremely intense meteorological forces or the causative force.

Whatever a scientist's attitude toward tornado

electricity, he will rarely admit the objective reality of curiosity and prankishness as tornado attributes. Inanimate nature cannot be animallike; this is a matter of definition and a dogma if there ever was one. Ball lightning also has been called "curious" and "prankish" as it does its eerie stunts. Even ordinary lightning behaves peculiarly on occasion and may be highly selective in what it hits and what it spares. A few courageous souls have examined these characteristics and postulated the existence of "electrolife." In their view, sentient electrical structures may be created during intense electrical activity, or perhaps the strong fields distort space and time so that "entities" pass into our universe from "elsewhere." Like UFOs, these entities are soon gone, leaving behind little besides smoke, smell, and memories. All that an objective individual can admit is that many of these phenomena are "strange."

THE TORNADO OF MONVILLE
Zurcher, Frederic; *Meteors, Aerolites, Storms, and Atmospheric Phenomena*, C. Scribner & Co., New York, 1876, pp. 154–155

[The heating and burning effects of the Monville tornado are of special interest, for they may indicate electrical or other forces at work.]

However, there was no tornado as yet, properly speaking; but, after receding to a distance and traversing some twenty-five miles, the storm suddenly returned into the valley near Malaunay and Monville, passing through a wood, the trees in which it broke off close to the ground. At that moment, an enormous cone, of sharply-defined outline and as black as coal-smoke, was seen to assume shape. The top of it was of a reddish-yellow, while it emitted flashes of lightning and a heavy rumbling sound. In a few seconds, the tornado hurled itself, with appalling velocity and by zigzag motion, through three considerable spinning-mills in succession, crushing them and all the working-people in them. The roofs were swept off, and not one stone left on another. The looms were twisted, the heavy pieces shattered, chiefly, too, where there were ponderous masses of metal. The trees in the vicinity were flung down in every direction, riven and dried up for a length of from six to twenty feet and more. While clearing away the ruins, in the attempt to rescue the unfortunate people buried beneath them, it was noticed that the bricks were burning hot. Planks were found completely charred, and cotton burned and scorched, and many pieces of iron and steel were magnetized. Some of the corpses showed traces of burning, and others had no visible cuts or contusions, but seemed to have been killed by lightning. Workmen who were hurled into the surrounding fields, all agreed in saying that they had seen vivid flashes and had noticed a strong smell of sulphur. Persons who happened to be on the adjacent heights, alleged that they saw the factories wrapped in flames and smoke as the cloud enveloped it. The breadth of the belt laid waste by the tornado was seven hundred and fifteen feet on the level of Malaunay, less than one and a half miles from the point where its ravages began, nine hundred and ninety-five feet in the middle, and one hundred and ninety-five feet near Cleres, where the cloud disappeared. The length of the belt, as the bird flies, was about ten miles.

One really very remarkable circumstance is, that *débris* of all kinds, such as slate, glass, planking, and pieces of woodwork, mingled with cotton, fell near Dieppe, at a distance of from fifteen to twenty-three miles from the scene of the catastrophe. These various objects were beheld in the air by several persons, who mistook them for the leaves of trees, so high were they above the ground. Among the scattered fragments carried thus far, was a scantling more than a yard long, five inches wide, and half an inch thick.

A FIERY WIND

Anonymous; *Symons's Monthly Meteorological Magazine*, 4: 123-124, 1869

Out in Cheatham county about noon on Wednesday—a remarkably hot day—on the farm of Ed. Sharp, five miles from Ashland, a sort of whirlwind came along over the neighbouring woods, taking up small branches and leaves of trees and burning them in a sort of flaming cylinder that travelled at the rate of about five miles an hour, developing size as it travelled. It passed directly over the spot where a team of horses were feeding and singed their manes and tails up to the roots; it then swept towards the house, taking a stack of hay in its course. It seemed to increase in heat as it went, and by the time it reached the house it immediately fired the shingles from end to end of the building, so that in ten minutes the whole dwelling was wrapped in flames. The tall column of travelling caloric then continued its course over a wheat field that had been recently cradled, setting fire to all the stacks that happened to be in its course. Passing from the field, its path lay over a stretch of woods which reached the river. The green leaves on the trees were crisped to a cinder for a breadth of 20 yards, in a straight line to the Cumberland. When the "pillar of fire" reached the water, it suddenly changed its route down the river, raising a column of steam which went up to the clouds for about half-a-mile, when it finally died out. Not less than 200 people witnessed this strangest of strange phenomena, and all of them tell substantially the same story about it. The farmer, Sharp, was left houseless by the devouring element, and his two horses were so affected that no good is expected to be got out of them in future. Several withered trees in the woods through which it passed were set on fire, and continue burning still.

TORNADO HEATING EFFECTS
Anonymous; *Nature,* 44:112, June 4, 1891

M. Teisserenc de Bort communicated the results of his inquiries respecting a destructive tornado which visited the town of Dreux on August 18 last. At 10h. 5m. p.m., Paris time, a sharp clap of thunder occurred, followed by heavy rain and hail for about a minute and five minutes later the tornado broke over the town with a noise resembling that of an express train, making a furrow in the ground, and in less than a minute tiles were flying about, trees uprooted, and several houses destroyed. After a short course the effects of the tornado ceased, and it appeared to rise to the upper strata of air, but descended again with equal violence near Epone about 60 kilometres distant, the rate of translation being about 29 miles an hour. The action of the electricity seemed to be of an unusual nature; although much damage was done by it, no metallic object was fused, but only traces of fusion could be found in bad conducting bodies. Among other incidents an iron bedstead was dismounted, without trace of fusion.

SEEING THE INSIDE OF A TORNADO
Justice, Alonzo A.; *Monthly Weather Review,* 58:205–206, May 1930

Although the incidents herein set forth occurred nearly two years ago, it is thought that they are sufficiently interesting to be reported even at this date. It was just 16 months to a day from the time the events happened that the writer heard a direct account of them from the man whose extraordinary experience forms the basis of this story.

Mr. Will Keller, a farmer of near Greensburg, Kans., is the man to whom reference is made, and the following is substantially his story:

It was on the afternoon of June 22, 1928, between 3 and 4 o'clock. I was out in my field with my family looking over the ruins of our wheat crop which had just been completely destroyed by a hailstorm. I noticed an umbrella-shaped cloud in the west and southwest and from its appearance suspected that there was a tornado in it. The air had that peculiar oppressiveness which nearly always precedes the coming of a tornado.

But my attention being on other matters, I did not watch the approach of the cloud. However, its nearness soon caused me to take another look at it. I saw at once that my suspicions were correct, for hanging from the greenish-black base of the cloud was not just *one* tornado, but *three*.

One of the tornadoes was already perilously near and apparently headed directly for our place. I lost no time therefore in hurrying with my family to our cyclone cellar.

The family had entered the cellar and I was in the doorway just about to enter and close the door when I decided that I would take a last look at the approaching tornado. I have seen a number of these things and have never become panic-stricken when near them. So I did not lose my head now, though the approaching tornado was indeed an impressive sight.

The surrounding country is level and there was nothing to obstruct the view. There was little or no rain falling from the cloud. Two of the tornadoes were some distance away and looked to me like great ropes dangling from the clouds, but the near one was shaped more like a funnel with ragged clouds surrounding it. It appeared to be much larger and more energetic than the others and it occupied the central position of the cloud, the great cumulus dome being directly over it.

As I paused to look I saw that the lower end which had been sweeping the ground was beginning to rise. I knew what that meant, so I kept my position. I knew that I was comparatively safe and I knew that if the tornado again dipped I could drop down and close the door before any harm could be done.

Steadily the tornado came on, the end gradually rising above the ground. I could have stood there only a few seconds but so impressed was I with what was going on that it seemed a long time. At last the great shaggy end of the funnel hung directly overhead. Everything was as still as death. There was a strong gassy odor and it seemed that I could not breathe. There was a screaming, hissing sound coming directly from the end of the funnel. I looked up and to my astonishment I saw right up into the heart of the tornado. There was a circular opening in the center of the funnel, about 50 or 100 feet in diameter, and extending straight upward for a distance of at least one half mile, as best I could judge under the circumstances. The walls of this opening were of rotating clouds and the whole was made brilliantly visible by constant flashes of lightning which zigzagged from side to side. Had it not been for the lightning I could not have seen the opening, not any distance up into it anyway.

Around the lower rim of the great vortex small tornadoes were constantly forming and breaking away. These looked like tails as they writhed their way around the end of the funnel. It was these that made the hissing noise.

I noticed that the direction of rotation of the great whirl was anticlockwise, but the small twisters rotated both ways —some one way and some another.

The opening was entirely hollow except for something which I could not exactly make out, but suppose that it was a detached wind cloud. This thing was in the center and was moving up and down.

The tornado was not traveling at a great speed. I had

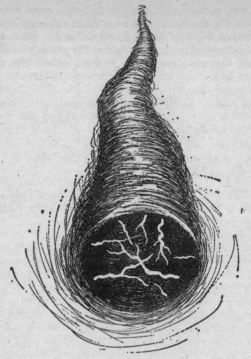

Looking up into a tornado funnel. One observer who lived through the ordeal saw lightning flashing from side to side of the hollow tube.

plenty of time to get a good view of the whole thing, inside and out. It came from the direction of Greensburg, which town is 3 miles west and 1 mile north of my place. Its course was not in a straight line, but it zigzagged across the country, in a general northeasterly direction.

TORNADOES AT BLACKWELL, OKLA., MAY 25, 1955
Montgomery, Floyd C.; *Monthly Weather Review*, 83:109, 1955

One lady who took cover under a stairway ended up one-half block away—still under the stairway, which was all that was left of her two-story house. She tells me the storm was a black wall and the lightning went up from the ground to the cloud—not from the cloud to the ground.

I stood in the door of my storm cellar and watched the storm go through town. The wind at my place, nine blocks west of the main path, was a dead calm. The storm sounded like a roaring freight train going through open country, only louder. As the funnel was directly east of me, the fire up near the top of the funnel looked like a child's Fourth of July pin wheel. It was something I will not forget for a long time.

FREAKS OF THE TORNADO
Walsh, George E.; *Harper's Weekly*, 57:25, May 17, 1913

The Weather Bureau at Washington has been collecting statistics and facts about cyclones and tornadoes for many years, and the experts have succeeded in securing considerable valuable data about the big winds; but, after all, the freaks of the storm are the things that give it special interest, and if all these were properly classified some remarkable reading would be furnished. Every visitation of a tornado adds to this valuable storehouse of queer freaks.

It is not uncommon for the whirling wind to cut a house in half, demolishing one side and leaving the other undisturbed. This happened in an Iowa tornado, and the part that was left intact was so little disturbed that the clock on the mantel continued ticking as if nothing had happened. In the Texas town of Sherman, which was visited by a tornado in 1896, two houses were picked up and carried into the air, where they exploded. Every one in them was severely injured except a baby, which did not receive so much as a scratch. A man milking a cow in a shed saw the cow and shed carried up in the air, but he was not so much as touched. Not a drop of the milk in his pail was spilled or disturbed.

In the St. Louis tornado of the same year a carpet in the parlor of one house was pulled up by the twister and carried away a few hundred yards without so much as a rent being torn in it. The tacks had been pulled up as neatly as if extracted by a careful carpet-layer. In another house the bed-clothing and mattress were lifted from the bed, and the bedstead was left intact. A resident was carried through the roof of another house with the bed and dropped a quarter of a mile away without injury. The mattress saved him in the fall, and he picked himself up in a vacant lot to dress without knowing exactly what had happened to him.

The "twisters" have been known to pull nails out of shingles and then go on to pick up a chimney bodily and carry it through the air. In Kansas one picked up a buggy and landed it in the branches of a tree. At another time it ripped the harness completely off a horse and left horse, buggy, and man uninjured. In Louisville, in 1890, a tornado carried the roof off a house and pulled a child from the mother's arms and carried it safely to another house six blocks away.

But these are merely among the harmless freaks of the big wind. There are others more heartrending. It has dismembered human beings, tearing arms and legs from the body, and twisted the hair of women into ropes. In Kansas it drove a piece of scantling six inches square through the body of a hog. At another time it blew in the door of a farmer's house and carried the owner away on the door, to drop him in the branches of a tree. The tornado did not hurt him, but he broke his neck falling from the tree to the ground. No one has succeeded in measuring the full force of a tornado, but it is known to travel at the rate of two hundred miles and more an hour.

Tornadoes are exciting more general attention than formerly because of the greater number of towns and villages located in the tornado belt. Each successive one is more dangerous than its predecessors because it is apt to find more human material to destroy. Formerly it might travel half the length of a continent without finding anything in its path to destroy except grass, trees, and occasionally the crops of a solitary farmer. To-day, if it followed the same route, it might pass over a dozen villages and towns.

The only thing that can possibly break the force of a tornado is a range of mountains. It may create wild havoc among the trees and boulders of a mountain, but it cannot carry the mountain itself away. It will uproot giant forest trees, suck the water from wells and streams, twist and demolish iron bridges, and carry up houses, but the mountains are proof against the mighty force of the wind. Until we know how to control the tornado or find some means of baffling it, its menacing danger must always be a source of considerable uneasiness in the great plain sections of the country. But, like earthquakes, the tornado and cyclone do not come every year, and sometimes they defer their visit for a decade or so, for which we may be thankful.

THE TALE OF—A GUST
Godden, William; *Symons' Meteorological Magazine,* 46:54, 1911

I hope you will see your way to take a similar course with reference to a report from Bradford, which appeared in the daily papers recently. A gust of wind is said to have carried a girl to a height of twenty feet or so, whence she fell with fatal result. Onlookers seem to have experienced no inconvenience at all. Surely on the face of it a more preposterous story never appeared in print. What was the strength of the gale: and did nothing else of consequence happen owing to the wind at Bradford on the morning of 23rd February? (William Godden)

Acting on this suggestion, we communicated with Mr. H. Lander, the rainfall observer at Lister Park, Bradford, who kindly sent us a copy of the *Yorkshire Observer* for February 25th, in which there was a fairly full report of the inquest on the school-girl who was undoubtedly killed by a fall from a great height in an extremely exposed playground during very gusty weather. One witness saw the girl enter the playground from the school at 8:40 a.m., and saw her carried in three minutes later. Another witness saw the girl in the air parallel with the balcony of the school 20 feet above the ground, her arms extended, and her skirts blown out like a balloon. He saw her fall with a crash. The jury found a verdict, "Died as the result of a fall caused by a sudden gust of wind." (Ed. S.M.M.)

SINGULAR PHENOMENON
Anonymous; London *Times,* July 5, 1842

Wednesday forenoon [June 29] a phenomenon of most rare and extraordinary character was observed in the immediate neighborhood of Cupar. About half past 12 o'clock, whilst the sky was clear, and the air, as it had been throughout the morning, perfectly calm, a girl employed in tramping clothes in a tub in the piece of ground above the town called the common, heard a loud and sharp report overhead, succeeded by a gust of wind of most extraordinary vehemence, and only of a few moments·duration. On looking round, she observed the whole of the clothes, sheets, &c., lying within a line of certain breadth, stretching across the green, several hundred yards distant; another portion of the articles, however, consisting of a quantity of curtains, and a number of smaller articles, were carried upwards to an immense height, so as to be almost lost to the eye, and gradually disappeared altogether from sight in a south-eastern direction and have not yet been heard of. At the moment of the report which preceded the wind, the cattle in the neighboring meadow were observed running about in an affrighted state, and for some time afterwards they continued cowering together in evident terror. The violence of the wind was such that a woman, who at the time was holding a blanket, found herself unable to retain it in fear of being carried along with it! It is remarkable that, while even the heaviest articles were being stripped off a belt, as it were, running across the green, and while the loops of several sheets which were pinned down and snapped, light articles lying loose on both sides of the holt were never moved from their position.

IV

GEOLOGY

21

Graveyards of the Mammoth

Throughout the Arctic, bones and carcasses of the mammoth are found in incredible profusion. Entire islands seem largely made from mammoth bones and the bones of related animals. Catastrophists, those who believe that the recent history of the earth had some violence-filled chapters, claim that these remains are proof positive that their concept of geology is correct.

Both catastrophists and their philosophical opposites, the uniformitarians, can agree that the deposits of organic and inorganic debris on Siberian and Alaska shores are a unique and vast storehouse of biological and geological information. The hundreds, perhaps thousands, of feet of muck are close packed with uprooted trees, decaying vegetable matter, jumbled bones, and rotting carcasses. The problem is explaining this geological junkyard.

At least three problems are involved:

1. The muck is very thick and widespread. How was it deposited and where did it come from?

2. Immense numbers of animal bones are strewn through the muck, mostly smashed and mixed as if by violent forces. Can these remains be explained without invoking a catastrophic cause?

3. Some carcasses, notably those of the mammoth, are well preserved, with surprisingly fresh plant remains in mouth and stomach. The implication is that these animals were quick-frozen by a catastrophic change in climate. Is this surmise justified?

The catastrophist immediately declares that the

muck was deposited by colossal floods resulting from a shift of the earth's polar axis, the impact of an immense meteorite, or some other earth-wrenching event. The uniformitarian counters that the deposits could only be the work of thousands of years of sedimentation in a very cold climate. Decide for yourself as you read the accounts below.

ON THE OCCURRENCE OF MAMMOTH AND MASTODON REMAINS AROUND HUDSON BAY

Bell, Robert; *Geological Society of America, Bulletin,* 9:369–390, 1898

[The frozen mammoth carcasses in the Arctic were controversial even in the 19th century—long before Sanderson, Price, Velikovsky, and other modern catastrophists. Here is an early condemnation of antiuniformitarians.]

Extinction of the Mammoth in Siberia. The mammoth in northern Siberia probably passed the winters within the forest-line, where he would find shelter from the chilling winds and where he might live well, browsing on the small branchy spruce, larch, birch, etcetera. With the advent of spring he would begin his northward march, taking advantage of the long daylight, and he would spend part of the summer and the autumn roving about the shore of the Arctic sea, enjoying the cool weather and finding abundant sustenance on the small trees and the alder, willow, and birch brushwood. Then, with the beginning of the severe weather, he would turn his footsteps toward his winter quarters and move south as the season advanced. The periods of their annual migrations having become settled, it would be difficult or impossible to overcome the inertia of long-fixed habit, and they would be obliged to endure the increasing severity of the climate on the borders of the Arctic sea. In the meantime their numbers would be greatly diminished from causes to be mentioned further on. At length, those which journeyed as far as the sea coast might be reduced to the single herd which migrated to the mouth of the Lena, where the climate of autumn would be the best on the coast, owing to the large quantity of warm water from the south which accumulates off the mouth of this great river.

At this stage, if an unusually early and severe season were to set in, accompanied by great snow-storms, before the herd had started for the south, the result might be disastrous to the remaining mammoths. The now stunted brush would be covered by the deep snow, on which perhaps a strong crust had formed, thus preventing the animals from obtaining any food, while the almost continuous darkness of the early winter would also operate against them. The same conditions would make it difficult or impossible for them to travel. Other individuals or herds which did not migrate so far north may have perished from a similar cause in various parts of the region. We know how completely helpless the deer of any species become in our northern woods when caught in deep snow with a crust upon it.

Under circumstances like these the last of the mammoths would soon perish, since creatures of their organization, living upon such slightly nutritious food, must have it continuously and in large quantities. That such a process of starvation is not imaginary, I may mention the fact that the reindeer sometimes perish over large areas in our northern barrenlands from this cause. Their lives depend upon a continuous supply of the reindeer-lichen, which they obtain by removing the snow or by finding the plant where the ground has been left bare by drifting. A striking instance of this occurred many years ago on Akpatok island, in Ungava bay. This large island had always swarmed with reindeer, but one winter, when the snow was deeper than usual, rain fell upon it (an almost unprecedented occurrence) and formed a heavy and permanent crust over both the bare ground and the snow, thus preventing the deer from obtaining their food. The consequence was that the whole number perished, and the island has never been restocked. If this former great herd had comprised the whole species then living, the reindeer would now be extinct.

Preservation of the Flesh of Mammoths in Siberia. The preservation till the present day of the flesh of some of the mammoths which perished in the region about the mouth of the Lena river and elsewhere proves that the carcasses must have become frozen immediately after death, and this circumstance may be accounted for in the following way: If the last of these creatures succumbed in the manner supposed, there may have been at that time a series of unusually cold years, as sometimes happens in high latitudes, and this, together with the increasing severity of the climate in general ever since, would account for the preservation of some of their carcasses in the snow and ice which have persisted in that region till the present time.

The occurrence of large numbers of the remains of mammoths in the alluvial deposits about the mouth of the Lena and other rivers may be explained by the supposition that the animals had broken through the too thin ice in attempting to cross the streams upon it on their southward migration in the autumn, and that their bodies had subsequently floated down to the still water. Indeed, it is highly probable that whole herds of these animals lost their lives in this manner. While the bison was abundant in our northwest territories it was a matter of common occurrence for large numbers of them to be drowned when attempting to cross the streams in compact droves before the ice was strong enough to bear the strain. The great abundance of bison bones in some of the fluviatile deposits in this region is easily accounted for in this way.

The mammoths, owing to their great weight, would be still more liable to such an accident. Professor Richard Lydekker, in "The Royal Natural History," lately published, speaking of the trade in ivory from Siberia, says that within a recent period, covering twenty years, 20,000 mammoths must have been discovered in that region.

Improbable Theories. The supposition that the mammoths of northern Siberia were frozen where we find them by a sudden change from a warm to a very cold climate, and which has remained permanently so, is as untenable as the other theory, which supposes the bones and tusks found there to be those of mammoths which were drowned in great numbers and at the same time within a limited area by a sudden cataclysm. If it were possible (which it is not) that such an abrupt change of climate could happen, it would require to be general around a great part of the globe, and there is no evidence that such a thing occurred at any time in the history of the earth. Again, to invoke the agency of sudden cataclysms to account for geological phenomena is an exploded notion which does not require discussion.

THE NEW MAMMOTH AT ST. PETERSBURG

W., A. S.; *Nature,* 68:297–298, July 30, 1903.

[So much sensational literature exists describing the frozen Siberian mammoths that this matter-of-fact account is refreshing.]

The new mammoth just mounted for exhibition in the Zoological Museum at St. Petersburg, is a triumph of the taxidermist's art. The frozen skin has been cleaned, softened, and prepared. The skeleton, and as many of the surrounding soft tissues as possible, have been carefully removed from its interior and preserved separately. The animal has been actually stuffed like a modern quadruped, and placed in the attitude in which it originally died. The skin of the head and the ears are artificial, copied from the famous old specimen obtained a century ago by Adams. A model of the base of the proboscis has also been added. The skin of the trunk and limbs, however, is nearly complete, only embellished in parts by the addition of a little wool and hair from other specimens; and some deficiencies are covered by the surrounding mount, which represents the morass into which the animal slipped. The well-preserved tail is especially noteworthy, and bears a large tassel of long black hair at its tip. The animal is a young male of rather small size.

The hopelessly-struggling aspect of this mammoth is very striking, and reproduces exactly the attitude of the carcass as it lay buried in the Siberian tundra. In fact, the chief value of the specimen depends upon the circumstance that it was scientifically disinterred, photographed at various stages in the excavation, and carefully preserved by the best modern methods. Great credit is due to Dr. Otto Herz, the leader of the expedition organised by the St. Petersburg Imperial Academy of Sciences, who undertook the arduous task of securing the carcass and transporting it to the Russian capital. His are the only photographs hitherto obtained of a mammoth buried in the tundra, and they throw important new light on the question of the conditions under which these large quadrupeds were destroyed and entombed. Some of Dr. Herz's photographs have lately been presented by Dr. Salensky to the British Museum.

The carcass in question was exposed by a landslip on the bank of the River Beresowka, an affluent of the Kolyma, in the Government of Jakutsk, in latitude 67° 32′N. The head was entirely uncovered, so that the foxes and other carnivores ate its soft parts, while the inhabitants of a neighbouring village removed a tusk. The Governor of Jakutsk, however, succeeded in keeping the remainder of the specimen undisturbed until the arrival of the expedition from the Academy. It was buried partly in ice, partly in frozen sand and gravel, and there was a sufficient covering of earth to prevent its naturally thawing.

According to the general report published by Dr. Herz,* he began to excavate the specimen from the front. In this manner he soon discovered the two fore limbs spread widely apart, and sharply bent at the wrist. Proceeding backwards on the left side, he unexpectedly met with the hind foot almost at once, and it gradually became evident that the hind limbs were completely turned forwards beneath the body. Dr. Herz then removed the skull, and found the well-preserved tongue hanging out of the mandible. He also noticed that the mouth was filled with grass, which had been cropped, but not chewed and swallowed. Further examination of the carcass showed that the cavity of the chest was filled with clotted blood. It is therefore natural to conclude that the animal was entrapped by falling into a hole, and suddenly died from the bursting of a blood-vessel near the heart while making an effort to extricate itself. As shown by the recent researches of Dr. Tolmatschow, the ice surrounding the carcass was not that of a lake or river, but evidently formed from snow. It is thus quite likely that the mammoth was quietly browsing on the grassland which formed the thin covering of a glacier, and fell into a crevasse which was obscured by the loose earth. On this subject, however, much more information may shortly be expected, when Mr. Ssewastianow publishes an account of the geological researches which he made in the neighbourhood of the Beresowka last summer.

---

*"Berichte des Leiters der von der kaiserlichen Akademie der Wissenschaften zur Ausgrabung eines Mammuth-Kadavers an die Kolyma-Beresowka ausgesandten Expedition" (St. Petersburg Academy of Sciences, 1902).

THE GLACIATED GRAVE OF THE MAMMOTH IN SIBERIA
Anonymous; *Current Opinion*, 61:330, November 1916

[Descriptions of the Siberian boneyards inevitably envoke claims of catastrophism, such as a sudden shift of the earth's pole of rotation.]

The whole of northeast Siberia is one vast graveyard filled with the bones of animals that have perished within comparatively recent times. Little does the traveler think, says the physical geographer, Doctor D. Gath Whitley, that the ground under him only a few feet below his sled is packed full of the bones of enormous animals which have perished in some mysterious manner since man appeared upon the earth.

The whole of northern Siberia, from the Ural Mountains to Bering Strait, is one vast graveyard filled with animal remains. The bones, teeth and skulls are those of elephants, rhinoceroses, buffaloes and musk-oxen. These bones occur everywhere. They are found on the banks of the rivers, in the plains, on rising ground and in frozen cliffs. On the shores of the Arctic Ocean there are sloping banks of ice. These are split and furrowed in all directions with deep chasms. As the traveler looks down into their dark depths from above, he sees that the lower portions of these icy chasms are filled with tusks, bones and skulls in countless abundance. We quote from *Chambers's*:

"In other places on the northern coast of Siberia fronting the Arctic Ocean the low cliffs which rise above the beach and are formed of earth and clay are full of the bones of elephants and rhinoceroses. In the brief summer, which hardly lasts for six weeks, portions of these earthy cliffs thaw and fall on the beach below. Then it is that the traveler who walks along the shore witnesses an astonishing spectacle. Not only does he observe icebergs stranded on the beach but he also sees the tusks, bones, and teeth of elephants (the mammoth) lying on the shore and whitening the beach for long distances! If he leaves the Arctic Ocean behind and journeys inland, the same signs constantly meet his astonished gaze. He comes, it may be, to a plain where for perhaps half a mile the whole ground seems to be formed of masses of tusks,

teeth, and bones of elephants and rhinoceroses welded together in one confused mass in the frozen soil. These
mighty beasts must have been destroyed in herds, but how
they perished no one knows.

"Still more amazing is the fact that the islands in the
Arctic Ocean north of Siberia are equally full of the tusks
and bones of elephants and rhinoceroses; and on the
shores of these islands in the Polar Sea the tusks of elephants can be seen sticking up like trunks of trees in the
frozen sand!

"Stranger still, actually the very bodies of these great
elephants, with flesh, fur and hair perfect, are seen standing upright in the frozen cliffs.

"When the cliffs thaw, the bodies of these great elephants fall to the ground, and are so perfect, after being
entombed for thousands of years, that the wolves eat the
flesh!"

RIDDLE OF THE FROZEN GIANTS
Sanderson, Ivan T.; *Saturday Evening Post*, 232:39+, January
16, 1960

[Most of Sanderson's article consists of surmises about
how mammoths (and other animals) were quick-frozen in
the Arctic muck. Our policy aims at presenting data rather than theory. Therefore, only Sanderson's intriguing, ca-
tastrophism-oriented summaries of the basic facts are reproduced below.]

About one seventh of the entire land surface of our
earth, stretching in a great swath round the Arctic Ocean,
is permanently frozen. The surface of some of this territory
is bare rock, but the greater part of it is covered with a
layer, varying in thickness from a few feet to more than
1000 feet, of stuff we call muck. This is composed of an
assortment of different substances, all bound together with
frozen water, which becomes and acts as a rock. While
its actual composition varies considerably from place to
place, it is usually for the most part composed of fine
sand or coarse silt, but it also includes a high proportion of
earth or loam, and often also masses of bones or even
whole animals in various stages of preservation or decomposition. So much of the last is there on occasion that
even strong men find it almost impossible to stand the

stench when it is melting. This muck is spread all across northern Asia and is exceptionally widespread in Northern Siberia. It appears again in Alaska, and lies right across the top of Canada almost to Hudson Bay.

The list of animals that have been thawed out of this mess would cover several pages. It includes the famous woolly mammoths and woolly rhinoceroses, horses like those still existing wild in Asia, giant oxen and a kind of huge tiger. In Alaska it also includes giant bison, wolves and beavers, and an apparently quite ordinary lion as well as many other animals now extinct and some which are still in existence, like the musk ox and the ground squirrel. The presence of the extinct species provides us with a fine set of riddles, and of those that are not extinct, with another set; and the absence of still others, like man, for instance, with a third set. The greatest riddle, however, is when, why and how did all these assorted creatures, and in such absolutely countless numbers, get killed, mashed up and frozen into this horrific indecency?

FROZEN MAMMOTHS AND MODERN GEOLOGY

Farrand, William R.; *Science,* 133:729–735, March 17, 1961 (Copyright 1961 American Association for the Advancement of Science)

[This selection should be contrasted with the preceding one by Sanderson to see how different camps view the same evidence. In 1961, scientists were very wary of catastrophic implications—much more so than in 1976. In any event, Farrand presents an excellent review of the subject.]

Frozen woolly mammoths have perplexed both scientists and laymen during the several centuries since the first direct description of a frozen mammoth was recorded, in 1692. In the records of Digby, a well-known mammoth hunter, "the gods must have enjoyed many a hearty laugh over humanity's attempt to account for the remains of mammoths." One of the biggest obstacles to complete interpretation of the frozen mammoths was, and to a lesser degree is still, the lack of detailed knowledge of the distribution, geologic context, and age of the beasts. Tolmachoff wrote a very complete summary of the information available in 1929, but no comprehensive paper has appeared since that time, although many more geological data are now at hand.

In contrast to scientific efforts, a number of popular and quasi-scientific articles have appeared in recent years, in which fragmentary knowledge, folk tales, and science fiction are combined under the guise of verity—much to the chagrin of scientists and the confusion of the public. The most recent of such articles is that of Sanderson, who comes to the conclusion that the "frozen giants" must have become deep-frozen within only a few hours' time. Such a thesis, however, consistently disregards the actual observations of scientists and explorers. Adding insult to injury, Sanderson proceeds to fashion a fantastic climatic catastrophe to explain his conclusions.

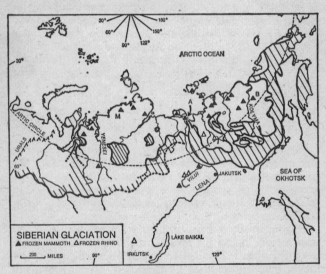

Locations of Siberian frozen mammoths. The letters indicate specific mammoth finds. The shading shows the maximum extent of glaciation, which was of the ice-sheet type west of the Lena and Alpine to the east.

* * * * * * * * * * * * *

Death and Preservation. All the evidence now at hand supports the conclusions of previous workers that no catastrophic event was responsible for the death and preservation of the frozen woolly mammoths. The cadavers are unusual only in that they have been preserved by freezing; the demise of the animals, however, accords with uniformitarian concepts. The ratio of frozen specimens (around 39) to the probable total population (more than 50,000) is of the order of magnitude expected among terrestrial mammals on the basis of chance burial. Furthermore, the occurrence of nearly whole carcasses is extremely rare (only four have been found), in spite of the numerous expeditions for fossil ivory and other exploration in northern Siberia.

There is no direct evidence that any woolly mammoth froze to death. In fact, the healthy, robust condition of the cadavers and their full stomachs argue against death by *slow* freezing. On the other hand, the large size of their warm-blooded bodies is not compatible with *sudden* freezing. In addition, all the frozen specimens were rotten and, in most cases, had been somewhat mutilated by predators prior to freezing. This is attested to by many first-hand accounts. Although some of the flesh recovered from the cadavers was "fibrous and marbled with fat" and looked "as fresh as well-frozen beef or horsemeat," only dogs showed any appetite for it; "the stench . . . was unbearable." Histological examination of fat and flesh of the Berezovka mammoth showed "deep penetrating chemical alteration as a result of the very slow decay," and even the frozen ground surrounding a mammoth had the same putrid odor, implying decay *before* freezing. Furthermore, the stories of a banquet on the flesh of the Berezovka mammoth were "a hundred per cent invention."

Soft parts of other fossils are not unknown in the geologic record, but sudden or catastrophic changes of climate have not been postulated to explain the preservation of these parts. Skin and hair of Pleistocene ground sloths are known from nonglacial areas. From more remote times we have mummified skin of Mesozoic dinosaurs and muscle fibers of Devonian sharks, still showing individual fibers and cross-striations. Such fossil evidence implies preservation of these soft parts of a considerable period of time—at least as long as was required for lithification of the enclosing sediments.

The only direct evidence of the mode of death indicates

that at least some of the frozen mammoths (and frozen woolly rhinoceroses as well) died of asphyxia, either by drowning or by being buried alive by a cave-in or mudflow. As stated above, sudden death is indicated by the robust condition of the animals and their full stomachs. Asphyxiation is indicated by the erection of the penis in the case of the Berezovka mammoth and by the blood vessels of the head of a woolly rhinoceros from the River Vilyui (Siberia), which were still filled with red, coagulated blood.

The specific nature of deposits enclosing the mammoths is not known well enough to be very helpful as an indicator of the mode of death or burial. Most of the remains are associated with river valleys and with fluviatile and terrestrial sediments, but whether the mammoths bogged down in marshy places or fell into "riparian gullies" or were mired in and slowly buried by sticky mudflows is not clear. Perhaps all three of these agencies and several others were involved. One point of fact helpful in this problem is the specificity of the frozen animals: in Siberia only mammoths and woolly rhinoceroses have been found frozen and preserved, and the former have been found in much greater numbers than the latter.

So far no other members of the contemporary Eurasian fauna—stag, horse, reindeer, antelope, musk ox, and so on have been found frozen and well preserved. That only the bulky and awkward "giants" of the fauna are so preserved points to some peculiarity of their physique as a contributing factor. The low-slung rhinoceros would have trouble negotiating marshy ground and snow drifts. Similarly, the mammoth, with his stiff-legged mode of locomotion, would have difficulty on such terrain and, moreover, would probably not be able to cross even small gullies. It would be nearly impossible for him to extricate himself if he had fallen into a snow-filled gully or had been mired into boggy ground. A modern elephant is unable to pass over any trench which barely exceeds his maximum stride because of the pillar-like leg structure which is required to support his vast body. Also, the mere weight of the mammoth's body would have been a dangerous attribute if the animal happened to graze too near the edge of a river bluff which had been softened by the summer sun.

The stomach contents of the frozen mammoths indicates that death occurred in the warm season, probably in late summer or early fall, when melting and solifluction would have been at a maximum and, accordingly, locomotion would have been difficult.

The several theories of entombment, which have been alluded to above, generally reflect the theorist's particular experiences or impressions in the mammoth-bearing terrain. Digby was impressed by "countless riparian gullies" which would have been ideal mammoth traps when filled with snow in the winter. Vollosovich was himself trapped in a slowly moving stream of very sticky mud and had to be rescued by his guides. He theorized that an animal so trapped might fall on its side and act as a dam, being slowly buried and suffocated by mud. The Berezovka mammoth is commonly regarded as having fallen as a cliff slumped beneath it; its broken bones attest to such a fall. Presumably it then suffocated as it was buried alive by the caving bluff. Popov believes the Mamontova mammoth perished in a bog while grazing on the floodplain of the ancient Mamontova River. Quackenbush believed that his specimen from Alaska perished on a floodplain and that most of the flesh rotted away before the corpse was naturally buried by floodplain sediments. Another possibility is drowning by breaking through river ice. All of these theories are credible and can be accepted as possibilities. There appears to be no need to assume the occurrence of a catastrophe.

MUCH ABOUT MUCK
Anonymous; *Pursuit*, 2:68–69, October 1969

In a fine report on a highly informative talk given by a Mr. E. M. Benson, Vice-President of the North American Producing Division of the Atlantic Richfield Oil Company, to the Long Beach Petroleum Club of California on the new oilfield in northern Alaska, there appeared a rather noteworthy quote. This read:—"Drilling down through the 1000-foot thick frozen earth can produce some surprises. One of our wells brought up an 18-inch long chunk of tree trunk from almost 1,000 feet below the surface. It wasn't petrified—just frozen," the oil company executive said. The reason this statement is noteworthy is not because the reporter seems to have been impressed but rather that a man of Mr. Benson's experience—and he started as a worker in the fields—should use the word "surprise" in this case.

We are going to hear a lot about this frozen earth or "muck" from now on because of this vast oil strike on the Arctic shores of the Alaskan peninsula. It is indeed full of surprises but a tree trunk in it, and even at a depth of a thousand feet, is not at all surprising. What surprise there was on this occasion was probably due to the fact that it came to light in an area devoid of trees today and hundreds of miles from any forest growth. The nature of muck is not generally understood, and the theories on its origin are even less widely known.

Frozen soil, as diametrically opposed to ice on the one hand and rock on the other, constitutes one of the greatest mysteries on our earth's surface. What is more it covers no less than one seventh of the land surface of the earth, and all of it encircles the Arctic Ocean and lies within the Arctic circle at what we consider the top side of our planet. Actually, it is a form of "rock," despite its very mixed composition, at least to the extent that a tillite or pudding-stone may be. The reason for stating this is that the material that binds it is water, and water in its solid form as ice is also technically a rock and behaves as such. When this frozen soil melts it results in an appalling and often stinking sort of soup composed of goo with silt, sand, pebbles, and boulders, often with masses of preserved, semi-decayed, or fully decayed vegetable and animal matter. This is what is called "muck."

A world map of the distribution of this frozen soil and muck reveals several very interesting things, the most outstanding aspect being that it lies on low, level plains or tablelands. Unless it was caused by some cosmic forces that we have not yet detected, it would appear to be a subaerial deposit derived from massive erosion of higher grounds and with steeper slopes. However, its depth in some places drilled down to over 4000 feet but still without reaching solid rock. The conundrum is, of course, how do you get that thickness of what is manifestly surface-derived material if it is the result of mere run-off? To this there would appear to be but one answer.

First, the lands now blanketed with this material must at one time have been much higher above sealevel, so that stuff could be deposited upon them, rather than running on beyond and out into the sea. Alternatively, the sea level would have to have been much below that of today; but in this case are we asked to suppose that universal sealevel was not too long ago, geologically speaking, more than 4000 feet lower? If neither of these situations pertained when the first, and lowest layers of this muck were laid down, just what were the conditions, since no such strata could be laid down even under shallow, tranquil coastal seas? To suggest that the uplands from which this stuff came were much once higher and had a steeper run-off is begging the question, and doesn't help at all. Yet, there is the bloody muck lying all over the lot and to enormous depths. It has to be accounted for.

Let us next turn back to Mr. Benson's remark. This was to the effect that finding a section of a fair-sized tree trunk a thousand feet down in this frozen muck was a "surprise." It may indeed be to the average person who has not had cause to investigate or read about this incredible natural phenomenon, but it comes as no surprise at all to geologists who have specialized in the surface constitution of the Arctic regions. A mere section of tree trunk is a mild relief compared to some of the things that the muck has yielded. In the New Siberian Islands, for instance, whole trees have turned up; and trees of the family that includes the plums; and with their leaves and fruits. No such hardwood trees grow today anywhere within two thousand miles of those islands. Therefore the climate must have been very much different when they got buried; and, please note, they could not have been buried in frozen muck which is rock-hard, nor could they have retained their foliage if they were washed far north by currents from warmer climes. They must have grown thereabouts, and the climate must have been not only warm enough but have had a long enough growing period of summer sunlight for them to have leafed and fruited.

Ergo, either what is now the Arctic was at the time as warm as Oregon, or the land that now lies therein was at that time elsewhere. Geophysicists don't go for an overall warming of this planet to allow such growth at 72 degrees north; otherwise everything in the tropics would have boiled! Thus, we are left with the notion that either the whole earth's crust has shifted, or bits of it have drifted about. But then comes another problem—the Time Factor.

Along with the plum trees, and other non-arctic vegetation there are found associated animal remains of many kinds. One of these is the famous mammoth. Now, everybody has somehow got the totally erroneous idea that these great hairy beasts are found in ice. Not one has ever been found in ice: they are all in this frozen earth or muck. Then, just because of their layer of fat and their covering of long hair everybody likewise thinks that they were arctic types. A moment's consideration will disclose just how ridiculous an idea this is. A large elephantine needs some half a ton minimum of fresh green food a day to maintain itself, and there were apparently (at least according to the number of their bones and bodies that have been found in the muck) hundreds of thousands of them up till only a few thousand years ago. For a minimum of eight months out of the year there is nothing for such large animals to eat north of the tree line in the Arctic, though some Barren Ground Caribou and a few Muskox get along by scratching through the shallow snow to get at tundra moss and lichens. Therefore these elephantines must have migrated far south for the winter or the climate must have been much milder than it is today, or the lands they lived in were elsewhere.

But not even this pinpoints the reason for the muck or explains just how all the junk that is found in it, even down to thousands of feet, got there. Mr. Benson's tree trunk may not have been a surprise but it is still a mystery in one way. And we should contemplate the many aspects of this mystery in order to be ready for the many more enigmas that we are going to be told about as our technicians slice into the far north.

22

Toads in Rocks

When a toad was discovered in solid rock by quarry-men or coal miners a century ago, it was as news-worthy as a UFO is today. Few rational people will admit publicly their belief in either phenomenon. At least with the toad-in-rock story some tangible evidence has been retained. But as the selections below testify, all critics claim that the unsophisticated work-men were careless and/or untruthful. Everyone *knows* that live toads *cannot* be found in rocks that are millions of years old.

Unfortunately, the toad stories refuse to go away. Like sea serpents they are a part of that continual background noise of anomalous events. Ignoring impossibility, suppose a toad actually did hop away from a cavity in a freshly split stratum of 100-million-year-old rock. Some possible implications are: (1) toads hibernate better than we thought and are essentially immortal under the right conditions; (2) our rock-dating methods are inaccurate by many orders of magnitude; and (3) something supernatural is forever creating anomalies either in fact or in our heads to keep us on our toes. If miracles do happen, then toads can be found in solid rocks. It may be that nature operates this way, violating the "logical" laws we try to impose with some low frequency, after the fashion of the "forbidden transitions" in quantum physics.

TOAD IN A HOLE
Wilson, A.; *Knowledge,* 1:136, 1881

[Before reproducing accounts of the discoveries of toads in rocks, consider the usual reaction of a scientist.]

In letter 87, "Arachnida" asks, "What is the construction of the common toad that enables it to be enclosed for many years in blocks of solid matter?" "Arachnida" should first of all have asked, is it true that toads are ever found so enclosed? The usual story is that of some quarrymen, who, blasting stones, see a live frog or toad hopping about, after the blast, among the *débris*. Because the toad is found thus, it is *assumed* that it came from the interior of the rock. Not a particle of evidence exists to show in such a case that the animal had anything whatever to do with the rock. If "Arachnida" will read in the "English Cyclopaedia" the account of Dean Buckland's experiments, he will find that the Dean enclosed healthy frogs and toads in holes cut in limestone and sandstone blocks. He buried the blocks in his garden three feet deep. At the end of the first year most had died, and the living ones, re-buried, all died long before the end of the second year. Common sense, apart from exact knowledge, would tell us that animal life of higher kind, with all its demands in the way of food, &c., could not exist under the circumstances of the popular tales and superstitions "Arachnida" inquires about. The oldest fossil toads and frogs occur in Tertiary rocks. If, therefore, a live toad hopped as has been alleged, out of a Cretaceous or Devonian rock, such a fact would amount to the declaration that the live toad could be ages and ages older than its fossil relatives, which declaration is, of course, the height of absurdity. There is no doubt that a frog or toad has an elastic constitution. It is cold-blooded; it can live under water for months; it can live for months after excision of its lungs, because the skin takes on the functions of lungs in such a case; and these animals (as in Dean Buckland's experiments) can live without food for a year or two, but, like all other animals (and plants), die *starved and meagre,* sooner or later. If "Arachnida" will only take the trouble to inquire into the *evidence* on which such stories as those he mentions are founded, he will find not one single, *proved* or *provable* fact which will warrant any belief in the utterly impossible existence of toads or frogs in rocks. I may refer him for a fuller account of such cases to the essay on "Some Facts and Fictions of Zoology" in my "Leisure Time Studies" (Chatto & Windus). As a naturalist, I stake my reputation on the correctness of the views stated above, and also repeated in my book.

AN EXTRAORDINARY TOAD
Birchall, E.; *Zoologist,* 23:9630, 1865

During the excavations which are being carried out under the superintendence of Mr. James Yeal, of Dyke House Quay, in connection with the Hartlepool Water Works, the workmen yesterday morning found a toad, embedded in a block of magnesium limestone, at a depth of twenty-five feet from the surface of the earth and eight feet from any spring-water vein. The block of stone had been cut by a wedge, and was being reduced by workmen when a pick split open the cavity in which the toad had been incarcerated. The cavity was no larger than its body, and presented the appearance of being a cast of it. The toad's eyes shone with unusual brilliancy, and it was full of vivacity on its liberation. It appeared, when first discovered, desirous to perform the process of respiration, but evidently experienced some difficulty, and the only sign of success consisted of a "barking" noise, which it continues invariably to make at present on being touched. The toad is in the possession of Mr. S. Horner, the president of the Natural History Society, and continues in as lively a state as when found. On a minute examination its mouth is found to be completely closed, and the barking noise it makes proceeds from its nostrils. The claws of its fore feet are turned inwards, and its hind ones are of extraordinary length and unlike the present English toad. The Rev. R. Taylor, incumbent of St. Hilda's Church, Hartlepool, who is an eminent local geologist, gives it as his opinion that the animal must be at least 6000 years old. The wonderful toad is to be placed in its primary habitation, and will be added to the collection of the Hartlepool Museum. The toad, when first released, was of a pale colour and not readily distinguished from the stone, but shortly after its colour grew darker until it became a fine olive-brown.

—Leeds Mercury, April 8, 1865. [Communicated, with the following paragraph, by Mr. E. Birchall.]

The Immured Toad.—It is stated in the 'Sunderland Herald' that the toad, lately found by some quarrymen at Hartlepool, and announced to be 6000 years old, is not a myth. The Rev. Robert Taylor, of St. Hilda's Parsonage, states that the toad is still alive, that it has no mouth, that it was found in the centre of a block of magnesian limestone, twenty-five feet below the surface of the earth, and that it differs in many respects from all ordinary toads.

A MUMMIFIED FROG
Shufeldt, R. W.; *Science,* 8:279–280, September 24, 1886

Not long ago Mr. James Stevenson of the U. S. geological survey visited me for a day or two at Fort Wingate, and while here invited my attention to an interesting specimen that had fallen into his possession during a recent trip he had made in the coal regions of northern Pennsylvania. The specimen consists of a mummified frog taken from the coalmine of McLean county Penn., and the following account of it is from a local newspaper loaned me by Mr. Stevenson for the present purpose. I quote the short notice in full; and the writer of it says, "One of the most curious finds unearthed lately in this region, and what may yet prove a valuable fact in the study of science and history, was singularly found by Eddie Marsh, the fourteen-year old son of Mr. D. B. Marsh, a book-keeper for Stevenson Brothers, hardware dealers. Eddie, becoming impatient at the fire in the stove, which was not burning vigorously, took the poker and began punching it. A large lump of coal lay smouldering, and he determined to break it; and, after punching at it for a moment, the lump burst open as if by explosion, and a number of pieces flew out of the stove. One piece he caught, and he was in the act of casting it back into the stove, when its lightness attracted his attention. On viewing it, he saw that it was nothing less than a perfectly formed frog. On last evening a large number of persons viewed the little curiosity. It had been embedded in the centre of the large lump of coal, and its bed was plainly discernible when the lump was laid open. The lump of coal came from the third vein of coal in the McLean county coalshaft, which is 541 feet under ground.

The curiosity apparently was not petrified. Apparently it had been mummified instead. It was shrivelled until it is about half the size of a full-grown frog, and it is light and soft. Its shape is perfect, and the warty protuberances of the skin are very plain. Its limbs are regular and properly shaped, including the finger-like toe of its feet, and its eyes and mouth are natural. There can be no doubt of its being a mummified frog, and now various and tough questions arise regarding it: How did it get that far under ground? How did it become embedded in that chunk of coal, which probably had been blasted from the centre of a thick vein? How many thousands of years had it been buried? and various other queries, which we will leave for the scientist to unravel and explain."

Mr. Stevenson tells me that he is personally acquainted with all the parties concerned in the discovery of this specimen, and has carefully examined the piece of coal whence the mummy was taken, and says, further, that it came from the vault, and not from either the sides or the floor of the mine.

He has done me the honor to turn the specimen over to me for diagnosis, as well as to take such steps as I saw fit to ascertain if there be any similar cases on record, and, finally, how geologists or paleontologists explain such finds as this. The specimen is now before me, and I at once recognized it as a species of Hyla, though I am unable to say which one. It apparently agrees in all its external characters with a specimen I have of Hyla versicolor, kindly diagnosed for me by Professor Cope last summer, though it is rather smaller. As will be seen from the life-size figure I have made of it, which illustrates this letter, it is in

A "mummified" frog found in a lump of coal taken from a vein 541 feet underground, according to Shufeldt.

nearly a natural position; its feet, however, are somewhat drawn up under it. I have figured it as viewed directly from above. It is completely mummified, and in a wonderfully perfect state of preservation, being of a dark, snuff-brown color, somewhat shrunken, and, in short, reduced to a condition, that, if properly excluded from the air, would keep for an indefinite length of time. I am aware that these tree-frogs very often climb into some of the most unheard-of places; but it struck me that it would be interesting to have some one tell us if they ever heard of a Hyla finding its way to the vault of a coal-mine 541 feet under ground, and climbing into the solid coal-bed after getting there.

A TOAD IN THE SOLID ROCK
Arnold, A. W.; *Scientific American,* 29:212, October 4, 1873

The other day Mr. Moses Gains of this place, while digging into a bank, found a toad embedded in the hard pan. He came to a stone some 2 feet square; and after digging this out, a man who was with him observed something black: taking his pickaxe, he carefully dug it out, and it proved to be a toad. It was some six inches below the surface of the stone, and its place of concealment was as smooth as if it had been made of putty. The toad was about 3 inches long and very plump and fat. Its eyes were about the size of a 3 cent silver piece, being much larger than those of toads of the same size such as we see every day. They tried to make him hop or jump by touching with a stick, but he paid no attention to them.

How came this toad embedded, 5 feet below the surface under a stone, in that hard pan? What did he subsist on? Will such toads live on being brought to the light? Is there any air in the ground, on which a toad could live, and how long must we suppose that he had been there?

HOW LIVING TOADS MAY OCCUR IN LIMESTONE
Worthen, A. H.; *American Naturalist,* 5:786–787, 1871

In the winter of 1853 the writer was informed by a gentleman of undoubted veracity, that in laying the foundation walls for a warehouse in the town of Naples on the

Illinois river, a living toad was found entombed in the limestone, which on coming in contact with the atmosphere soon resumed its wonted activity, though torpid when first discovered.

Having occasion to pass through Naples a few days afterwards, I examined the walls of the buildings to see if I could discover any clue that might serve to explain so improbable an occurrence. I found the walls constructed out of the brown dolomite of the lower St. Louis, or Warsaw limestone, and observed that the rock had been more or less fissured, the fissures cutting the strata at right angles to the lines of bedding, and varying from a mere line to an inch or more in width. Many of these fissures had been filled wholly or partially with a deposit of stalagmite, and in some places the exposed surface of the rock had been coated for an inch or more in thickness with the same material.

These facts seemed to me to afford an easy explanation of the reported phenomena; the toad had sought shelter in one of these crevices as his home for the winter, where he remained in a dormant condition, until the constant dripping of water holding carbonate of lime in solution sealed him in completely. Here he remained until he was released by the hammer of the workman, which broke the crust of his stony mausoleum, and restored him to liberty. Persons who had paid no attention to the manner in which limestones are formed, would make no distinction between the original dolomite which was formed beneath the ocean, eons of ages ago, and the incrusting stalagmite whose formation is still going on, and to them it would be all alike, *solid limestone*. As these comparatively recent calcareous deposits are of very common occurrence, it would not be surprising that living batrachians should be found in them, even more frequently than they are.

TOADS IN A TREE
Daniels, C.; *Zoologist,* 2:11:4805, 1876

[Reports often place toads and frogs in closed cavities in trees as well as rocks of various kinds. So here, for the sake of completeness, is a tree tale.]

Perhaps the enclosed cutting from the "Uitenhage Times" (South Africa) of December 10th may not be uninteresting to some of your readers:—"A few weeks ago, at the Umgawali Forest, a tree with a trunk of sixteen feet long being on the saw-pit, when the bark and the first plank had been sawn off, a hole was found going inwards, the size of a wine-glass, from which the sawyers scraped out sixty-eight small toads. They were each the size of the upper joint of one's little finger, of a light brown, almost yellow colour, and perfectly healthy, hopping about and away as if nothing had happened. All about them was solid yellow wood, with nothing to indicate how they could have got there, how long they had been there, or how they could have lived without food, drink or air."

23

Musical Sands

Along the seacoasts of the world travelers occasionally encounter a peculiar variety of sand—sand that emits loud noises. It goes under various names: musical sand, barking sand, sonorous sand, and whistling sand, to name the most common. Regardless of the name applied, these sands squeak, roar, hum, or rumble when walked upon or otherwise disturbed by man or nature.

No deep dark secrets are implied by this chapter on musical sand, although some intriguing local legends have grown up around the phenomenon. Musical sands are merely geological curiosities, like ice caves or petrified trees. They may, of course, be the sources of some anomalous sounds, such as the "morning cry of the Sphinx," or the notorious Bell of Nakous, or possibly the droning hums heard near the seacoast in some areas.

Despite its lack of mystery, no one really understands the details of sound production in musical sand, including the veritably deafening roars emanating from some deposits. And just why are musical sands so localized; what special geological conditions are conducive to their formation? We will all survive if these questions remain unanswered, as they have during a century of scientific study, but the whole idea of musical sands is just too tantalizing to ignore in this sourcebook.

RESEARCHES ON SONOROUS SAND IN THE PENINSULA OF SINAI

Bolton, H. Carrington; *American Association for the Advancement of Science, Proceedings,* 38:137–140, 1889

Leaving New York, January 2, 1889, I reached Cairo January 31st, and in March entered the desert of Sinai; the village of Tor which is the starting point for *Jebel Nagous* is on the Gulf of Suez, but cannot conveniently be visited by water owing to contrary winds. Jebel Nagous is off the regular caravan routes and is not popularly known, hence has been visited but nine or ten times in eighty years by scientific travellers. About four and one-half hours northwest of Tor is the long detached mountain known as Jebel Nagous (or Abu Suweirah). On the steep slopes of this mountain rest several large banks of sand; one of these, which I distinguish by the name Seetzen's Bell Slope, after its discoverer, emits distinct musical sounds whenever the sand slides down the incline either spontaneously or through the agency of man. The mountain consists of massive white sandstone carrying quartz pebbles and veins; it is about three miles long and 1,200 feet high. The huge Bell Slope measures 260 feet across the base, five or six feet across the top and is 390 feet high; it is bounded by nearly vertical walls of sandstone. The yellowish white sand rests on the rocks at the high angle of 31°, is very fine grained, and composed chiefly of quartz and calcareous sandstone. The grains are well rounded to subangular, and silt is notably absent. As the sand reposes at a high angle it possesses a curious mobility which causes it to flow down the incline like soft pitch or molasses; the sand above the point of disturbance falls into the depression and this depression advances up the slope at the same time. This downward flow takes place spontaneously whenever the sand, forced up the incline by the violent winds, accumulates in such quantity as to exceed the angle of rest. The movement is accompanied by a strong vibration and by a musical tone resembling the lowest bass note of an organ with a tremolo stop. The larger the bulk of sand moved the louder the sound; it is by no means so sensitive as the sand of so-called singing beaches (which I have described elsewhere), and fails to emit sounds when struck with the hand or clapped together in a bag. The vertical cliffs on either side yield an echo that may magnify and prolong the sounds, which were loud enough to be heard several hundred feet. The peak of Jebel Nagous rises above the Slope to the height of 955 feet above the sea level.

The sand of the slope is derived partly from disintegration of the rock itself and partly from the more distant plain below, from which violent winds blow it up on to the mountain side.

The Bedouins of the region account for the acoustic phenomenon by attributing it to the *Nagous* or wooden gong of a subterranean monastery in the heart of the mountain, and claim the sounds can only be heard at the hours of prayers.

Several other sandbanks presenting a similar appearance to the eye were tested but gave out no musical sounds whatever. Microscopical examination of these sands shows that they contain much silt, which prevents the vibrations necessary to yield the sounds. After careful study, however, of Seetzen's Bell Slope I became convinced that the phenomena could not be unique in the desert as supposed, and I made systematic search for another locality. After testing many sandbanks on the journey northward to Suez I discovered, April 6th, banks of sonorous sand resting on low cliffs a quarter of a mile long. This new locality is in Wadi Werdan about a day and a half from Suez, by camels, and is on hillocks called Ojrat Ramadan.

The sand blown from the extensive plains to the north, falls over the southern face and rests at two angles, 31° at the top and 21° or less near the base. Wherever it possesses the mobility before described it emits a distinct musical note on being disturbed. The highest bank measures only sixty feet on the incline, and it is not probable that the sounds can occur spontaneously. Dr. Julien has named the new locality Bolton's Bell Slope, and reports that microscopical examination shows the sand to consist chiefly of quartz grains, and a larger proportion of calcareous sandstone than at Jebel Nagous. The size of the grains of quartz varies from 0.11 to 0.42 mm. and of sandstone 0.11 to 0.34 mm., the average being smaller than that of the sand grains on Jebel Nagous. Like the latter it is very free from silt.

SONOROUS SAND IN NEVADA
Anonymous; *Knowledge,* 3:63–64, 1883

The Reno, Nevada, *Gazette* describes a remarkable hill of moving sand in the eastern part of Churchill County, Nevada, about sixty miles from Land Springs Station. It is about four miles long and about a mile wide. In the whole dune, which is from 100 to 400 feet in height, and contains millions of tons of sand, it is impossible to find a particle larger than a pin head. It is so fine that if an ordinary barley sack be filled and placed in a moving waggon, the jolting of the vehicle would empty the sack, and yet it has no form of dust in it, and is as clean as any sea-beach sand. The mountain is so solid as to give it a musical sound when trod upon, and oftentimes a bird lighting on it, or a large lizard running across the bottom, will start a large quantity of the sand to sliding, which makes a noise resembling the vibration of telegraph wires with a hard wind blowing, but so much louder that it is often heard at a distance of six or seven miles, and it is deafening to a person standing within a short distance of the sliding sand. A peculiar feature of the dune is that it is not stationary, but rolls slowly eastward, the wind gathering it up on the west end, and carrying it along the ridge until it is again deposited at the eastern end. Mr. Monroe, the well-known surveyor, having heard of the rambling habits of this mammoth sand-heap, quite a number of years ago took a careful bearing of it while sectioning Government lands in that vicinity. Several years later he visited the place, and found that the dune had moved something over a mile.

MUSICAL SAND IN CHILE
Gray, M. H.; *Nature,* 81:126–127, July 29, 1909

Some few miles to the west of the town of Copiapo, in Chile, and, so far as my recollection of the locality carries me, about half a mile to the southward of the railway line, there is a tailing off of a ragged hill-range, which runs about north and south. In a ravine—it is too small to be called a valley—the sand which covers the greater part of that portion of Chile has, blown doubtless by the sea-breeze, been carried up the gully to which I refer, and lies there at a slope equal to the flowing angle of dry sand. The place is locally known by the name of "El Punto del Diablo," as, given conditions of wind and weather, which time did not allow me to study, a low moaning sound, varying in intensity, can be heard for quite a quarter of a mile away. Amongst the superstitious natives the place is avoided. Thinking it worth a visit, I went there with the late Mr. Edwards, who was then the British Consul in that district. On our arrival we found that the sands were quite silent, but on making a glissade down the slope a gradually increasing "rumble" was heard, which increased in volume as the sand slid away before us. As the sound increased we were subjected to an undulatory movement, so decided that it was difficult to keep one's balance, and as we both had heard that this sand had swept over an old silver mine, there was a clear impression on the minds of both that the vibration might break in the roof of the old workings. I write of this experience for what it is worth. I do not know whether the ground under the sand was hollow or solid, and although I have ventured to theorise on the subject, as yet I have found no satisfactory solution of this, to me, quite unique experience.

THE SINGING BEACH OF MANCHESTER, MASS.
Bolton, H. C., and Julien, A. A.; *American Association for the Advancement of Science, Proceedings,* 32:251–252, 1883

Abstract. The authors describe the acoustic phenomena observed by one of them at Manchester-by-the-Sea, Mass., and on the island of Eigg, Hebrides, together with the results of microscopical examination of the sands. The beach at Manchester forms a small crescent about three-quarters of a mile long, and is terminated at each end by bold promontories of granite, rich in feldspar, and intersected by numerous dykes of igneous rocks among which porphyritic diorite is noticeable. The beach sand resembles at first sight ordinary sea-shore sand, but when struck by the foot, or stroked by the hand, yields a peculiar sound which may be likened to a subdued crushing; the sound is of low intensity and pitch, and is not metallic nor crackling. This phenomenon is confined to that part of the beach lying between water-line and the loose sand above the reach of ordinary high tide. Some parts of the beach emit a louder sound than others. The sounding sand is near the surface only; at the depth of one or two feet the acoustic properties disappear, probably owing to the moisture. Only the dry sand has this property. The sounds occur when walking over the beach, increase when the sand is struck obliquely by the foot, and can be intensified by dragging over it a wooden pole or board. A slight noise is perceptible upon mere stirring by the hand, or upon plunging one finger into the sand and suddenly withdrawing it.

The character of the sounds obtained by friction on the beach at Manchester, Mass., is decidedly musical and we have been able to indicate the exact notes on a musical staff. The shrillness and lowness of note depend chiefly on the quantity of sand disturbed; by plunging both hands into the sand and bringing them together quickly with a swoop a large quantity of the sand vibrates and we hear a tone of which the dominant note is

By stroking the sand nearer the surface and with less force very high notes are heard somewhat confused. The following were heard at different times.

By rubbing firmly and briskly a double handful of the sand several notes on a rising scale are heard, the notes rising as the quantity of sand between the hands diminishes. We do not hear each note of the scale separately, but the ear receives an impression something like that formed by sliding a finger up a violin string at the same time that the bow is drawn.

Similar beaches occur in various parts of the world. One of us visited the island of Eigg, Hebrides, in July and found the acoustic phenomena quite similar to those of Manchester. The Eigg locality has been described by its discoverer Hugh Miller. One of the most famous localities in the world is on the island of Kauai, of the Hawaii Islands. There the sounds are said to be so loud as to resemble distant thunder, when any great weight is dragged over it. As elsewhere dampness prevents the sound. The sand is almost wholly calcareous and has been examined by Dr. Blake of San Francisco.

In other places sonorous sand is associated with high dunes or steep hills; of these the most famous is Jebel Nakous on the Gulf of Suez, in Arabia Petraea, which has been described by many European travellers. A similar hill exists near Cabul in Afghanistan. The sand of these hills is silicious. In Churchill Co. Nevada, a somewhat similar phenomenon is described, the sound being likened to that produced by telegraph wires when the wind blows through them.

Microscopical examination of the sands from several localities shows them to be unlike in constitution, in form, and in structure. The sand of Manchester is about fifty per cent feldspar, that of Kauai is calcareous, that of Eigg silicious. The latter is peculiar in containing dark granules of chert (to about three or four per cent of the whole) which has a cellular structure. The quartz is present in various sizes, some rounded and others angular.

To explain the sonorous properties of these sands several theories are considered. That of equality of size of the grains is rejected. Reasonance due to cellular structure probably accounts for the sound in the sands of Kauai and of Eigg, but this structure does not occur in other cases. Effervescence of air between moistened surfaces does not apply to the Manchester sand. Sonorous mineral or rock, such as clinkstone, is not present. There is no evidence of electrical phenomena being concerned. The hypothesis adopted is based upon the structure of the sand which, instead of being composed of the usual rounded particles, is made up of grains with flat and angular surfaces. In the Manchester sand, the plane surface of feldspar is apparent in many of the grains. Probably a certain proportion of quartz and feldspar grains is adapted to give the sound, while less or more of either component would fail of the result.

It is concluded that different conditions are concerned in the production of the sound in different localities; as, for example, cellular structure, intermixture of grains having cleavage planes, parallel arrangement, slight cementation of the grains, etc.

THE "BARKING SANDS" OF THE HAWAIIAN ISLANDS
Bolton, H. Carrington; *Nature*, 42:389–390, August 21, 1890

About a year ago *Nature* printed my letter from Cairo giving a condensed account of an examination of the Mountain of the Bell (*Jebel Nagous*) on the Gulf of Suez, and of the acoustic phenomenon from which it is named. In continuation of my researches on sonorous sand, which are conducted jointly with Dr. Alexis A. Julien, of New York, I have now visited the so-called "barking sands" on the island of Kauai. These are mentioned in the works of several travellers (Bates, Frink, Bird, Nordhoff, and others), and have a world-wide fame as a natural curiosity; but the printed accounts are rather meagre in details and show their authors to have been unacquainted with similar phenomena elsewhere.

On the south coast of Kauai, in the district of Mana, sand-dunes attaining a height of over one hundred feet extend for a mile or more nearly parallel to the sea, and cover hundreds of acres with the water-worn and wind-blown fragments of shells and coral. The dunes are terminated on the west by bold cliffs (*Pali*) whose base is washed by the sea; at the east end the range terminates in a dune more symmetrical in shape than the majority, having on the land side the appearance of a broadened truncated cone. The sands on the top and on the landward slope of this dune (being about 100 yards from the sea) possess remarkable acoustic properties, likened to the bark of a dog. The dune has a maximum height of 108 feet, but the slope of sonorous sand is only 60 feet above the level field on which it is encroaching. At its steepest part, the angle being quite uniformly 31°, the sand has a notable mobility when perfectly dry. And on disturbing its equilibrium, it rolls in wavelets down the incline, emitting at the same time a deep bass note of a tremulous character. My companion thought the sound resembled the hum of a buzz saw on a planing mill. A vibration is sometimes perceived in the hands or feet of the person moving the sand. The magnitude of the sound is dependent upon the quantity of sand moved, and probably to a certain extent upon the temperature. The drier the sand the greater the amount possessing mobility, and the louder the sound. At the time of my visit the sand was dry to the depth of four or five inches; its temperature three inches beneath the surface was 87°F., that of the air being 83° in the shade (4:30 p.m.).

When a large mass of sand was moved downward I heard the sound at a distance of 105 feet from the base, a light wind blowing at right angles to the direction. On one occasion horses standing close to the base were disturbed by the rumbling sound. When the sand is clapped between the hands a slight hoot-like sound is heard; but a louder sound is produced by confining it in a bag, dividing the contents into two parts and bringing them together violently. This I had found to be the best way of testing sea-shore sand as to its sonorousness. The sand on the top of the dune is wind furrowed, and generally coarser than that of the slope of 31°, but this also yielded a sound of unmistakable character when so tested. A bag full of sand will preserve its power for some time, especially if not too frequently manipulated. A creeping vine with a blue or purple blossom (kolokolo) thrives on these dunes, and interrupts the sounding slope. I found the main slope 120 feet long at its base; but the places not covered by this vine gave sounds at intervals 160 paces westward. At 94 paces further the sand was nonsonorous.

The native Hawaiians call this place *Nohili,* a word of no specific meaning, and attribute the sound caused by the sand to the spirits of the dead, *uhane,* who grumble at being disturbed; sand-dunes being commonly used for burial-places, especially in early times, as bleached skeletons and well-preserved skulls at several places abundantly show.

Sand of similar properties is reported to occur at *Haula,* about three miles east of Koloa, Kauai; this I did not visit, but, prompted by information communicated by the Hon. Vladimar Knudsen, of Waiawa, I crossed the channel to the little-visited island of Niihau. On the western coast of this islet, at a place called *Kaluakahua,* sonorous sand occurs on the land side of a dune about 100 feet high, and at several points for 600 to 800 feet along the coast. On the chief slope, 36 feet high, the sand has the same mobility, lies at the same angle, and gives when disturbed the same note as the sand of Kauai, but less strong, the slope being so much lower. This locality has been known to the residents of the island for many years, but has never been before announced in print. This range of dunes, driven before the high winds, is advancing southward, and has already covered the road formerly skirting the coast.

The observations made at these places are of especial interest, because they confirm views already advanced by Dr. Julien and myself with regard to the identity of the phenomena on sea-beaches and on hill-sides in arid regions (*Jebel Nagous,* Rig-i-Rawan, &c.). The sand of the Hawaiian Islands possesses the acoustic properties of both classes of places; it gives out the same note as that of Jebel Nagous when rolling down the slope, and it yields a peculiar hoot-like sound when struck together in a bag, like the sands of Eigg, of Manchester (Mass.), and other sea-beaches—a property that the sand of Jebel Nagous does not possess. These Hawaiian sands also show how completely independent of material is the acoustic quality, for they are wholly carbonate of lime, whereas sonorous sands of all other localities known to us (now over one hundred in number) are siliceous, being either pure silex or a mixture of the same with silicates, as feldspar.

The theory proposed by Dr. Julien and myself to explain the sonorousness has been editorially noticed in *Nature,* but may properly be briefly stated in this connection. We believe the sonorousness in sands of sea-beaches and of deserts to be connected with thin pellicles or films of air, or of gases thence derived, deposited and condensed upon the surface of the sand grains during gradual evaporation after wetting by the seas, lakes, or rains. By virtue of these films the sand grains become separated by elastic cushions of condensed gases, capable of considerable vibration, and whose thickness we have approximately determined. The extent of the vibrations, and the volume and pitch of the sounds thereby produced after any quick disturbance of the sand, we also find to be largely dependent upon the forms, structures, and surfaces of the sand grains, and especially upon their purity, or freedom from fine silt or dust (*Proceedings Am. Assoc. Adv. Sci.,* 38, 1889).

ROARING SANDS OF THE KALAHARI DESERT
Anonymous; *Nature,* 140:285, August 14, 1937

Mr. A. D. Lewis has recently given an interesting account of these sands (*S. African Geog. J.,* 19, 33–49; 1936). They lie at the south end of an elongated patch of whitish sand dunes near the south-east corner of the Kalahari desert, and the roars are heard most intensely along the southern face, which rises nearly 100 ft. at a slope of about 1 in 2. Compared with the rest of the desert sands, the grains are perhaps more rounded and of a more uniform size and shape. Mr. Lewis describes two types of noise, a roar caused by pushing the sands forward in a heaped-up manner and a hum by keeping the sand moving slowly down the slope. A very loud roar is produced by sitting on the slope and sliding down it in slow jerks. In the still of the early evening or morning, such a noise is easily heard, like the rumbling of distant thunder, at a distance of 600 yd. Merely moving the fingers up and down the sand produces a roar, the upward motion giving a higher note than the downward. Samples of the sand were taken in bags to Pretoria, and it was found that a roar was obtained by tilting the bag over sharply when half empty. If the bags were left open, the roar was lost after a few weeks, though it could be restore for a short time by heating the sand in an oven.

24

Carolina Bays by the Million

Upward of a million shallow, water-filled depressions dot the eastern seaboard of the United States. They are concentrated on the coastal plain of the Carolinas, thus the name Carolina Bays. A tremendous amount of material has been written about the bays, even complete books. Most of the good articles are too long to reproduce in full here. The first selection, by Prouty, providing an excellent summary of the geological facts, is only part of his lengthy defense of the meteorite hypothesis for the bays' origin. The second selection, by Kelly, is included for two reasons: (1) he brings the oriented lakes of Alaska into the discussion (they may have a similar origin); and (2) he offers his own, rather intriguing theory for the formation of the Carolina Bays.

The big mystery of the Carolina Bays has always been their origin. They have been thoroughly mapped, measured, dredged, and magnetically surveyed, and still no one is certain how they were created. The meteorite theory is highly favored today even though no meteorites have been found that are specifically associated with any of the bays. This does not rule out the meteorite theory, because the site of the famous 1908 Siberian meteor event reveals no large chunks of meteoric material either. If the meteorite theory is correct, the Carolina collision must have shaken the earth to its foundations, perhaps reversing its magnetic field and causing biological extinctions. The main mass of the meteorite could have landed offshore in the Atlantic sending colossal tidal waves around the world. Such catastrophism, however, may never have transpired. The Carolina Bays may have been formed unspectacularly by the action of wind-driven currents, springs, of freezing and thawing action during an ice age. The Alaskan oriented lakes, for example, are now thought to be a type of "patterned ground" formed in arctic climes. But did arctic weather reach clear down to the Carolinas and Georgia in recent geologic time?

CAROLINA BAYS AND THEIR ORIGIN
Prouty, W. F.; *Geological Society of America, Bulletin,* 63: 167–224, 1952

Distribution, Coverage, Number, and Grouping of Carolina Bays. The Carolina Bays are entirely confined in their occurrence to the Atlantic Coastal Plain and a few coastal plain outliers. The large percentage of these rimmed, elliptical depressions are found in South Carolina and southeastern North Carolina. The bays also occur in rather large numbers for some distance to the west of the Savannah River in Georgia. Scattered bays also occur in the south and north central parts of the Georgia Coastal Plain in groups and clusters, as they do in the north central part of the Coastal Plain of North Carolina. A very few scattered bays are to be found even in extreme northeastern Florida and in the Chesapeake Bay Region of Virginia and Maryland, and three or four questionable bays exist in New Jersey.

Concentration of large bays occurs in some localities as does the concentration of small bays in other localities, but in general there is a fairly uniform mingling of sizes in the distribution. In some parts of the bay area, a number of overlapping bays occur in a northwest-southeast line, giving elongated "multiple bays." In other parts of the area, several bays overlap, making broad, more or less pear-shaped or heart-shaped "multiple bays." Roughly speaking the larger bays occur in greater proportion in two large districts, one in the southeastern North Carolina-northeastern South Carolina district and the other in the southwestern South Carolina-northeastern Georgia district. The North Carolina district includes the large Lake Waccamaw bay which has a length of over 6 miles, a sand

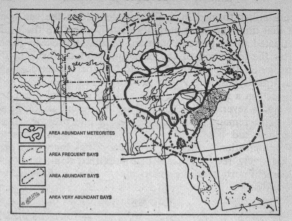

Geographical relation of Carolina Bay area with area of abundant meteorites.

rim at the southeast end about 23 feet above the lake level, and a width of over 2000 feet. At several localities in the Carolinas, small bays are found within a few hundred yards of the inner edge of the coastal plain. In a few localities in Georgia, "ghost" or remnant bays are found on coastal plain outliers a little distance into the Piedmont from the unbroken coastal plain line. These outliers were formerly part of the Coastal Plain before streams removed much of the sand cover from the underlying Piedmont rocks.

Some bays were without doubt formed in the lowlands, in many cases river bottoms, as well as in the interstream areas and valley slopes. Skeleton bays can be seen in a few places in the floodplain of the Cape Fear River and partially destroyed bays can be seen along the present river banks. Some bays project across waterways or are partly concealed by river swamps. There are no bays to be seen in the more recently formed portions of the Coastal Plain and for 7 miles inland from the coast town of Myrtle Beach, South Carolina. Going inland and north toward Conway, South Carolina, the first bays to be seen show signs of having been partially destroyed by wave action. It is logical to conclude that the bays

were either formed in shallow water along the sea coast
of that time and were partially destroyed before the ocean
retreated to its present position, or that the ocean raised
after the formation of the bays and migrated back to the
position of the partially destroyed bays before retreating to
its present position. Partial destruction of bay rims is to
be seen in a number of places along the coastal areas and
in places several miles back from the present shore. Study
of plant remains in the sediments of the present coastal
swamps and beach ridges by Professor Wells (personal
communication) confirms the theory that there has been
a relatively recent sea advance and retreat along a considerable portion of the coast line of the Carolinas. In the
Wilmington, North Carolina, area, as pointed out also by
Wells, peat deposits in Blythe Bay which have been covered by several feet of marine sediments are now ex-

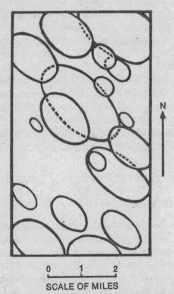

SCALE OF MILES

*Concentration of bays in portion of Bladen County,
North Carolina. About 65 per cent of the area is
covered by bays, including overlap. Bays smaller than
1900 feet long are not shown.*

posed by stream erosion. This seems to show a marine invasion and retreat some time after the formation of the peat in the bay.

As far as known the Carolina Bays were formed under both geographical and time limitations, later than the formation of most of the Pamlico Terrace.

The area of distribution of the bays is about 83,000 square miles. Of this area, perhaps 43,000 square miles have very few or no bays. The bays cover, including overlap, roughly about 10 per cent of the surface. Where bays are large and thickly distributed, they may cover more than 50 per cent of the surface. Two large areas in Bladen County, North Carolina, were measured. In one of these, 7 miles long by 4 miles wide, the area covered by bays was found to be a little over 50 per cent. Another section of Bladen County, 5 miles by 4 miles, had a bay area of 67½ per cent. In places, 20 bays to the square mile, each longer than 500 feet, have been counted. Some of the large bays cover several square miles. These, in some cases, may be made up of several overlapping bays. Many bays are concealed in heavily wooded, swampy, or river-bottom lands.

A conservative estimate of 3.5 bays to the square mile, each longer than 500 feet, gives an estimate of 140,000 bays of moderate and large size. It is almost impossible to estimate the number of small bays. One might be justified in roughly guessing that the total number of bays, large and small, is about half a million.

THE ORIGIN OF THE CAROLINA BAYS AND THE ORIENTED LAKES OF ALASKA
Kelly, Allan O.; *Popular Astronomy*, 59:199–205, April 1951

[Kelly has long belonged to the school that claims many topological features of the earth were caused by the impact of large meteorites. Thus it is surprising to find him advocating a radically different origin for the Carolina Bays and the oriented Alaskan lakes, although his theory does depend ultimately upon catastrophism.]

The origin of the Carolina Bays and the Oriented Lakes of Northern Alaska is a problem that has long intrigued the scientific world. Probably the great interest in this scientific puzzle arises from the fact that Melton and Schriever, geologists from the University of Oklahoma, who first discovered the Carolina Bays, attributed them to a gigantic shower of meteorites. This interpretation was made in 1933. Such a spectacular theory immediately aroused the interest of the Press and several articles appeared in popular magazines describing the fearful holocaust that must have occurred. Following this introduction to the public, the scientific world began to investigate. Many different hypotheses were proposed but none seemed to fulfill all the requirements. Dr. Douglas Johnson, a geologist of Columbia University, said of these bays or depressions: "They are without doubt one of the most remarkable geomorphic features on the surface of the earth. They share with submarine canyons the distinction of being among the most difficult of earth forms to explain." Johnson was unaware of the Oriented Lakes of Alaska.

The Oriented Lakes of Northern Alaska were first investigated by R. F. Black and W. L. Barksdale of the United States Geological Survey. They published a rather complete article about these lakes in the *Journal of Geology* in March of 1949. They did not propose a complete theory of origin but they did give a table of comparisons between the Carolina Bays and these lakes. It was shown that out of 17 items of comparison, the two groups were similar in all but five. Among other things they concluded that "The Carolina Bays and the Oriented Lakes of Alaska are so strikingly similar that it is believed that the conditions operating to produce them must have been, at least in part, similar." No one else, so far as we know, has made any investigation or any proposal as to the origin of these lakes.

It is not our purpose in this short article to criticize other theories of origin but rather to advance one which we believe answers all of the requirements, so far as we know them.

This theory is based on cosmic collision as the motivating energy that produced these bays or lakes, and, in fact, the force that has produced most of the physical features of the earth. Such collisions and the oceanic floods that must have followed, can explain every unexplained problem of modern geology, including submarine canyons.

Many thousands of these collisions have occurred in the earth's long history and the last major one caused the Biblical Flood which is also recorded by many other races of people. The physical evidences of this last great flood are found all around the world, in tremendous gravel deposits in unusual locations; in old shore lines high above the present levels of inland lakes such as Great Salt Lake and the Dead Sea; in recent glaciation and evident change of climate; in prehistoric animals found frozen in the Arctic, and a vast array of other physical evidence that cannot be mentioned here.

The Carolina Bays and Oriented Lakes of Alaska are only a small part of this great array of collision evidence, but they are the immediate concern of this article and one more step in proving the collision theory. Our reasoning is as follows: Before this last great catastrophe, the North Pole was located near Apatak Island in Hudson Strait. This fact is proved by drawing an arctic circle around this point, which is then found to contain all the glaciated area of North America, including Greenland and Iceland. These two islands were in practically the same relative position to the old arctic circle as they are today, so that their ice conditions have not changed.

It will be seen, then, that a considerable part of the North Atlantic was well within this old arctic circle and so must have contained large quantities of sea ice and glacial ice. On the other side of the circle, the Arctic Ocean also was in a position suitable to the production of ice.

The meteorite or asteroid, which caused this last cataclysm, struck the earth at a point which was then just outside the arctic circle but now off our South Atlantic Coast. It formed a great under-sea crater whose outlines can be traced for hundreds of miles as a nearly perpendicular wall. When this collision occurred it moved the surface of the earth in relation to the rays of the sun and at the same time changed the axis of the earth to its present location. A new alignment would certainly follow if the striking body penetrated the crust of the earth and added its weight to one side of the earth flywheel. On the other hand, if it only struck a glancing blow, the earth would probably wobble a little like a spinning top and soon regain its former axis. All the evidence seems to indicate that this object did penetrate the crust of the earth.

Such a collision would, of course, cause a terrific earth shock felt all over the world. The polar ice cap would have been shattered and the oceanic flood that followed would have floated vast quantities of ice far away from its source. Geologists have estimated the ice over Hudson Bay to have been over two miles thick. This ice and the ice in the Great Lakes apparently melted in place but the old polar cap was elevated and the ice moved off the land in all directions as the grooves in the rocks so plainly indicate. The glacial ice and sea ice that was floated by this flood must have rushed back with these waters to fill the impact point. This ice would have melted quickly in such an inferno* but some of the sea ice far away near the coast of Greenland might have trailed far behind and missed this hot water bath. This ice could have been stranded like a great fleet of ships, for wind and tide would have tended to orientate them to some degree. When they grounded on the coastal plain, the seaward end of each berg or cake of ice would float more easily. Thus the bergs were grounded or anchored like ships in a harbor and would swing with the tide, all pointing in the same direction as the outgoing tide. As the tides receded, there came a time when the bergs failed to float on the incoming tide and so remained in this fixed position until melted.

Once the stranded bergs were firmly fixed on the bottom, the tides began to shape the land surfaces between. Since ice floats with about nine-tenths of its mass below the surface, this grounding would take place while the tidal floods were still quite deep for these cakes of ice might have been several hundred feet thick, judging by Antarctic sea ice. The ice in the Carolina Bay region probably remained for a year or so after the tides had returned to normal but in Alaska, they may have remained hundreds of years before melting completely.

The length of time that might have passed before the tides returned to normal would be difficult to determine by geological observation but the Biblical account of the Deluge tells us that the waters were "Going and returning

---

*The Finns have a legend of a hot water flood.

continually for one hundred and fifty days." This seems like a reasonable estimate of the time that might have been required.

Major Chapman Grant, of San Diego, California, who visited the Carolina Bays in 1948, describes the area as not really a flat plain but a region in which low gravel hills are interspersed with bays of a little lower elevation and with stream channels a little lower than the bays. He also pointed out that seldom, if ever, does a stream flow from one bay to the next as is the case in all other lake country, but always around the bays. In like manner the gravel hills do not encroach upon the bays nor do the so-called beach ridges. Johnson and others were at a loss to explain why these old surf lines or beach ridges, as they called them, did not cross the bays for the ridges are no higher than the bay rims. All these questions are easily answered if we imagine a cake of ice in each bay and tidal waters flowing in and out among these obstructions.

At first, when the tides were deep and strong, the gravel hills were deposited in the larger open areas between bergs. At the same time, channels were eroded out where the bergs were closer together and the current stronger. This kept the gravel hills from approaching too close to the bergs and produced the "kettle holes" or basins around each berg. Big bergs usually produced the dominant current and so the bays formed by little bergs close by seldom overlap the rims of bays made by bigger bergs. There are exceptions to this overlapping of rims, but, in general, the rule holds good. There are, in fact, exceptions to every general feature of uniformity in the Carolina Bays but all of these exceptions can be explained by the varying shape of the bergs, by distance of separation, and by the varying current of water flowing between them. Aerial photographs show this flow pattern around fixed objects so plainly that one wonders why this explanation was not forthcoming long ago.

Another characteristic feature of the bays is the occurrence of rows or chains of bays. Many chains of three or more are found nearly touching one another and with stream channels on either side. Usually these chains are made up of bays of nearly equal size and may have resulted from a large berg breaking up after grounding. In any event, such a chain would force the water to flow parallel to the sides of such group and the current would tend to arrange them in better alignment. These chains occur so frequently in the Carolina Bay region that they became a stumbling block to the advocates of the meteoritic theory, for it seemed beyond the realm of chance that meteorites should fall in many rows.

Since the ice probably remained long after the tides receded, the final melting took place without any passing current. Thus the final melt-water overflowed the bowl in which each berg was sitting and produced the delicate sand rims, even improving upon the symmetry that the tidal current had produced. Later, small channels were cut in the rim of each bay, allowing the greater part of each lake to drain into the stream channels.

The Oriented Lakes of Alaska show greatest deviation from the Carolina Bays in that the water drains from one lake to the next. This may be explained by the fact that Alaska was moved from a north temperature climate into the arctic; that the ice bergs stranded there did not melt for many hundreds of years; and that the streams and vegetation built up the land around them so that when the bergs did finally disappear, the streams were forced to flow from one lake to the next.

The Alaskan Lakes cover an area somewhat larger in size than the Carolina Bays, being about 450 miles east and west and extending from Point Barrow south about 100 miles. As in the Carolina region, the biggest lakes are found near the coast for the largest bergs grounded first. Farther inland the lakes become more scattered, less elongated, and more erratic in orientation. A few scattered lakes of smaller size are also found near the coast, but on higher ridges and plateaus, apparently because smaller bergs were thrown to greater heights by the first great tides and were less well orientated because of the shallower tidal currents following.

In outline, the Alaska Lakes are more rectangular than the Carolina Bays. This was probably due to a different fracture pattern and to the different orientation relative to the sun. The Carolina Bays are oriented in a northwest-southeast direction and therefore the northeast and east side of most bergs received more sunlight and melted faster. This difference in exposure to the sun produced the curious ovoid shape with the straighter side on the shady side. Where bergs were close together so that one might shade the other, the curvature on the shady side fits the theory. Another point bearing this out, is the fact that in large bays with multiple rims, the outer older rim is always a more perfect oval, showing that as the berg melted faster on the sunny side the new formed rims changed in shape with the berg. No other theory has ever been able to account for these multiple rims or the ovoid shape.

In Alaska the lakes are pointed more nearly north and south, the average trend being 12 degrees west of north. Being well above the Arctic Circle (most of them above 70 degrees north) the summer sun shone on all sides of the bergs with little favoritism, so that a more even rectangular shape was achieved.

Another possible reason for the uniformity in outline of these bays and lakes would be that the shock waves from the collision, through the water and through the earth, produced a uniform pattern in cracking the ice. This same collision shock pattern may be seen in the grid-like pattern of the mountains on the moon, especially in the mountain rim around Mare Imbrium. Shock waves traveling outwardly and upwardly might fracture ice floating on a sphere, in boat-shaped forms. In Alaska, which was much more distant from the point of collision than the Atlantic ice, the shock might have cracked the ice in a more rectangular pattern. Such a shattering of ice would almost surely produce a uniformity of some shape but there would be many minor variations. Such is the case, in both Alaska and Carolina, and, as the old proverb goes, "The exception proves the rule."

Conclusion. We believe that the Carolina Bays and the Oriented Lakes of Alaska were formed by strong tidal currents flowing around fixed objects that have since disappeared, that cakes of sea ice are, so far as we know, the only large objects in nature that could have fulfilled all the requirements, and that cosmic collision flood is the only possible force that could have moved them into place. We therefore rest our case and await the onslaught of our critics.

25

Mima Mounds: Also by the Million

A Mima mound is the upside-down counterpart of a Carolina bay—a hill rather than a depression—low in profile, and extremely abundant in some areas and totally absent in others. The name Mima mound is usually applied only to the mounds on the Mima Prairie in the state of Washington. But we also have the pimpled plains of Oklahoma; the San Diego hillocks; hogwallows; and mounds by other names elsewhere. A map of some of these formations is reproduced with the second selection. For some unknown reasons, North America seems to have more than its share of natural mounds. Australia has its "puffs," but reports from elsewhere are conspicuous by their absence. Possibly mound formations exist on other continents but have been unknowingly filtered out by the Sourcebook Project's preoccupation with literature in English.

As with the Carolina Bays, the Mima mound controversy centers on origin and not the basic facts. Are the mounds a type of patterned ground caused by repeated freezing and thawing, a southern representative of the Arctic's strangely contoured flatlands? Wind action and the incessant labors of the pocket gopher have also been suggested. The latter idea is the target of much ridicule when the size of the gopher is compared to the rather impressive mounds; but consider Africa's anthills and, of course, the Egyptian pyramids.

The hundreds of thousands, probably millions, of mounds and hillocks have more than curiosity value. Their immense numbers reflect wide-scale geological processes we do not understand. If their origin is the same as that of arctic patterned ground, their existence in the southern United States tells us much about the continent's climate during their formation. Other kinds of evidence has been accumulating suggesting that the ice age (if it actually occurred) left its marks far to the south of the ice sheet's terminal moraines that stretch across the midsection of the United States.

THE MYSTERY OF THE MIMA MOUNDS

Scheffer, Victor B.; *Scientific Monthly*, 65:283–294, October 1947 (With permission of the American Association for the Advancement of Science)

[This is one of the classic articles on the Mima Mounds. However, the reader should be warned that many scientists do not concur with Scheffer's "gopher theory," as the subsequent selections show.]

On the prairies of western Washington near the southern tip of Puget Sound are scattered thousands of large earth mounds whose origin has puzzled observers for more than a century. On Mima Prairie some of the mounds are higher than a man's head and have a content of 50 cubic yards. The mounds are smooth and round, like great spheres nearly buried in the earth. In many cases, the hollows between the mounds are filled with cobblestones up to the size of a football. In the spring of the year, when the mounds are covered with white-and-yellow daisies and green bracken ferns, they stand out clearly from their duller surroundings.

Wherever a mound has been sliced open by a roadway, a peculiar cross section is revealed. The typical mound is made up of soft black prairie silt mixed with pebbles up to the size of a walnut. The mound rests in a slight depression, or bed, in coarse, stratified glacial gravel, which continues downward for an unexplored distance. Thus, the typical mound is a biconvex lens, with the greater curvature exposed to the sky and the lesser curvature pressed against the gravel. At the base of the mound, armlike structures of black silt extend into the gravel. These have been called "mound roots" by certain investigators.

The origin of the mounds has long been disputed. A few years ago, a student at the University of Washington suggested a novel theory to account for the mounds and invited me to join him in a search for supporting evidence. How we approached the problem and attempted to fit our findings into a convincing pattern has been described in a preliminary paper.

As we delved into the mystery of the Mima Mounds, it dawned on us that these formations are kindred to similar, though less spectacular, mounds strewn by the millions over the Western states from the Mexican border to northern Washington. Thus, the theory accounting for the mounds of Puget Sound—which we now accept—embraces also the countless mounds of similar shape and structure in the Western states. Because of certain peculiar features, Mima Prairie has served as a Rosetta stone in explaining the origin of other mound prairies.

More than a century ago mound prairies drew the attention of travelers in the new West. In July 1842, Commander Charles Wilkes made a special trip to "Bute Prairie," south of Olympia, Wash., and dug into three of the mounds in an attempt to unlock their secret. He finally concluded that "they bear the marks of savage labour, and are such an undertaking as would have required the united efforts of a whole tribe." As indeed they would!

On the famous railroad survey of 1853–56, naturalists Gibbs and Cooper examined some of the mounds, and Gibbs suggested that "they might have been produced by the immense growth of the 'giant root,' (*Megarhiza* (*Echinocystis*) *Oregana*), forming a nucleus around which the soil has been gradually washed away." Cooper— a more conservative scientist—believed that the mounds were perhaps the result of eddy and whirlpool action at a time when the prairies were submerged beneath Puget Sound. When Gibbs returned to the East he described the mounds to Louis Agassiz, who "unhesitatingly" pronounced them the nests of a species of sucker. Professor Agassiz may be forgiven this opinion in view of the fact that he had not seen the mounds, some of which rise to a height of seven feet.

Joseph LeConte, geologist of the University of California, first saw the Puget Sound prairies in 1871. He was the first to point out the similarities among the mounds in California, Oregon, and Washington and he tried to show that their origin was due to "surface erosion under peculiar conditions." As he reconstructed their geological history, the prairies were left by a retreating body of water with a blanket of fine topsoil and a coarse subsoil; erosion started to remove the finer topsoil everywhere but in certain spots; weeds, shrubs, and ferns immediately seized upon these spots, or islands, and anchored the soil; then when the climate grew drier, vegetation was able to survive only on the higher (and richer) islands while erosion continued to gnaw at their bases.

Interest in the American earth mounds was aroused in faraway England, Geologist Alfred R. Wallace discussed a letter from his brother in California describing the "hog-wallow" region of the San Joaquin Valley.

The surface thus designated [he wrote] may be represented on a small scale by covering the bottom of a large flat dish with eggs distributed so that their longer axes shall lie at various angles with one another, and then filling the dish with fine sand to a little more than half the height of the eggs.

The California brother attributed the mounds to "innumerable rills that issued from the retiring sheet of ice" of a glacier long since disappeared. (It is now well established that the San Joaquin Valley was at no time covered by ice.)

Soon afterward, G. W. Barnes discussed the small hillocks that lie on the old sea terraces back of San Diego. He concluded that the San Diego mounds were produced —and are still being produced—by a peculiar combination of wind and water erosion in the presence of vegetation, as follows: prevailing winds deposit dust and leaves at the base of a shrubby desert plant; rain-water erosion cuts faster at the base of the mound than at the top; the shrub eventually dies; and, "deprived of its protection, the summit is reduced and the base widened as it is lowered, till finally a remnant of the deposit has become so assimilated and compact as to constitute a more permanent summit." Accompanied by Dr. K. O. Emery, I examined the San

Diego mounds in 1943 and found them very like the mounds of Puget Sound.

In a resume in 1905, J. C. Branner disposed of a number of theories to account for the Western mounds and concluded: "The ant-hill theory seems to me the most plausible, but with our present knowledge it is far from satisfactory." He also dwelt on the concept that the mounds are the result of differential solution and concretion on a large scale.

Marius Campbell, of the Geological Survey, followed shortly with a paper summarizing the various hypotheses for the mounds that lie on the plains from Arkansas to the Pacific coast. He showed that naturalists had laid the origin of the mounds to the agency of humans, burrowing mammals (ground squirrels, gophers, and prairie dogs), ants, fishes, water erosion, chemical solution, wind action, physical and chemical segregation, glacial action, uprooted trees, and spring and gas vents. Campbell suspected the importance of burrowing mammals and ants, especially the latter, although he confessed his inability to understand their methods of operation.

In 1913, J. Harland Bretz, of the University of Washington, published an article on glaciation of the Puget Sound region and therein described his careful studies of Mima Prairie. He concluded that the mounds were probably the result of water and ice action. In retrospect, it seems logical that Bretz should have associated the mounds with glacial activity since the region under scrutiny, where the mounds are better developed than anywhere else in the United States, marks also the farthest point reached by the Vashon Glacier, last of the Western ice sheets.

Ellis and Lee, in 1919, laid the origin of the San Diego mounds to "the action of wind as it sweeps through the sparse desert vegetation and blows away the loose soil except where it is held by plant roots." These investigators, like certain others before them, apparently did not realize that wind-built mounds are invariably *oriented* with the direction of the prevailing wind, whereas the mounds in question are either round or, if elongated, are aligned in no common direction.

The theory has been suggested, with variations, that the great power of freezing water has been instrumental in creating the mounds. The proponents of this theory may have studied the mound prairies of the North, but surely not those of the warm coastal plains of southern California.

In 1941, soil-scientist C. C. Nikiforoff published a long report on his studies of mounds in the Central Valley of California, principally in Tulare County. The mounds here are so similar in shape, size, and arrangement to those of Puget Sound that certain photographs from the two areas appear to have been taken from the same station. In two respects, however, the regions are different: in Tulare County the mounds are underlain by a stiff clay hardpan and in the rainy season may be surrounded by water a foot or two deep, whereas in Puget Sound the mounds are underlain by coarse gravel and rarely, if ever, stand out as islands. Nikiforoff concluded that the "hog-wallow microrelief" was perhaps the result of ground-water pressure from the Sierra Nevada pushing up through countless "windows," now represented by mounds, in the hardpan of the valley.

The mounds in the Central Valley are so numerous, or were when the pioneer farmers arrived on the scene, that a special implement, the "Fresno Scraper," has been devised for the purpose of leveling them off and making the ground fit for cultivation. The machine is still widely used.

The foregoing statements high-light the history of research on Mima-type mounds. In 1941, Walter W. Dalquest was engaged in a survey of the mammals of the state of Washington. As he extended his field observations to the prairies near Mima, he was at the same time enrolled in a course in glacial geology at the University of Washington. Here he learned that the origin of the prairie mounds was a mystery. About then the idea struck him that the mounds are the handiwork of a pocket gopher over untold periods of time. When he broached the idea to old-timers born and raised on the prairies, they commonly put tongue in cheek and cautiously remarked, "W-e-e-l, they must have been pretty big gophers." This is a not illogical conclusion in view of the fact that the Mima Mounds are mong the most spectacular—if not the largest—structures created by any mammal.

The gopher of the Western states, *Thomomys,* is a rat-like, brownish rodent that burrows in the soil of prairies and mountain meadows and along stream channels in the desert. It seldom ventures aboveground (as does the ground squirrel) and never enters the shade of the forest (as does the mole). It feeds on fleshy roots and often pulls an entire plant, root-first, into its subterranean chamber. The "pocket" part of the gopher's name refers to a deep, fur-lined pouch in each cheek. The pouch is about the size of an ordinary thimble and is used for carrying food, nesting material, and dirt. With this pouch to serve as a hod, with a pair of powerful forepaws for digging, and with the ability to run backward as well as forward in its burrow, the gopher is well equipped to excavate its labyrinthine tunnels.

Our theory of the origin of the Mima Mounds by gopher activity may be summed up as follows: A few tens of thousands of years ago, the Puget Sound prairie was laid down by rivers draining from the Vashon Ice Sheet. At first, the rivers were powerful and were able to carry the large boulders now found in the substratum of the prairie. Later, the rivers were quieter and were able to carry only the fine silt that, richened and darkened by the addition of grass-root humus, now composes the topsoil.

As soon as vegetation captured the raw new soil, we suppose that pocket gophers came in from the unglaciated country to the southward, advancing perhaps a few hundred feet in a gopher generation. By the time they reached the southern end of Puget Sound they encountered a barrier, the evergreen forest that had been racing against them to occupy the new land. There they were stopped, and, to the present day, no gophers are found on the lowlands of the Pacific coast north of southern Puget Sound. To be specific, the northern limit of the gopher range is Point Defiance Park, in Tacoma.

We can picture then, thousands of years ago, gophers rooting through the thin silt of the Puget Sound outwash in search of plant roots. At certain places they dug deeply into the gravelly subsoil in order to make nest chambers well protected from prowling bear, wolf, or wildcat. Areal spacing of the nest chambers corresponded to the size of the "territory" of each animal. The center of an old territory now marks, we believe, the center of a modern mound.

In excavating for its nest chamber, the gopher was instinctively led to dig deep into the bedded gravel, regardless of the effort involved. When the animal ran into a large boulder it undermined the obstruction and allowed it to settle. Thus, we now find, at the base of most mounds, a concentration of coarser materials. On the other hand, in foraging daily for food over its home range, the gopher was driven by less powerful instincts. When it encountered a bothersome rock in its path, it simply passed around it, shoving dirt along as it went. Thus, we find plainly exposed in the intermound hollows large boulders that were doubtless at one time buried in the topsoil.

Where the mound and its bed are in contact, there are found "mound roots," long a puzzle to geologists, which are simply abandoned gopher tunnels now filled with black silt contrasting in color with the yellow gravel around it. (They call to mind the peculiar devil's corkscrews, or *Daemonelices,* of the Nebraska sediments. Once described as fossil plants or animals, the corkscrews are now generally believed to be the casts of burrows of extinct rodents.) We can imagine that, in cases where a gopher mound was abandoned by its owner for some reason or other, the nesting chamber collapsed and caused a depression at the crest of the mound, a characteristic feature of many of the mounds on Mima Prairie.

In fancy, it is easy to picture the start of a Mima Mound. It is less easy to account for its growth. For reasons that may never be known, the gophers carried more dirt toward the nest than away from it. Perhaps some biologist will suggest an experiment whereby the growth of a Mima-type mound can be studied from start to finish. At present, we do not know whether the mounds on the Puget Sound and other prairies are still growing, whether they are in equilibrium with the forces tending to reduce them, or whether they are shrinking.

In reviewing our evidence in support of the gopher-origin theory, we realize that most of it is indirect. We cannot say that we have seen a gopher, or a family of gophers, build a giant mound. Yet, as each new fact with regard to the mounds is uncovered, it seems to strengthen the gopher theory. And, what is perhaps more important, no counter-theory based on the action of nonliving forces (such as wind and water) approaches a satisfactory explanation of the peculiar structure and arrangement of the mounds. The following facts have led us to our conclusions:

1. Mima-type mounds are distributed along the Pacific Coast exclusively in the range of the pocket gopher. On the north, both the mounds and the gophers terminate abruptly in the vicinity of Puget Sound.

2. Burrowing animals with habits similar to those of the gopher, namely, the ground squirrel (*Citellus*) and the mole (*Scapanus*), are known to occur on many of the mound prairies. We may deduce, however, that these animals are not pertinent to the formation of mounds since there are no ground squirrels in western Washington and no moles on most of the mound prairies of Califonria.

3. Mima-type mounds are found only where there is a thin layer of workable soil on top of a dense substratum. It is significant that the substratum is of no particular geological formation. Thus near San Diego and Fresno, the substratum is a hardpan of cemented soil; a few miles southeast of Mount Hood, in Oregon, the substratum is basaltic rock; and in Puget Sound it is bedded gravel.

4. Where gophers are working in deep sandy soil unlimited by a basement they never form Mima-type mounds. In other words, their up-and-down movements are not restricted or localized. In deep soil near Olympia, Wash., only fifteen miles from the mound display at Mima, gophers have been working for untold years, and the surface of the ground is still so level that it is used as an airfield.

5. The usual agent in the formation of hillocks and mounds is geological deposition of one kind or another. This agent can hardly be responsible for mounds of the Mima type. Deposition, whether by ice, wind, or water, depends on a moving vehicle, and movement always results in a deposit which is aligned in one general direction. Mima-type mounds, as may be seen from aerial photographs, are unoriented. Also, deposition does not produce round mounds on a sloping terrain, as are occasionally seen on the gopher prairies.

6. For similar reasons, the agency of erosion may be dismissed. Erosion is generally the result of a moving vehicle. We may point out, further, that on the Puget Sound prairies, the mounds are draped the year around

with a mossy turf that protects them from wind and rain-water erosion. And, in countless cases, the hollows between the mounds are completely closed depressions from which there is no rapid outflow of water—simply drainage through the porous gravel bed.

7. Only by a liberal use of the imagination can we conceive of a set of geological forces capable of producing the elaborate structure of the mounds, namely: the fluffy, unstratified soil of the mound adjoining a distinctly bedded substratum; the presence of "gopher-size" rocks in the mound as compared with the heavy cobbles beneath and beside the mound; the curious dip in the substrate beneath the sound; the mound roots; and the sunken depression usually found on the summit.

The reader may be disturbed to learn that *there are no gophers on Mima Prairie,* where climax examples of the mounds appear. This fact is of little importance, however, since there is clear evidence that gophers once lived there. Through some unknown agency—fire, flood, or pestilence—they were wiped out. Once gone from the prairie, they would not return, for the prairie is now isolated from surrounding gopher range by a river and a forest. Since the Mima Prairie Mounds are identical in structure with others only a mile away where gophers *are* found, at the present time, we feel confident in stating that both series of mounds are of common origin. And, as we have pointed out, Mima Prairie is only one among scores of plains along the coast where Mima-type mounds occur.

Finally, we should like to pose three questions, the answers to which some interprising naturalist may be led to seek:

First, what are the dynamics of mound formation? Were the present mounds built in a matter of years? Centuries? Do conditions of the environment favor their growth at the present time?

Second, does ground water at certain times of the year and in certain localities act in the same way that a soil hardpan does, to force the gophers into mound-building activity?

Third, how widespread in North America are gopher mounds of the Mima type? Shortly before his death in 1942, government naturalist Vernon Bailey told us that he had puzzled over Mima Prairie for years and wondered whether some giant gopher might have lived there long ago. He also said that in his extensive travels he had seen similar formations in southwestern South Dakota, southwestern Louisiana, eastern Texas, and many other parts of the West. Only in California, Oregon, and Washington have we had an opportunity to study them.

PIMPLED PLAINS OF EASTERN OKLAHOMA
Knechtel, Maxwell M.; *Geological Society of America, Bulletin,* 63:689–700, 1952

[Knechtel does not believe the pocket gopher theory. Rather, he feels that mound formations are more closely related to the patterned ground of the Arctic regions.]

Introduction. Low-relief topography, or microrelief, formed of innumerable closely spaced small hummocks or mounds, is a conspicuous feature of many large tracts of nearly level to gently sloping land in some states west of

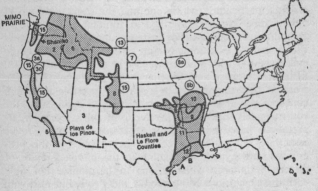

Map of United States showing geomorphic provinces in which pimpled plains occur. (1) Puget trough; (2) Columbia plateaus; (3) scattered localities in Basin-and-range province; (4) California trough; (5) Pacific Border terraces; (6) southern Rocky Mountains; (8) areas in Central Lowlands; (9, 10) Ozark-Ouachita region; (11, 12) parts of Gulf Coastal Plain; (13 and probably 7) river terraces at low altitudes in the Great Plains.

the Mississippi River, as well as in some other parts of the world. The figure, based on a map constructed by Price, shows a number of physiographic provinces wherein such mounds are reported to occur in the United States.

Such mounds are known as "prairie mounds," "hogwallows" (California), "Mima mounds," (Washington), and "puffs" (Australia). The origin of the mound-studded surfaces, which in this country are commonly called "pimpled plains" has been a subject of much discussion for more than 100 years and has been attributed to various natural processes. Interpretations of their genesis set forth in the references cited involve such concepts as erosion by networks of rivulets, "mud-volcano" phenomena, hydrostatic pressure of ground water, "concretionary action", frozen-ground phenomena, construction by ants, termites, rodents, or aborigines.

The diversity of interpretations suggests that such natural-mound systems may have originated in various ways. Eventual agreement may nevertheless be attainable with reference to the origin of individual systems, or groups of systems, particularly where one and the same example of mound relief has been ascribed to different and seemingly incongruous processes. For instance, mound systems near Puget Sound, Washington, were attributed by Newcomb and Pewe to melting of ice wedges in networks of vertical fissures; Dalquest and Scheffer believed them to be the work of pocket gophers. It is scarcely possible that both concepts would survive a thorough-going analysis of the controversial phenomena involved. In other cases, interpretations based on dissimilar processes may prove to be essentially compatible—a contingency implicit in the writer's working hypothesis relating to the pimpled plains of eastern Oklahoma which seems to harmonize not only with the suggestions of Newcomb and Pewe, but also with the soil-erosion hypothesis of LeConte.

The Pimpled Plains of Eastern Oklahoma. Pimpled plains are extensively developed in the Arkansas River valley and the Ouachita Mountains. They appear on air-photos as multitudinous small, rather uniformly spaced, bright or dark patches of ground, most of which are sub-circular. The center of each patch coincides approximately with the apex of a mound 2 to 4 feet high. The distance from center to center, generally between 50 and 100 feet, is rather uniform for any one locality, and commonly the margins of the patches are separated by approximately half that distance. Locally, however, the patches are much broader than the interspaces and are of various polygonal shapes.

Many road cuts expose the materials of the mounds and the surfaces on which they rest. A typical mound consists of loesslike material that is partly clay and contains small pellets of limonite, as well as a few subangular fragments of sandstone lithologically like that of local bedrock units of Pennsylvanian age. Most of the rock fragments are 2 inches or less in greatest dimension and are distributed at random. The loesslike material rests with a sharp contact on a flat, nearly level floor that commonly consists of heavy clay, or claypan, lighter in color than the material composing the mound. In places the floor material approaches the consistency of hardpan. The origin of the materials of the mounds and the deposits immediately underlying them calls for more study and is not dealt with here. Additional information concerning them, including a number of mechanical analyses and descriptions of soil profiles, is given by Knobel, Boatright, and Boatright in describing the *Conway very fine sandy loam* and the *Le Flore silt loam,* the only mound-forming soil materials mentioned among the various units shown on their map.

The writer has commented as follows upon the bedrock associated with the pimpled plains of eastern Oklahoma, their range of altitude and the time of their origin:

"Many of the mounds occur within areas of bedrock exposure but their areal distribution bears no direct relation to that of any of the different bedrock units. Some of them occur also on ancient gravel terraces and others on the higher parts of the Recent alluvial plains along the larger streams . . . Those in Le Flore County occur at altitudes ranging through several hundred feet though they are present only on nearly level surfaces and gentle slopes. For example, on the gently sloping upper surface of a prominent hogback a mile south of Bokoshe mounds occur approximately 400 feet above the Arkansas River level; within half a mile of these and 300 feet lower are others on the higher parts of the alluvial plain along Buck Creek.

"Clearly, the mounds on all such plains were formed since the region attained essentially its present stage of geomorphic development and can therefore scarcely be older than late Pleistocene."

Summary. The pimpled plains of eastern Oklahoma are evidently assignable to a category of surficial phenomena, sometimes called *Polygonboden,* which in some parts of the world includes features attributable to permafrost. The intermound furrow networks visible on airphotos of localities in eastern Oklahoma are comparable in pattern and coarseness of texture to the great polygonal networks of ice-filled fissures that commonly form in perennially frozen ground, but the eastern Oklahoma patterns bear an equally close resemblance to those of fissure networks caused elsewhere by desiccation and are comparable in some respects to inter-mound furrow patterns that appear to have originated, in some other parts of the United States, as a consequence of columnar jointing in the bedrock under the furrows. The data at hand offer little, if any, support to the possibility that the Oklahoma patterns are associated in origin with jointing in bedrock; they do, however, appear to establish desiccation as a possible agency in the origin of these patterns.

The transformation from systems of prismatic blocks enclosed by fissures to systems of mounds comparable to those of the pimpled plains may, apparently, be accomplished by one or more of three processes: (1) expansion of material that accumulates in the fissures; (2) subsidences of the ground along the fissures; and/or (3) erosion by rivulets which may form along the fissures. Assuming that the inter-mound furrow systems of eastern Oklahoma are related in origin to systems of fissure polygons due to desiccation, the mound relief there may be attributable to widening of grooves that have resulted from subsidence of the ground along the fissures of the polygonal networks.

Because of the mound systems are present at various altitudes and occur locally on alluvial surfaces close to the present stream levels, the mound relief of eastern Oklahoma is improbably not older than late Pleistocene.

THE MIMA MOUNDS

Kelly, Allan O.; *Scientific Monthly*, 66:174–176, 1948 (With permission of the American Association for the Advancement of Science)

I read with a great deal of interest the article in the October number by Dr. Scheffer, "The Mystery of the Mima Mounds."

Excepting the gopher theory, I have heard all the other explanations he says have been advanced for the origin of these mounds and some others that he did not mention, including buffalo wallows, bearer mounds, prehistoric elephant wallows, and that they were made by shovel-nosed sharks when the land was submerged. The last theory was advanced by an oil driller who had found shark's teeth in the area around Bakersfield, California, where these mounds cover hundreds of square miles. The gopher theory is new to me, but I think I can disprove it.

First, gophers do not work in a manner that would tend to form such mounds. The University of California found at its cattle experiment station near Fresno that gophers, when fenced off from their natural enemies so that they are unmolested, work the soil quite evenly, so that each year the mounds of soil they pile up tend to make a sort of summer fallow job of cultivation. This cultivated soil produces a better crop of grass the following year, and hence gophers do not deplete the soil. They cultivate one part of an area one year and another part the next. They do not move the soil or other material toward a central point.

Second, gophers and squirrels will not live in these mound areas, commonly called "hog wallows," if there is any other more suitable terrain, the reason being that these mounds provide their natural enemies, coyotes and foxes, with a good cover for close approach. It is not nature's way—that gophers could have survived for long ages by building good cover for their enemies.

Dr. Scheffer mentions these mounds being found near San Diego, California. This is true. They are found on most of the coastal mesas from San Diego northward into Orange County and southward into Lower California. San Diego County also provides examples of these mounds

The San Diego hillocks, another variety of "pimpled plains."

under different conditions and different terrain. They are found in a number of inland valleys with narrow canyon outlets and at elevations of 200–4,500 feet. El Cajon Valley near San Diego is about 200 feet in elevation; San Marcos Valley, 350 feet; Ramona Valley, 1,500 feet; and Mendenhall Valley, 4,500 feet. All these inland valleys in San Diego County have one thing in common: they have narrowly restricted drainage outlets. The great Central Valley of California has the same characteristics, only on a larger scale.

It is my contention that these mounds are gigantic ripple marks made by deep water flowing slowly out of these valleys through the narrow openings. The same thing can be seen on a small scale in any tidal basin where the outgoing tide leaves mud flats. The size of the ripple marks on these mud flats will be found to vary with the depth of the water and the rate of flow. The deeper the water, the larger the mounds, provided there is a wide expanse of flats where the water begins to flow faster in channels; then the bottom will be smooth or in ridges paralleling the direction of flow.

If we could view the floor of the ocean between Florida and Cuba where the Gulf Stream moves quite swiftly (for an ocean current), then we might see such giant ripple mounds as we now see on dry land. Again, if we could fill any of the valleys mentioned above, or the great

Central Valley of California, with muddy water several hundred feet deep and allow that water to drain out through its narrow outlet to the sea, we would get the same sort of mounds we see there today. A scale model of one of these valleys should prove this point. The ripple mounds in these valleys are never found on the steeper slopes or in the channels where the current moved too swiftly but on the gentle slopes and flats where the current was gentle.

I agree with Dr. Scheffer that these mounds may be found on any type of substrata, glacial gravel, basaltic rock, clay, hardpan, etc. This proves that their origin had nothing to do with ground water or drainage. He asks how widespread are these "gopher mounds of the Mima type." I have not heard of their existence elsewhere in the world, but if I am correct in my theory of their origin, they should be found all over the world wherever the land was suitable in topography for their formation.

INDEXES

All indexes in this volume apply to *both* volumes G1 and G2. Subsequent volumes in the STRANGE PHENOMENA series will be self-contained with cumulative indexes available separately to those who wish them.

Proper names are so profuse in the sourcebooks that a thorough index of them would overwhelm the book. Therefore, only the most important proper names, such as "Barisal guns" are indexed.

Subject Index

Date-of-Event Index

Place-of-Event Index

331

Author Index

Source Index

ABOUT THE AUTHOR

WILLIAM R. CORLISS received a B.S. in physics from Rensselaer Polytechinc Institute in 1950 and an M.S. in physics from the University of Colorado in 1953. After nine years in industry working on space power and propulsion projects, he began a career in freelance writing. He has since authored or coauthored sixteen books in space technology, power generation, astronomy, geophysics, and man-machine systems. He has also written several dozen booklets and articles on a wide range of scientific and technical subjects for the National Science Foundation, the National Aeronautics and Space Administration, and the Energy Research and Development Administration. In 1974, Corliss founded the Sourcebook Project which has now published six volumes of anomalous data in astronomy, geology, biology, geophysics, and archeology. Corliss, his wife and four children and the Sourcebook Project are quartered in Glen Arm, Maryland.

PSYCHIC WORLD

Here are some of the leading books that delve into the world of the occult—that shed light on the powers of prophecy, of reincarnation and of foretelling the future.

- ☐ THE GOLD OF THE GODS
  by Erich Von Daniken   8477—$1.75
- ☐ SETH SPEAKS
  by Jane Roberts   8462—$1.95
- ☐ THE DEVIL'S TRIANGLE
  by Richard Winer   8445—$1.50
- ☐ PSYCHIC DISCOVERIES BEHIND THE IRON
  CURTAIN by Ostrander & Schroeder   7864—$1.50
- ☐ GOD DRIVES A FLYING SAUCER
  by Robert Dione   7733—$1.25
- ☐ NOT OF THIS WORLD by Peter Kolosimo   7696—$1.25
- ☐ WE ARE NOT THE FIRST
  by Andrew Tomas   7534—$1.25
- ☐ CHARIOTS OF THE GODS?
  by Erich Von Daniken   5753—$1.25
- ☐ LINDA GOODMAN'S SUN SIGNS
  by Linda Goodman   2777—$1.95
- ☐ BEYOND EARTH: MAN'S CONTACT
  WITH UFO'S by Ralph Blum   2564—$1.75
- ☐ EDGAR CAYCE: THE SLEEPING PROPHET
  by Jess Stearn   2546—$1.75
- ☐ YOGA, YOUTH & REINCARNATION
  by Jess Stearn   2398—$1.50
- ☐ THE OUTER SPACE CONNECTION
  by Alan Landsburg   2092—$1.75

Buy them at your local bookstore or use this handy coupon for ordering:

Bantam Books, Inc., Dept. PW, 414 East Golt Road, Des Plaines, Ill. 60016

Please send me the books I have checked above. I am enclosing $_____
(please add 35¢ to cover postage and handling). Send check or money
order—no cash or C.O.D.'s please.

Mr/Mrs/Miss_____

Address_____

City_____State/Zip_____

PW—7/76

Please allow three weeks for delivery. This offer expires 7/77.

OUT OF THIS WORLD!

That's the only way to describe Bantam's great series of science-fiction classics. These space-age thrillers are filled with terror, fancy and adventure and written by America's most renowned writers of science fiction. Welcome to outer space and have a good trip!

☐	FANTASTIC VOYAGE by Isaac Asimov	2477	$1.25
☐	STAR TREK: THE NEW VOYAGES by Culbreath & Marshak	2719	$1.75
☐	THE MYSTERIOUS ISLAND by Jules Verne	2872	$1.25
☐	ALAS, BABYLON by Pat Frank	2923	$1.75
☐	A CANTICLE FOR LEBOWITZ by Walter Miller, Jr.	2973	$1.75
☐	RAGA SIX by Frank Lauria	7249	$1.25
☐	THE MARTIAN CHRONICLES by Ray Bradbury	7900	$1.25
☐	HELLSTROM'S HIVE by Frank Herbert	8276	$1.50
☐	HIERO'S JOURNEY by Sterling Lanier	8534	$1.25
☐	DHALGREN by Samuel R. Delany	8554	$1.95
☐	20,000 LEAGUES UNDER THE SEA by Jules Verne	8569	95¢
☐	STAR TREK XI by James Blish	8717	$1.75
☐	THE DAY OF THE DRONES by A. M. Lightner	10057	$1.25
☐	THE TOMBS OF ATUAN by Ursula LeGuin	10132	$1.75

Buy them at your local bookstore or use this handy coupon for ordering:

Bantam Books, Inc., Dept. SF, 414 East Golf Road, Des Plaines, Ill. 60016

Please send me the books I have checked above. I am enclosing $_____ (please add 35¢ to cover postage and handling). Send check or money order—no cash or C.O.D.'s please.

Mr/Mrs/Miss_____

Address_____

City_____ State/Zip_____

SF—8/76

Please allow three weeks for delivery. This offer expires 8/77.

Bantam Book Catalog

It lists over a thousand money-saving best-sellers originally priced from $3.75 to $15.00 —bestsellers that are yours now for as little as 60¢ to $2.95!

The catalog gives you a great opportunity to build your own private library at huge savings!

So don't delay any longer—send us your name and address and 25¢ (to help defray postage and handling costs).
